ISLAM

ISLAM

A GUIDE FOR JEWS AND CHRISTIANS

F. E. PETERS

PRINCETON UNIVERSITY PRESS · PRINCETON AND OXFORD

Copyright © 2003 by Princeton University Press
Published by Princeton University Press, 41 William Street,
Princeton, New Jersey 08540
In the United Kingdom: Princeton University Press,
3 Market Place, Woodstock, Oxfordshire OX20 1SY
All Rights Reserved

Library of Congress Cataloging-in-Publication Data

Peters, F. E. (Francis E.)
Islam: a guide for Jews and Christians / F.E. Peters.
p. cm.
Includes bibliographical references and index.
ISBN 0-691-11553-2 (alk. paper)
1. Islam — Relations — Christianity.   2. Christianity and other religions —
Islam.   3. Islam — Relations — Judaism.   4. Judaism — Relations —
Islam.   5. Islam — Origin.   6. Islam — Essence, genius, nature.   I. Title.

BP172 .P455 2003
297 — dc21   2002042464

British Library Cataloging-in-Publication Data is available

This book has been composed in Sabon Typeface
Printed on acid-free paper. ∞
www.pupress.princeton.edu

Printed in the United States of America

10   9   8   7   6   5   4   3   2   1

For Charlie and Bonnie

TAKEN MUCH TOO SOON,

GONE FAR TOO LONG

Contents

Prophetic Reports; From Prophetic Tradition to Law; A
Growth Industry; A Skeptical Reaction; Islamic Justice: The
Qadi; Islamic Morality and Islamic Jurisprudence; A Society
of Law — and Lawyers; Judgments and Opinions; Priests and
Rabbis; Jewish Rabbis and Islamic Ulama: A Comparison
with a Difference; The Schools; Ijtihad; The Closing of the
Gate; Consensus on Moral Matters

Identity Markers; Building the Umma: Conversion; The
Making of a Muslim; An Arab, and Arabic, Islam; "There Is
No Coercion in Religion"; Dhimma and Dhimmis; The Mil-
let System; Defining the Truth; The Umma Divided: Early
Muslim Sects and Sectarianism; Innovation and Heresy;
Sunnis and Shiites; The Enemy Without: Jihad; Just Wars
and Crusades; The Enemy Within: Ibn Taymiyya; Funda-
mentalists As the Faithful Remnant

To Be a Muslim; Women in the Ritual Life of Islam; Muslim
Prayer; Friday Prayer and the Mosque; The Hajj; To Mount
Arafat and Back; Intercalation Prohibited; The Enshrine-
ment of Jerusalem; The Distant Shrine; The Christian As-
sault on Jerusalem; Muslim Jerusalem in the Middle Ages;
The Pious Visit al-Quds; Muslim Devotions; The Friends of
God; The Passion and the Death of Husayn; Islam and the
Graven Image; The Word as Decoration

The Beginnings of Muslim Asceticism; The Sufi Way; The
Path to God; Salvation; The End and What Follows; End
Time Scenarios; The Muslim Dead; The Cosmology of the
Other World; A Heavenly Journey; The Quranic Eschaton;
Intercession in Islam; The Vision of God and Other Rewards

of Paradise; Are the Martyrs in Paradise? A Savior Returns; Shiite Messianism; The Mahdi

Introduction

THE POINT of this book is simple and rather direct: to provide a reader whose cultural and religious formation has been Jewish or Christian with a way of approaching the body of belief and practice called Islam. In *The Monotheists* I place Islam as an equal at the side of Judaism and Christianity and attempt, in considerable detail, to contextualize each with the others in the hope of illuminating all three. Here, the primary focus is Islam, and the other two monotheistic systems are cited only to the extent that they cast light on the faith and practices of the Muslims, the least known and certainly least understood of the three monotheistic faiths.

My objective is not to reduce Islam to Judaism or Christianity (or some combination of them) in order to make it intelligible to non-Muslims, but to enter Islam through the same door Muhammad did. After he had had his first experience of the supernatural, he went, puzzled and frightened, to a relative of his wife, who had "read the Scriptures and learned from those that follow the Torah and the Gospel." You have experienced, the man explained to him, what Moses had before you. And, Muhammad himself would later add, Abraham and Jesus as well.

The Quran, the book of revelations given to Muhammad by God, makes no attempt to disguise the affiliation of its contents with what was found in the sacred books of the Jews and Christians. Indeed, Muhammad was instructed by God to refer those who doubted the revelations in the Quran to the Jews and the Christians, who would confirm that what was in the "clear Arabic Quran" was likewise the Word of God. In the Muslims' own view, the Quran is, quite simply, the same God saying the same things to his often heedless creation.

That is the theological basis of the approach here. There are equally convincing historical grounds for going down this way. Christianity is clearly an "offshoot" of Judaism. The image is Paul's, an olive tree branch that Christians claim has replaced the trunk, but a branch nonetheless. Branch and trunk, stem and offshoot, parent and offspring, the two have grown up and out together, each dissembling, as suited its purposes, the family resemblance. No such easy image occurs with Islam. It is neither a branch nor a child of either Judaism or Christianity, though some Jews and many Christians used to think so. Rather, it is their successor, according to the Muslims. A child not of Moses or Jesus but of Abraham, and of God.

We will leave the quarrel over rank orders to the respective communities. What is incontestable is that Islam, almost from its inception, was a party in the great religious competition that took place for many centuries among the monotheists around the Mediterranean, eastward into Asia and southward into Africa. It was indeed a confrontation as much as a competition, often hostile in intent and act, but it was also the great growth period for the three communities, an extraordinarily rich era of interaction when the practices, institutions, and religious ideals of Judaism, Christianity, and Islam grew into what would long be their standard form, in many cases into our own lifetime. Jews, Christians, and Muslims not only worshiped the same God; they also shared many, though by no means identical, ideals and aspirations, operated often in the same social and economic environment, and at certain times and in certain places lived side by side within the same culture, indistinguishable in language, costume, and manners.

Little of that reality is apparent today. Judaism and Christianity have evolved in the public consciousness into "Western" religions, while Islam remains at best a "Middle Eastern" or at worst an "oriental" religion, and in any event an exotic one. But it did not always appear so, least of all to the millions of Sephardic Jews and Eastern Christians who lived out their lives in Muslim lands, spoke Arabic, Persian, Turkish, and were largely indistinguishable from their Muslim compatriots. And perhaps it will not appear so to the reader at the end of these pages.

The enterprise is delicate, to be sure, to explain Islam in terms that are familiar to a Jew or Christian — "practicing" is not terribly much to the point here — and are at the same time faithful to the historical givens of Islam. As the Christians once did regarding the Jews, Muslims of the modern era have invested enormous energy in fighting their way clear of what they too now perceive as their Western siblings. This book, in any event, has not been written from the perspective of a Muslim but from that of a student of Islam (and of Judaism and Christianity). Nor is it a Jewish or Christian critique of Islam or a rationalist's take on that religion. I have tried to present the matter in an intellectually rigorous and yet accessible manner, and I have done my best to avoid what has been called, in a somewhat different context, "parallelomania." The book is what it says it is: a guide for Jews and Christians to the beliefs and practices of their fellow monotheists, their siblings and rivals for the affection of the Father, the Muslims.

ISLAM

1. *Discovering Scripture in Scripture*

THERE is only one way to approach Islam and that is to open and read from the pages of the Quran. The Muslim will prefer to hear it, but for the non-Muslim, the Muslim Scripture is almost always a book and not the "recitation" (*al-quran*) that its Arabic title announces it to be. It is by no means an easy read. The Quran, or Koran, as it is sometimes spelled, bristles with obscurities and ambiguities. Highly emotive poetry—or so it appears; the non-Muslim is normally relying on a translation, which is not very kind to poetry—alternates with an often pedestrian didacticism. Even in translation, the Quran has the sound, look, and feel of a patchwork, an assemblage.

These are aesthetic judgments made by a palate unused perhaps to another culture's high delicacies, and as such they are of no matter. Or they would be save that this book itself, or the person speaking through it—its "voice"—challenges others who doubt its authenticity to try to duplicate it. The Quran is, on its own testimony, nonpareil, or to use its own term, "inimitable." But there are other elements of this fundamental Islamic text that attract the attention, often the surprised attention, of the Jewish or Christian reader. On those same pages unfolds a terrain that is at once familiar and alien. The familiar is quickly characterized: the Quran is *biblical*, and biblical in the expanded sense favored by the Christians. Across its pages pass Adam and Noah, Abraham, Isaac, and Jacob,

David and Solomon, and yes, John the Baptist, Jesus, and the Virgin Mary.

"IN THE BEGINNING . . ."

The Quran's account of Creation is similar to that of the Bible in intent and some detail: both insist on an omnipotent creation from nothing, for example, and on the Creator's fashioning of humankind. It is not laid out here in the linear narrative fashion of Genesis (or of other books of the Bible), however. It is immediately apparent that the Muslim Scripture is a collection of revelations, which Muslims claim were given by God to Muhammad over the last twenty-two years of his life. In our copies of the Quran these revelations are divided into 114 suras, or chapters, although some of the suras almost certainly contain more than one revelation, and they are arranged not in the order they were delivered but according to their descending length. Rather than a single narrative or story, the Quran is an assembly of "occasional" revelations bestowed under particular circumstances, some of which we can plausibly identify and many others we cannot. Thus, the events of God's Creation are introduced at various appropriate points — appropriate to God's purpose of warning and instructing — rather than at the very outset on the linear narrative model of Genesis. Genesis tells the story of Creation; the Quran simply alludes to it. When Creation events are cited in the Quran, they are generally in résumé form and presented as moral examples, to underline God's power, for instance, or his goodness.

THE NAME(S) AND NATURE OF GOD

Who is this deity? In Exodus 3:14 Moses boldly asks God his name and the response is (in Hebrew) *ehyeh* ("I am") *asher* ("who" or "that which"), whose meaning — "I am who I am"? "What I am"? "What I will be"? — is by no means clear. The Israelites called him something very similar, Yahweh, which shows up as early as Genesis 2:4. Here God is called Yahweh Elohim, perhaps "the divine Yahweh," but the two names often appear apart as individual names of God, with Yahweh usually translated into English as "Lord" and the plural Elohim as "God." The Creator is chiefly called Allah in the Arabic Quran, though Muslims later counted ninety-nine appellations for the deity in that book, a phenomenon that gave rise to a variety of practices and beliefs in Islamic circles. Allah was well known in pre-Islamic Mecca — his shrine was the chief one in the town — and to the Arabs generally before Islam. Muhammad thought of him — and preached him — as the same God worshiped by the Jews and Christians. Some Muslims prefer to leave the name untranslated in English, but that gives the impression of Allah's being alien or exotic instead of the same deity referred to by most English speakers as God (capitalized), the Divine Creator and Final Judge of monotheism.

Whereas Jews shied away from using any of the names of God available from Scripture and increasingly resorted to circumlocutions like *ha-Qodesh barukh hu* ("The Holy One, Blessed be He"), Muslims followed the Quran's lead that God's were "the most beautiful names" (7:180, etc.), and they developed numerous cult practices, devotional, mystical, and magical, around the quranic names. Most directly, God's names could be recited as a form of prayer, sometimes counted out by means of a *subha*, thirty-three or ninety-nine beads strung out in the form of a chaplet — the Eastern Christian prayer rope and Western Christian rosary were modeled on the Muslims' subha — though among more profane Muslims this handheld prayer calculator eventually degenerated into the omnipresent Middle Eastern worry beads. Sufis incorporated the litany of divine names into their regular *dhikr*s, or group "séances," and mystics eagerly sought out the unique "true" name of God, assumed to be one among the canonical ninety-nine, that would reveal his inner being. Finally, the most beautiful names, because of their formulaic nature, were frequently used on amulets and in other forms of apotropaic magic.

The Quran insists, Muslims believe, and historians affirm that Muhammad and his followers worship the same God as the Jews (29:46). Conceptually, at least, this is true. The Quran's Allah is

the same Creator God who covenanted with Abraham and dispatched the prophets to their tasks, and although he is perhaps
more dominantly central to the Quran than Yahweh to the Bible,
he is not portrayed in the same manner as his biblical prototype.
The Allah of the Quran is at once more powerful yet unmistakably
more remote than Yahweh. Allah controls all, but from a distance;
he is a universal deity quite unlike the Yahweh who in the early
books of the Bible follows close on every step of the Israelites.
Allah had his own, quite different history, which we can to some
extent construct from the cult of the deity of that name who in pre-
Islamic days was worshiped all across the Fertile Crescent and
Arabia by the polytheistic Arabs. Though both the Quran and its
Meccan audience knew at least part of that history, very little of it
is laid out in the Quran. Later Islamic generations, who cared
nothing about Allah's pre-Islamic career, had the quranic portrait
of their God filled out by Muslim authors, many of them converts
from Judaism or Christianity, who were well aware of Yahweh's
biblical history, but the Muslims' notion of God, though in its
main lines identical with the Bible's, has very different nuances of
detail. The portrait of Yahweh that unfolds in the Bible is both
more complex and psychologically nuanced and more directly engaged in history, if not in secondary causality, than the majestic but
rather abstract and remote Allah of the Quran. *Allah: A Biography*
is not a very plausible project.

THE BIBLE IN THE QURAN

The Quran's links to the Bible continue well beyond Creation. Before the Quran ends, it has touched on Adam, Cain and Abel,
Noah and the Flood, Abraham and his sons Ishmael and Isaac,
Lot, Jacob, Joseph and his brethren, Moses and Aaron, the Pharaoh, the escape of the Israelites from Egypt, Saul, David, Solomon, Jonah, and Job. Jesus and Mary have their own considerable
place there as well, as we shall see. This is a fairly extensive repertoire, but the absences are equally interesting. Though the Quran
was obviously interested in prophecy and the prophetic office, and

many of the early biblical figures from Adam to Solomon are treated as prophets, the classic prophets of the biblical canon like Jeremiah and Isaiah—two of the prophets most favored by Christians—are not mentioned at all. The Exile and the Return are likewise ignored, as is all subsequent Jewish history. The Quran was interested in history in a very narrow sense. When Muhammad speaks in Scripture, he is not so much explaining the past as he is using it, and the biblical stories in the Quran are generally told for a reason: sometimes as signs, demonstrations of God's power, justice, or goodness, or, more commonly, as punishment stories about the consequences of ignoring prophets, particularly when they refer to the people of Abraham, of Lot, of Noah or Moses.

The Quran speaks often and at times at length of the Children of Israel—the Banu Israil, who in its eyes constituted both a community (*umma*) and a religion (*din*). Unlike the legislation of the Christian Roman Empire, which reserved the designation *religio* uniquely for Christianity and characterized Judaism as *superstitio*, the Quran recognizes multiple religions in the world, of which Islam is one, along with that of the Children of Israel, the Christians, and the pagans, "those who associate (others) with God." Of these latter Muhammad is made to say in the Quran, "To them their religion and to me, mine." The community of the Children of Israel is tribal—it takes Muhammad some time, and probably some Jewish assistance, to sort out the correct progenetic sequence of Abraham, Isaac, Jacob/Israel—but its religion is scriptural. Like Christianity and Islam after it, the din of the Children of Israel is founded on the contents of a divinely revealed Book. Jews and Christians are in fact often characterized in the Quran simply as "People of the Book" without further description or distinction.

Although there were other divine books, like that given to Abraham (Quran 87:19), the primacy of honor in the Israelite revelation belongs to the Torah (*Tawrat*) sent down to Moses. Moses is central to Muhammad's closure with Judaism, and this is true from the very earliest of the quranic revelations. The Torah revelation, its prehistory, form, and modalities, is the prototype of the quranic one. And it is Moses' example, particularly in his dealings with the Pharaoh, that provides the moral paradigm—persecution, then vindication—of Muhammad's own mission. Muhammad also understands that his Book is a confirmation of what has been sent beforehand to the Jews through Moses (2:41). Indeed, early in his career, the Prophet had been instructed by God to turn to the Jews if he had any doubts about the revelation sent down to him, and the Meccans are offered as a proof of the truth of Muhammad's message the fact that "the scholars of the Banu Israil know it" (26:196–197).

The presence of so much biblical matter in the Quran has prompted suspicion among non-Muslims that from the outset Muhammad was in contact with Jews who served, wittingly or unwittingly, as his informants. We have no evidence that there was a permanent Jewish colony at Mecca, as there certainly was at Medina, but it seems likely to think, given the considerable presence of Jews in the Yemen to the south and in the oases to the north of Mecca, that Jews passed through the town and that their beliefs and practices were familiar, to some degree, to Muhammad and his contemporaries—more familiar indeed than they are to us since we have little idea of the shape and heft of seventh-century Arabian Judaism. The issue of whether Muhammad "borrowed" anything from that quarter for his own message may come down to the degree of originality one is willing to grant to prophets, or, more pertinently, to other people's prophets. Islam was, and is, not simply a warmed-over version of Judaism, or of Christianity, for that matter, although some earlier Christians thought so. It was a unique vision—whether from God or inside Muhammad's own head is precisely what separates the Muslim from the non-Muslim—preached with great conviction, and in the end with great success, over the course of twenty-two years.

HISTORY BEGINS

Islam is quite obviously a biblical religion. But it is not such merely because echoes of biblical stories sound throughout the Muslims' own sacred book, and certainly not because Muslims follow the Christian practice of reading the Jewish Bible, which they assuredly do not. Islam is biblical in a more profound sense: the theological premises of Islam, the very ontological ground from which it springs, find their first expression in the Hebrew Bible and in that same Book of Genesis that begins with Creation. The eleventh chapter of Genesis provides a broad prospect of cultural history — "Once upon a time all the world spoke a single language and used the same words" — which is followed by a detailed list of Noah's descendants. The genealogy comes to an abrupt halt, however, and the book's broad focus narrows down to the person of one Abram — later he will be called Abraham. From chapter 12 onward, the Bible is nothing else than the story of Abraham and his descendants or, more properly, the story of the playing out of a contract God made with the same Abraham and whose terms were to bind his descendants as well.

At the beginning of the twelfth chapter of Genesis, Abraham is living in Haran, in what is now southern Turkey, a recent migrant, along with his father and other relatives, from "Ur of the Chaldees." Without prelude and with no indication of the circumstances, God tells Abraham to leave Haran, "your country, your kinsmen and your father's house," and to go to a land God will show him, where "I will make you a great nation" (Gen. 12:2). The details are still sparse, but in the country called Canaan, Abraham is told by God that this land will be his. Abraham "built an altar there to the Lord who appeared to him" (12:7), and a little later, in another place in that same land, "he built an altar to the Lord and invoked the Lord by name" (12:8). He was apparently not the only one there to do so. In chapter 15 of Genesis, what had before been a promise is ceremonially formalized into a covenant (*berit*), when God appears to Abraham "in a vision" (15:1) — a common form of divine communication in such circumstances. The Bible now explains: "Abram put his faith in the Lord and the Lord counted that faith as righteousness" (15:6). For his part, God spells out that Abraham, for all his and his wife's advanced age, will have heirs, who will grow into a great people, and that these present nomads will possess a land of their own that will stretch "from the River of Egypt to the Great River, the river Euphrates" (15:18).

THE COVENANT AND THE COVENANTS

The Bible makes it perfectly clear that the Israelites, later called Jews, are the Chosen People, and why not, since they transcribed and preserved it. Why, then, do the Christians and Muslims think *they* are? First, recall that the Christians *were* themselves Jews, and that when they claimed they were Abraham's heirs they were earmarking themselves, like other Jewish sects, as the one faithful remnant among God's own. They were following Abraham in faith in their conviction that Jesus was the promised Messiah, an argument spelled out at some length in Paul's Letter to the Romans. There were also plentiful suggestions scattered through the Bible that God was more than a little displeased with his people. There were even hints, like those dropped in Jeremiah 31, that the Covenant might be renegotiated, which is, the Christians claimed, exactly what happened. Finally, the Christians also maintained that this was a "new covenant" (Gk. *nea diatheke*; Lat. *novum testamentum*) for an eschatological moment in the history of Israel, one that justified the Gentiles' (the goyim, or non-Jews) being drawn into "the Kingdom," to use Jesus' own preferred image for the End Time. Faith, then, was at the base of the Christians' claim to the Covenant, faith in Jesus, and not mere obedience of the Law.

The Quran seems to have seen it quite differently. It knows a number of different divinely initiated covenants (*ahd, mithaq*) from Adam (20:115) onward through all the prophets; including Jesus and Muhammad (33:7). Though a covenant was made with the Christians (5:14)—there is no sign that it was "new" in any Christian sense of that word—it is the one made with Moses on Sinai that appears to have a special significance in the Quran. It is mentioned several times (e.g., 2:63, 93), and in one of its presentations (2:83) it is spelled out in terms that faintly echo the Ten Commandments, albeit with a distinctly Muslim cast: "Worship none save God, be good to parents and to kindred and to the orphans and the needy, and speak kindly to humankind and establish prayer (*salat*) and pay the tithe (*zakat*)."

From one perspective, there is no difference among these covenants that God "exacts" from his chosen prophets and their followers, save that Muhammad is the last of those messengers (33:40), and hence Islam will be the last covenant of all. But the Muslim covenant is more than that. It is not a "new testament" in the Christian sense but rather a return to an older one — not to the primordial covenant with Adam, which was for all humankind, but to the more confessional covenant that God took from Abraham. Islam is nothing other than the "religion of Abraham," the Quran announces (2:135), but it is in fact not very different from what was given to, and sworn to by, the other prophets (2:136).

Why the religion "of Abraham"? The biblical precedent is clear: when Jews and Christians refer to the Covenant, they mean the one that God concluded with Abraham. But the Quran's firm insistence on the point has something more behind it. The context is almost certainly polemical. When Muhammad promulgated his divinely revealed message of an absolute and purified monotheism in seventh-century Mecca and Medina, many simply turned their backs on him, as had Jesus' audience when he began to speak of his body as the "bread of life" (John 6:58–61). But for some of the more acute listeners, the message raised a question. "Why then," they asked Muhammad, "should we not just become Jews or Christians?" God himself instructed his prophet on what to respond. "Say: No, we follow the religion of Abraham, the monotheist, who was not one of the polytheists" (Quran 2:135). Islam is, then, older than either Mosaic Judaism or Jesus Christianity; it is a return to the father of believers professing his faith at the dawn of monotheism.

ABRAHAM

Abraham is clearly a transcendentally important figure in the Muslim revelation. He is mentioned, sometimes at length, in thirty-five chapters of the Quran, more often than any other biblical personality except Moses. Moses, like Jesus, is a key figure in the Muslim view of Sacred History as it is laid out in the Quran. They were the divinely designated founders of the communities of Jews and Christians, and each was the bearer of a Book sent down from on high. Abraham too had a book, as we have just seen, but that is not his importance. Abraham, who "paid his debt" (53:37) and whom God himself made his "friend" (4:125), stands at the head of the file of believers in the One True God. He was already a *muslim*, a "submitter," and a *hanif* (3:67). The latter is a somewhat mysterious word, but since the Quran frequently glosses it with the expression "he was not one of the idolaters," *hanif* may reasonably be understood as "monotheist."

For all his obvious significance, the Quran's message regarding Abraham is, like the Bible's own, somewhat mixed. The narrative passages on the patriarch put great stress on his repudiation of his father's and relatives' pagan idolatry (so, for example, 6:75–79; 26:72–80), and yet, when the outlines of a theology of Abraham emerge — and they are no more than an outline — Abraham merits well of his God because he has been tested and not found wanting (2:124). The test was no less than God's command to Abraham to sacrifice his unnamed son (37:102–107). Thus, it was by reason of Abraham's obedience in this matter that God had established his Covenant (*ahd*) with the man who is now his friend, a contract that will extend to Abraham's descendants (2:128, 132).

The Bible's own account of the Covenant gives grounds for thinking that either Abraham's "submission," that is, his adherence to the One True God, or his extraordinary act of obedience (or perhaps both) was the reason for the concordat. The two rival groups of Abraham's children later strenuously debated whether it was, as the rabbis maintained, Abraham's obedience — the "binding of Isaac" became a powerful motif in Jewish circles — or, as Paul and the Christians argued, the patriarch's faith that rendered him just in God's eyes. The Quran sounds no discernible echo of that dispute and credits both Abraham's belief and his obedience, though there is a manifestly greater interest in the story of his breaking free of the idolatry of his kinsmen.

What was truly revolutionary in the covenant offered to Abraham, and later in more detail to Moses, was its exclusivity clause. Abraham and his descendants were to worship no other god, to pay no dues, to give no respect, honor, or even acknowledgment to the deities of other peoples. This appears to us, who define mono-theism as the denial of *belief* in any god save one, as at best henotheism, the recognition of a primary god above all others. But it is, in practice, true monotheism. Where it really counted, in sac-rifice and invocation, Abraham and his heirs were required to be-have as if there were only one god. It would take centuries for that radical liturgical disregard of the other gods to be fully concep-tualized into a denial of their very existence, a process immeasur-ably aided by the fact that this god, astonishingly, had no image or effigy. Boldly, Yahweh could only be imagined.

A HOLY LAND

> Raise your eyes and look into the distance from the place where you are, north and south, east and west. All the land you can see I will give to you and your descendants for ever. I will make your descen-dants as countless as the dust of the earth; if anyone could count the dust upon the ground, then he could count your descendants. Now go through the length and breadth of the land, for I give it to you. (Gen. 13:14–17)

So the Lord pledged to Abraham in Genesis, and later in that same book the promised land is grandly defined as all the territory "from the River of Egypt to the Great River, the river Euphrates" (15:18). The "Promised Land" has had a long history in Judaism, but both Christians and Muslims also view this terrain — which they prefer to call, after the Roman fashion, "Palestine" — as holy soil, though for quite different reasons. Very early on Christians had begun to disassociate themselves not only from the main body of Jews but also from the Jewish Holy Land in general and their Holy City, Jerusalem, in particular. The Muslims, who see no vi-sions of a "heavenly Jerusalem," have no particular religious claims on Palestine as such, though they do on certain of its holy places, and, what is quite a different matter, some Arabs of the region obviously have a political claim on Palestine. Neither Chris-tianity nor Islam fosters the notion of a "return" to their Palestinian holy land, however — not, at least, in the sense of a migration. What Christian and Muslim devotion generated instead was, first, a powerful desire to visit the places esteemed holy in that land — the practice we call "pilgrimage" — and second, the more overtly political wish to control those same holy places. In Western Christendom this impulse led in the eleventh century to the first of the Christian holy wars against Islam, the Crusades, and in Islam, to a powerful Counter-Crusade under the famous hero Salah al-Din (Saladin), who in 1187 retook Jerusalem and Palestine from the Christian Franks. In both these events the land and its most celebrated and sacred city mingled in the minds and motives of the combatants, but it was Jerusalem that stood as a convenient and moving symbol for what each side wished to possess for itself in that holy land.

HAGAR AND ISHMAEL

To return to the Bible, it is his wife Sarai who in the opening verses of Genesis 16 suggests to Abram that perhaps he can and should father a son by her Egyptian slave-girl, Hagar. So indeed he does. There is quickly, and perhaps inevitably, a falling-out between the two women. Hagar flees and returns only after a divine apparition promises that her son will have many descendants, though he himself will ever be an outcast. At his birth this first son is called Ishmael; Abram is by then eighty-six years old (Gen. 16:10–16). Some thirteen years later, the Lord appears once more to Abram. He repeats the promise of numerous heirs and a land to possess, but now the promise is connected with a reciprocal act on Abram's part: as a sign of the covenant, he must circumcise all the males of his household, kin and foreigner alike, the newborn on the eighth day. It is on this occasion too that, in an act symbolizing the transformation of their state — it happens often in these three communities — Abram's name is changed to Abraham and Sarai's to Sarah. Abraham is puzzled, however. He and his wife are far beyond parenthood; perhaps it is Ishmael, after all, who will inherit the promise. No, the Lord insists, Ishmael will be the father of a great nation, but it is the son of Abraham and Sarah who will inherit. Abraham has himself, Ishmael, and the other males of his household, kin and slaves, circumcised without further comment (Gen. 17).

The promise will be offered once again by God before it is finally fulfilled in Isaac's birth in chapter 21 of Genesis. Sarah and Hagar are still at odds, however, and it is at Sarah's insistence that Hagar and her son Ishmael are driven out of Abraham's camp near Beersheba to wander in the desert, where the child would surely have died had not God heard Hagar's prayer and caused the miraculous appearance of a well. "God was with the child," the account concludes, "and he grew up and lived in the wilderness of Pharan" (21:20–21).

This is almost the last we hear of Ishmael in the Bible. Ishmael himself marries an Egyptian wife (Gen. 21:20–21), and one of his daughters marries Esau (Gen. 25:13–15), from whom the Edomites — later the Idumeans — of the Negev are descended. In Genesis 25:9 Ishmael is somewhat unaccountably present with Isaac to bury Abraham at Hebron, and there is a list of his sons in Genesis 25:12–18. They dwell somewhere to the east of the Israelites.

ISHMAELITES AND ARABS

Although at his death, at age 137 (Gen. 25:17), Ishmael disappears from the Bible, he remained in the consciousness of the Jews. We cannot follow the full gestation of the story, but we can read its denouement. The source of Genesis may have thought the Edomites of the Negev, one of Israel's inveterate enemies, were the nation descended from Ishmael, but a later generation of Jews thought otherwise. The second-century B.C.E. Book of Jubilees, which is largely a retelling of Genesis from a slightly different perspective, informs us that Abraham before his death summoned all his sons and grandchildren, including Ishmael and his twelve offspring, and bade them to continue to observe circumcision, to avoid ritual uncleanness and marriage with the Canaanites. Then, at the end of the same passage, a crucial identification is made, though almost certainly not for the first time. The sons of Ishmael, and their cousins, the offspring of Abraham and another wife, Keturah, with whom they intermarried, did indeed become a great nation, as God had promised: they were the Arabs. Abraham sends Ishmael and his offspring to settle "between Pharan and the borders of Babylon, in all the land to the East, facing the desert. And these mingled with each other, and they were called Arabs and Ishmaelites" (Jubilees 20:11–13).

Both the name and the identification stuck, first among the Jews and then among the Christians of the Middle East. The Middle Easterners of the pre-Islamic era, the Arabs were either Ishmaelites or Saracens, and even the latter word, whose actual origin is uncertain, was parsed in biblical terms: "Saracen" came from "Sarah" and the Greek *kene*, "empty" or "void," thus "Sara-is-barren." None of this had anything to do with the origins of Islam, however. The identification of the Arabs as Ishmaelites was strictly ethnic — everyone knew the Arabs were polytheists — and it was an ethnic identification based on a similarity of customs. One who was *not*, apparently, aware of the identification was Muhammad. Ishmael appears several times in the Quran, first as a somewhat indistinct Hebrew prophet, and then, in the later chapters, he is identified as Abraham's son. But nowhere is it suggested or even hinted at that Muhammad knew Ishmael was widely recognized elsewhere as the ancestor of the Arabs. Nor is it ever asserted that Islam's claim to be the new version of the True Faith was based on the Arabs' blood descent from Abraham through Ishmael, as the Jews' was by their descent through Isaac and Jacob. Muslims are not, in any event, the "Children of Ishmael."

ABRAHAM AND ISHMAEL IN MECCA

The Quran passes directly from Abraham's conversion to God's command to construct the Kaaba (2:127). There is no mention in the Muslim Scripture of Hagar or Sarah, nor of the Bible's elaborate story of the births of Ishmael and Isaac. It was left for the later Muslim tradition, which had access to a variety of Jewish and Christian information, to spell out the details of how Abraham and Ishmael got from the land of Palestine to Mecca. There was more than one Muslim version of how that occurred, but the chief events were understood as follows: As Isaac, Abraham's son by Sarah, grew up, his mother began to be jealous of her bonds-woman Hagar and the boy Ishmael. She planned to mutilate her rival, and in the end Sarah chose to circumcise her. "Hagar took a piece of cloth to wipe the blood away. For that reason," the historian al-Tabari (d. 923) explained, "women have been circumcised and have taken pieces of cloth (as sanitary napkins) down to to-day." In the biblical account, Sarah forces Abraham to drive Hagar and Ismael into the wilderness. In the Muslim tradition, or at least one version of it, Abraham takes the two by God's command, and with Gabriel's guidance, to Mecca, which explains the quranic verse 14:27, where Abraham says, "My Lord, I have settled some of my posterity in an uncultivable valley near Your Holy House." Then Abraham leaves the two of them there and returns to Palestine, and to the biblical narrative.

At his expulsion from Abraham's household, Ishmael must have been about sixteen old, certainly old enough to assist his father in the construction of the Kaaba, as described in the Quran and implicit from the last line of the preceding. The traditional version of what next occurred is derived from Genesis 21:15–16, transferred from a Palestinian setting to a Meccan one. Mother and child barely survived in the inhospitable environment of Mecca. With her son nearly perishing from thirst, Hagar rushed back and forth between the two hills called Marwa and Safa—the origin of the running between the two hills on the eastern side of the Meccan Haram that became part of the Muslim pilgrimage ritual—until God caused the spring called Zamzam to gush up from the valley floor to save them both. The object of the story is now clearly to provide an "Abrahamic" explanation for some of the landmarks of the Mecca sanctuary and features of the pilgrimage. The helpless Ishmael sounds much younger than sixteen in the tale, and some Muslim versions of the story do in fact make him a nursing infant, which means, of course, that Abraham will have to return on a later occasion to build the Kaaba with a somewhat older Ishmael.

ISRAELITE TALES

The Quran's earliest references to these and other biblical events and personages are allusive in the extreme, though there was an effort in the Medina sections of the Quran to supply further — and more accurate — details on such matters as well as to sharpen their exegetical thrust. If the Quran's brief but pointed biblical references were enough to ground the faith of the first believers, they by no means satisfied the pious curiosity of succeeding generations of Muslims, at least some of whom had been Jews or Christians and so, presumably, had a fuller knowledge of the Bible, and, we may suspect, of the midrashim, the later Jewish explanations, retellings, and expansions of the Bible. Jewish converts in particular served as informants for this body of biblical amplification later known to the Muslims simply as *Israiliyyat*. The word means not "Judaica" or "stories from Jews," whom the Muslims called Yahud, but rather, from their content, "biblical stories" or "Israelite tales." If Abraham and Ishmael built the Meccan Kaaba, for example, as the Quran asserts, how did Ishmael, much less Abraham, find himself in that remote Arabian town? The quite elaborate and, on the face of it, quite plausible answer is provided in the Israelite tales. Driven from the Negev, Hagar took the young — actually infant in this version — Ishmael into Arabia and finally settled at Mecca, where Abraham later sought out and discovered his former concubine and firstborn son. Many more details follow in the tale, though the Quran itself shows no awareness of them. Ishmael grows to manhood at Mecca, marries a local Arab princess, and raises a family. The career of his descendants was not brilliant: they were forced to yield control of Mecca to outsiders and, more, they ignominiously lapsed from the monotheistic faith of their illustrious grandfather into a litholatrous paganism.

If the Israelite tales began innocuously enough as Bible amplifications, once attention began to be directed more to their origins than to their content, the fact that they had been supplied by Jews, albeit converts, bothered some Muslims and the Israiliyyat began to be excluded from serious consideration as history — "It is reported by the Jews; it is prohibited (to be used) . . ." — even though they were never really intended as such. But well before this reaction, the Israelite tales had worked themselves deep into the Muslim view of the prophets who had received and spread God's message in earlier times. Indeed, much of Louis Ginzberg's collection of rabbinic stories on Scripture, *Legends of the Jews*, can be echoed, if not duplicated, directly out of the Muslims' "Tales of the Prophets."

ABRAHAM THE BUILDER

The verse where God recalls his command to Abraham and Ishmael to build the Kaaba in Mecca appears rather abruptly in the Quran. There is no mention of an earlier shrine there, much less that Adam built it. Nor does the Quran offer any explanation of how the patriarch got from Palestine to the distant Mecca. It was not difficult for a later generation of Muslims to figure out what had happened to Adam's original construction. When the Flood came upon the earth, God raised the Kaaba to heaven and hid the holy Black Stone embedded in its side on nearby Mount Abu Qubays. The Quran knows nothing of these stories. Of the Kaaba it says, quite simply (2:125–127):

> Remember We made the House a place of assembly and a place of security. Take you the station of Abraham as a prayer place. And We covenanted with Abraham and Ishmael that they should sanctify My House for those who circumambulate it, or those who are in retreat or those who bow or those who prostrate themselves (there).

> And remember Abraham said: Lord, make this land secure, and sustain its people with fruits, those, at least, among them who believe in God and the Last Day.

And remember Abraham and Ishmael raised the foundations of the House, (saying) "Our Lord, accept this from us."

And again (22:26):

Behold, We gave to Abraham the site of the House; do not associate anything with Me (in worship)! And sanctify My House for those who circumambulate, or those who take their stand there, those who bow or those who prostrate themselves there.

By all the available indices, verses 2:125–127 were pronounced by Muhammad not in the shadow of what is elsewhere referred to as "this sacred House" (5:100) or "this ancient House" (22:29), which we assume to be the Kaaba in Mecca, but in distant Medina, and perhaps even in the last year of his life, when his attention turned more directly back to his native city and particularly to the rituals practiced there. The verses in question are the effective Islamization of the cult practices that had long gone on—from Abraham's day, the Quran asserts—in and around Mecca, its sacred precinct (*haram*), and the cubical building (*kaaba*) that stood in its midst.

What the Muslims were told on divine authority about the ancient cult center at Mecca is summed up in those few verses, and once more it was left to later generations of Muslims to seek out additional information on the shrine's early history. And many of them did. It was said that Gabriel himself pointed out the Kaaba's location and gave directions on its dimensions; and that the Black Stone, the white sapphire that had come from heaven in the Adam stories, had not been destroyed in the Flood but had been hidden within Abu Qubays, a mount rising over the vale of Mecca on the east. Abraham restored it to the Kaaba, though later it turned black because it had been touched by menstruating women during the pagan era that preceded Muhammad's coming.

This, then, is how most later Muslims understood the proximate origin of the Kaaba, whose building was alluded to in the Quran. The patriarch Abraham, on a visit to his son Ishmael in Mecca, put down, on God's command, the foundation of the House on a site already hallowed by Adam.

THE ORIGINS OF THE MECCAN PILGRIMAGE

Abraham's work in Mecca was not complete, however. In Muhammad's day, numerous pilgrimages were being performed in and around Mecca — performed, that is, by a population still immersed in paganism. But the Quran announces that it was not always so. The pilgrimage (*hajj*) was in fact instituted by Abraham, as the Quran tells us (22:27–30), and at God's explicit command.

It is clear from these and similar quranic texts that the original pilgrimage rituals were not so much described to Abraham as alluded to for the benefit of a Meccan audience that was already quite familiar with them. Most of the quranic texts referring to the hajj as a matter of fact have Muhammad and not Abraham as the speaker. It was once again left for later commentators to fill in the details, not of the hajj, to be sure, but of Abraham's and Ishmael's connection with it. The chief authority here is al-Azraqi (d. 858), who was not a quranic commentator but one of the earliest historians of Mecca, and so an expert whose interests were somewhat different from those of exegetes: al-Azraqi is writing history. He describes how Abraham, at God's urging and under Gabriel's direction, performs the first hajj, which is an almost exact replica of what every Muslim has done there from the moment that the Quran and its messenger rescued this ritual from the pagans who were so mindlessly performing it, unaware that they were quite literally following in Abraham's footsteps.

THE BINDING OF ISAAC (OR ISHMAEL)

The famous episode of God's command to Abraham to sacrifice his own son, Abraham's unquestioning obedience, the relaxation of the command, and the Lord's final reward to his obedient servant — "All nations on earth will wish to be blessed as your descendants are blessed because you have been obedient to Me" — are described with dramatic and brilliant economy in Genesis 22:1–18. The binding of Isaac is likewise described in the Quran (37:101–107). In the immediately preceding verses (37:83–100), Abraham is portrayed arguing with his father and his people about their idolatry. When Abraham insults their gods, they say, "Build for him a building and fling him in the red-hot fire. And they designed a trap for them but We made them the undermost." Then, without transition, the text turns to a new topic, Abraham's unnamed son: "We gave him glad tidings of a son. And when he was old enough to work with him, he . . . [presumably Abraham; the Quran is not always generous in identifying its pronouns] said: 'O dear son, I have seen in a dream that I must sacrifice you. So look, what do you think?' He said: 'O my father, do that which you are commanded. God willing, you will find me steadfast.'" And then, "when they had both submitted (*aslama*)," God tells Abraham that it was merely a test, and concludes, "And We ransomed him with a momentous (*azim*) victim."

The entire incident is a good example of the Quran's allusive style. The story is filled with spaces and moves uncertainly to its point — "Thus do We reward the good" — stripping off all the biblical details of time and place, the journey, the servants, the fuel, the altar, the ram caught in the thicket, while adding the dream vision and his son's urging Abraham to do what he had to do. As it stands, the story is comprehensible, but only barely so, and only if we assume that the listeners already had, as we do, some idea of what was being talked about. Two points are worth noting, however. One is that the text does not say which son was being sacrificed, and the earliest Muslim commentators on this quranic passage were uncertain whether it was Isaac, as in the Bible, or Ishmael, as his importance in the Muslim Abraham tradition seemed to require. Second, the Quran, unlike the Bible's account but in agreement with many later Jewish treatments of the subject, makes that son, whether Isaac or Ishmael, both aware and approving of Abraham's willingness to sacrifice him at God's command. His self-sacrifice was voluntary, as it was not in the Genesis text but only in the later Jewish reading of that text.

THE JEWS IN THE QURAN

The Quran betrays a deep ambivalence toward the Jews of history. The Children of Israel were indeed the people whom God chose "in His knowledge" in preference to all the world (44:32; 45:16) and were destined to dwell in the land God gave them (7:137; 10:93; 17:104). But the Israelites were not content with their destiny. They did "mischief on the earth" and they were twice punished by an awful destruction of their temple (17:4–8; which destructions are meant is not clear from the text). But more consequential to the Quran is the Israelites' persistent habit of contention and disputation. The Children of Israel fell out among themselves as soon as "the knowledge" was given them (10:93; 45: 16–17). Indeed, Muhammad's view of contemporary Judaism, even before he went to Medina and had firsthand experience of a Jewish community — and of Jewish rejection — was that it was and remained a religion wracked with schism and sectarianism. God will judge among their factions at the Resurrection, but in the meantime, Muhammad has been sent to the Jews as an arbiter in religious matters. Only the Quran can explain the things on which they continue to disagree (27:76–78; 45:16–18).

For the Muslim, for whom the Quran is the revealed Word of God, the presence of all these stories, motifs, and judgments on the ancient Israelites and the more contemporary Jews present no problem of sources or derivation. But the non-Muslim, who perforce reads the Quran as the work of Muhammad and not of God, knows little of what to make of either Muhammad's information about the Bible and the Jews or of his attitudes toward them. Mecca had no fixed Jewish or Christian population, though members of both groups may have passed through it from Abyssinia across the Red Sea or from the Yemen in the south. There was, then, probably no lack of informants for both Muhammad and the Meccans, since his audience seems to have shared to some degree — how else would his preaching have made sense? — his biblical knowledge. It is the quality of that knowledge that defies exact definition. The shape and tone of the Quran's biblical stories suggest that we are dealing with orally transmitted midrashim rather than direct textual acquaintance. As far as the Bible is concerned, Muhammad may indeed have been retelling "old stories," as his Meccan opponents claimed (6:25; 8:31; 16:24; 23:83), but they owe far more to Genesis Rabbah than to Genesis. Nor is there any evidence that the Prophet was reading the Bible (or anything else, for that matter; he obviously was, as the Muslim tradition insists, an *ummi* [7:157–158], a "scriptural illiterate"). What he got, he heard at Mecca, though we do not know precisely from whom.

Was the midrashic background buzz that provided the Quran's richly textured version of the history of monotheism Jewish or Christian? Both groups shared the same biblical accounts, of course, and given the syncretizing tendencies of religious communities on the margins of culture, as the Jews and Christians of the Hejaz were, there is little to choose between them as sources for the biblical perspectives on view in the Meccan suras of the Quran. But there are clues. The notion that the Jews were highly factionalized, the repeated insistence that Jesus was of the Banu Israil (43:57–59), and Muhammad's own exalted, though hardly mainstream Christian, view that Jesus was both mortal and the prophetic Messiah (3:59; 4:171–172) all suggest that we are dealing in the Meccan environment, and perhaps at Medina as well, with some version of a Judeo-Christian remnant surviving in Arabia in the early seventh century.

JESUS IN THE QURAN

Jesus (Isa ibn Miryam) is often spoken of in the Quran, some thirty-five times in all, though never in an extended or consecutive account, since he was, like the other prophets, being cited merely as an example. The Quran sometimes echoes the canonical Gospel accounts and in other places diverges from them quite remarkably. We are told, for example, that Mary, who is identified as the daughter of Imran — which is also the name of Moses' father and suggests to some, chiefly Christian polemicists, that the Quran has confused the two Marys, the mother of Jesus and the sister of Moses — enjoyed the protection of God. Zachariah, the father of John the Baptist, whom the Quran also regards as a prophet and speaks of at some length, was chosen to be her guardian — Mary's father is called Joachim in the Christian Apocrypha — and she lived in the temple, where God miraculously provided food for her (Quran 3:33–37, 44).

The Gospels' annunciation scene appears twice in the Quran. Once, it is described briefly and to the point (3:42–47). An unnamed angel comes from God and tells Mary that she has been chosen — "God has made you pure and exalted above other women" — to bear the Messiah. She protests: "How can I bear a child when no man has touched me?" None ever will; there is no Joseph in the quranic narratives, though the Quran elsewhere angrily dismisses a Jewish calumny (4:156) that Jesus was illegitimate. The angel replies: "God creates whom He will. When He desires a thing He need only say 'be' and it is." Among the things the angel then predicts of the still unborn Jesus is that he will preach from his cradle, which may be an echo of the Gospels' portrait of the child Jesus teaching in the temple.

The second account is in the sura named "Mary" (19:16–22) and is more circumstantial. God sends to Mary his spirit "in the semblance of a full-grown (or perfect) man" who makes the announcement of her pregnancy. It is not said how this takes place, but the Quran is steadfast in maintaining that Jesus is in no sense the "son of God." Elsewhere, however, it is twice remarked that God "breathed into Mary of His Spirit" (21:91; 66:12). The account of Jesus' birth (Quran 19:22–35) bears little resemblance to that described in the canonical Gospels. Mary retires to a far-off place. When she feels her first labor pains she lies down by a palm tree and cries out in despair. God consoles her and miraculously provides water to drink and dates to eat. Mary is instructed to speak to no one. Her own people accuse her of unchastity, and when she keeps silent the infant Jesus defends her from his cradle (19:26–33), finishing with, "May peace be upon me when I am raised to life."

Jesus' life and teachings are not described in any detail in the Quran, although he too was instructed to pray and give alms to the poor (19:31). The same covenant was made with him and the other prophets (33:7), and of course with Muhammad as well (42:13). It is predicted that Jesus will provide signs for his mission by healing the blind and the leper and make come alive birds he has made from clay — a vivid story that also occurs in the Infancy Gospel of Thomas. When again a sign was demanded of him, God sent down from heaven a table spread with food (5:112–115), an event some Muslims (and non-Muslims) have seen as a reference to the eucharistic Last Supper and others to the miraculous feeding of the multitudes. Jesus will confirm the truth of the Torah and make lawful some of the things forbidden to the Jews (3:50–51; 5:46; 61:6). His message was chiefly that of monotheism, a double of Muhammad's own: worship the One True God and eschew polytheism. Indeed, he predicted the coming of Muhammad: "I am God's messenger to you, . . . announcing the good news of the messenger who will come after me, bearing the name Ahmad" (61:6).

Note: Once Muslims came in contact with Christians, they had to meet the challenge of finding Jesus' prediction of the coming of "Ahmad" (i.e., Muhammad) in the Christians' own Scripture, and in the Jewish as well since Jesus' messianic case was made by reading him out of the Bible. The challenge was sometimes met by finding texts that might serve. Muhammad's first preserved biographer Ibn Ishaq (2. 767) thought that John 15:23 ff., with its promise of a Paraclete — with some vowel changes *parakletos* can become *periklytos*, close enough to the Arabic "Ahmad" to be plausible — filled the bill. Isaiah 21:6–9, the call of the watchman announcing the fall of Babylon to newcomers on "a column of camels," was also occasionally cited from the Bible. The other method was to finesse the entire question by pointing out that the Peoples of the Book had tampered with their Scriptures, including, of course, removing all references to the coming of the prophet Muhammad.

Where the Quran departs most markedly from the canonical Gospel accounts is in its version of Jesus' last days. In 3:54–55 it is said that the unbelievers schemed against Jesus but that God had a better scheme: "I am gathering you up [*or* causing you to die?]," God says, "and causing you to ascend to Me." Elsewhere the Quran declares that God has set a seal on the Jews' disbelief, "so that they believe not, save a few" (4:155). It then continues: "And because of their disbelief and because of their terrible calumny against Mary and because of their saying that they killed the Messiah, Jesus, son of Mary — they did not kill him nor did they crucify him but he was counterfeited for them [*or* it just seemed so to them]. . . . They did not kill him certainly; rather, God raised him to Himself" (4:156–158). But all the Jews will believe in him before his actual death, and on the Day of Judgment he (Jesus) will be a witness against them (4:159).

In the end, then, Jesus is, despite his miraculous birth, a human prophet like God's other messengers (Quran 5:75), who ate earthly food like other men (25:22). He denies that he ever asked anyone to worship him (or his mother) as gods (5:116–117). Christians are wrong in making Jesus God (5:72) and part of a Trinity. He was only a messenger (4:17; 5:72).

CHRISTIANS AND CHRISTIANITY IN THE QURAN

The Quran casts Christians as occasional interlocutors with Muhammad at Medina, but as in the case of almost all the "they say" speakers in the Holy Book, their exact identity and the occasion of their remarks is left unspecified. We do not know of any permanent body of Christians at Medina, nor do the Muslim commentators on the Quran, so both they and we are hard-pressed to supply local, social, or sectarian context for "the Christians" who are referred to in the Quran, whether they were actual Christians who stood before the Prophet as he spoke, or whether "Christians" actually means "Christianity," some general notion of the Christian faith or the Christian community.

Supplying context is a problem for anyone who attempts to understand the Quran, and not least for the classical Muslim commentators who stood far closer to the events than we do. But the chapters in the Quran are not arranged chronologically, and it was as important for medieval Muslims as it is for modern historians to attempt to sort them into the order in which the revelations were pronounced. Then, with some modest assurance that at least the gross distinctions are correct—that these suras were delivered early on, or somewhat later, at Mecca, and these at Medina—we can attempt to put the quranic references to Christians somewhere along the time line of Muhammad's life.

Christians and things Christian—Christian dogma, institutions, and personages—are often referred to in the Quran. The Quran's Christianity is, of course, a construct, but unlike the later Christians' construct of Islam, this one bears for Muslims a divine patent: it is God's construct and so, by definition, undeconstructible. And what is it? Christianity, what is professed by Christians, is, in some very large areas, sheer falsehood. As the Quran explains, Jesus was *not* the son of God, although the Christians think so, and the Trinity does not express divine unity but tritheism, although the Christians deny it. This is theology at loggerheads, and, as has recently been observed, there is probably no more to be said about it.

In one area at least, theology leads back into history. The Quran denies the central Christian dogma of redemption, not explicitly, but implicitly, by its apparent denial of Jesus' death on the cross. It occurs in the already cited difficult passage that occurs in the Medina sura 4 (154–159). It is the Jews who are being referred to:

> For their [the Jews'] not fulfilling their covenant, for their unbelief in the signs of God, for their slaying the prophets unjustly, for their saying "Our hearts are uncircumcised"—nay, God has put a seal upon them for their unbelief, so that they believe not, save a few. And because of their disbelief—and because of their terrible calumny against Mary and because of their saying that they killed the Messiah, Jesus, son of Mary—they did not kill him nor did they crucify him but he was counterfeited for them [*or* it just seemed so to them]. Those who differ in regard to him are in doubt for that reason. They have no knowledge thereof beyond following their own opinion. They did not kill him certainly; rather, God raised him to Himself. God was mighty and wise. There shall not be any of the People of the Book but shall believe in him before his death.

Overwhelmingly the medieval Muslim commentators read these lines as a denial not merely of Jesus' crucifixion by the Jews, but of his very death. According to their understanding, what the Quran meant to say is that Jesus will die only on his second, eschatological coming. The classic commentator al-Tabari, for example, sums up the sources available to him as follows: Jesus will be sent down to earth and will kill the Antichrist. He will remain here for some time, though its duration is a matter of dispute. Finally, however, he will die a mortal death and will be buried by the Muslims next to Muhammad at Medina. This version of Jesus' past and future clearly contradicts the New Testament accounts, but the matter is of little concern to medieval exegetes, who thought the Christian versions were corrupt. Early in the twentieth century, however, another reading of these and parallel verses begins to be put forward by some Muslims: Jesus was not crucified by the Jews but rather he died a natural death at about the same time as the supposed crucifixion. His ascension, God's "raising up" of him referred to in 3:55, is perhaps to be understood metaphorically.

So the Quran on *matters* Christian, but what of the Christians themselves — the community called *Nasara* in the Quran, the add-on to "Jesus and those who followed him," or those concealed under the rubric Peoples of the Book? There is, to put it simply, both praise and blame for Christians in the Quran. Consider, for example, the famous verse 82 from sura 5:

> You will find the most vehement of mankind in hostility to the believers to be the Jews and the idolaters. And you will find the nearest to them [that is, to the believers] in affection those who say "Behold, we are Christians." That is because there are among them priests and monks, and because they are not proud.

The celebrated commentator Zamakhshari (d. 1144), after citing a Prophetic saying to the effect that "if a Muslim is alone with two Jews, they will try to kill him," glosses the second part of the text just cited by explaining that the Christians are both humble and men of learning, just the opposite of the Jews. "Here is a clear example," Zamakhshari goes on, "showing that the struggle for knowledge is very useful, leading first to good and then to success, even among the (Christian) priests. The same is true about concern for the hereafter . . . possibly another characteristic of the monk, just like humility, even though it is a Christian who is involved here."

Sura 5 continues in verse 83:

> And when they [that is, the Christians] listen to what has been re-
> vealed to the Messenger, you see their eyes overflow with tears be-
> cause of their recognition of the Truth. They say, "O Lord, we be-
> lieve. Inscribe us among the witnesses."

There are other such benign passages, but there is criticism of the Christians too, fairly extensive and some of it quite pointed. The Christians' assertion of the reality of the Incarnation or the Trinity is tantamount to disbelief (*kufr*) (5:75–76), and their unique claim to salvation is vanity (2:111). Finally, the Muslim is advised: "Do not take the Jews and the Christians as your friends and protec-tors. They are but friends and protectors to each other. And who-ever among you turns to them is one of them. In truth, God does not give guidance to an unjust people" (5:54).

The Quran, then, is apparently of two minds about Christians, and even about Jews. How are we to understand these differing views? Non-Muslim scholarship favors an evolutionary solution. The verses favorable to or in praise of the People of the Book are generally early ones: they date from a period when Muhammad was still feeling his way, still expecting, perhaps, an acceptance on their part of his mission and his message. With his more intimate exposure first to the Jews, and then, later, to the Christians, his favor changed to the harsher and more critical attitude exemplified in the Medina revelations. The Quran's final word on the subject, for example, is very likely this pragmatic and hardheaded pro-nouncement in sura 9:29, when Muslim arms had spread across the peninsula and encountered Jewish and Christian oasis commu-nities and tribes, some of whom resisted Islamic sovereignty: "Fight against those who do not believe in God or in the Last Day, . . . (even) among those who have been given the Book, until they pay the poll-tax from their hand and are humiliated.

Like Jews and Christians, Muslims are committed to the total and simultaneous truth of Scripture; thus their exegetes tend to be harmonizers no less than their traditional Jewish and Christian counterparts. So they not unexpectedly addressed the apparently discordant quranic views about Christians with the distinction just noted, a distinction suggested by the Quran itself, first in 2:62 — since the Muslim commentators always addressed the Quran verse by verse in the received order of the text rather than in the chronological order of the revelations, this would be the first mention of the Christians they would encounter, albeit in a Medina sura. There were, in fact, two types of Christians: the true followers of Jesus, the few "balanced people" who are praised and accounted among the believers, and the rest of the Christians, those who tampered with Scripture and willfully misunderstood Jesus' message, who are the object of the Quran's frequent and forceful denunciations. Contrary to what the non-Muslims assert, Muhammad did not change his mind in the course of his revelations — a theological impossibility, in any event — nor did God abrogate the praise verses by later condemnatory ones. The Quran is talking about two distinct groups of Christians (2:137).

What the Quran says is fixed in the memory of Muslims, but what the Quran really means is perhaps known only to God. Over the centuries, an enormous amount of energy has been poured into the task of elucidating the Quran, verse by verse, including all the ones that have been cited here on the subject of Christians and Christianity. The Quran had its own notion of Christianity, and Christians, but in the dense pages of the Muslim commentators, medieval and modern, the construct of the other faith called "Christianity" — the one used by both early and late Muslim polemicists and latter-day Muslim "dialoguers" — was continuously assembled and reassembled.

2. *The Past Remembered*

ALTHOUGH if many of the figures mentioned by name in the Quran are familiar from the Bible, the rhythms of the Recitation are not biblical, even across translation: the style of the Quran is that of neither the Old nor the New Testament. And it is not merely the voices and rhythms that differ: the structure, the *mise-en-scène* in which these familiar figures now appear, is different from their earlier presentations in the Scriptures of the Jews and the Christians. We are hearing something else in the Quran, a second, somewhat foreign accent we can discern, only after close inspection, as coming from the time and place the Recitation was first recited, in seventh-century Arabia, in a place called Mecca, from the lips of a man called Muhammad.

There appear to be, then, two levels of sensibility in the Quran. One of these has already been identified as "biblical," and it is chiefly characterized by its content and assumptions. The other is discernible, to be sure, but it is much more difficult to define; we can call it for the moment "Arabian." It is reflected in the work's expressive style, in many of the Quran's social, economic, and political concerns, and finally in another, not terribly well articulated belief system that lies next to the biblical and is either repudiated or reformed. Where the biblical sensibility came from is an open question, but it is natural to think that the Quran's Arabian quality is the product of the society in which Muhammad lived.

The Muslim would strenuously deny that these two elements present in the Quran, the biblical and the Arabian, have anything to do with the work's authorship. God is the sole author of the Recitation, not Muhammad, who merely repeated, or "recited," what he had been told, and God is not conditioned by the environmental circumstances that work on human authors. The issue may be allowed to pass — the answer to the question "Who composed the Quran, God or Muhammad?" is precisely the difference between Muslims and non-Muslims — since it can be addressed in other, less divisive terms. Even if the text of a divinely revealed Quran should not suffer from the constraints of history, its audience, the frequent "they" and "you all" of the Quran, certainly did. "They" heard and "they" understood, even if they did not all believe; even if they thought Muhammad was making it up or had lifted if from someone else, the Meccans and later the Medinese "got" this "clear Arabic Quran," perhaps better than a later generation of Muslims who had to labor over the text and certainly more perfectly than we who are so distant from them not only in faith but in culture.

If we are to attempt to understand this founding document of Islam unaided by faith, we must try to grasp in some fashion the two fields of religious sensibility within which the Quran's original audience operated. This is no easy task. Ernest Renan, the nineteenth-century former Catholic seminarian, Jesus quester, skeptic, and *orientaliste extraordinaire*, when he grew discouraged about discovering anything verifiable about the historical Jesus, thought that the odds might be better in the case of Muhammad, who was, after all, born "in the full light of history." He was grievously mistaken. We know a great deal more about first-century Galilee and Judaea than we do about Mecca and its inhabitants in the seventh century. We know who Jesus was talking to; we even know about some other messiahs of that time and place. We have good information on the Herods and even better information on the Romans because we have the contemporary Josephus, not the noblest of souls perhaps, but a decent historian and a very detailed one. We have archaeology, and we have the Dead Sea Scrolls, sectarian and very authentic. Behind Jesus there unfolds an extraordinarily rich tapestry of information that tells us what it was to be a Jew in Judaea or Galilee in the first century of the common era. It doesn't answer all the questions about Jesus, but it certainly puts that elusive messiah in context.

Behind the Quran there is nothing. It rises without warning like a mysterious continent from an Arabian sea. There is no Josephus to give us our bearings, no Scrolls, no archaeology. For this Book's setting we must turn elsewhere, and the prospect does not excite optimism. The northern and southern regions of western Arabia, that is, the Syro-Palestinian frontier in the north and the Yemen to the south, have preserved archaeological and even literary traces of their pre-Islamic religious past; the physical remains of shrines, inscriptions, the interested observations of Greco-Roman authors, the information collected by church historians or remembered by Christian missionaries, and the experiences of holy men who fecklessly wandered the frontiers of the Bedouin lands all help construct at least an outline of the forms, modes, and vagaries of pre-Islamic worship and belief in those regions. For the central stretch of western Arabia, however — the Red Sea's Arabian coastal areas and their steppe and mountain uplands between Madain Salih in the north and Najran in the south — the very birthplace of Islam, no such resources are available.

What the Arabs Thought, Remembered, or Imagined

This was the nomads' terrain, remote, rocky, and inhospitable, supporting a meager settled population in a few scattered oases like Yathrib — later Medina — and Khaibar, an occasional stretch of fertile garden land like the Wadi Fatima or Taif, and, of course, the shrine settlement of Mecca set down uncertainly in its parched arroyo. Oasis dwellers and Bedouin alike were illiterate — or nearly so. Various Arab peoples have left their scrawled traces throughout almost all of western Arabia from about 500 B.C.E. well into the Roman era. But none of these graffiti, which all date from Mecca's remote past, is in the language of Muhammad and the Quran, and the Hejaz was just beyond the eager reach of both

Greco-Roman imperialist-entrepreneurs and the equally literate and historically minded Christian missionaries. No contemporary was informed or interested enough to write a history of Muhammad's hometown or even to make note of its existence.

The remembered past of this region of pre-Islamic Arabia is preserved only in local oral traditions that, even after the coming of Islam, still recollected and savored the old genealogies, the tribesmen's poetry of love and war, and even, it would appear, some dim memories of other gods worshiped in the times the Muslims called "the age of barbarism" (*al-jahiliyya*). The later biographers of the Prophet and historians of Mecca drew upon these memories to piece together Arabia's history as Muhammad doubtless understood it, but as the Quran never spells out: how the Holy House and the town of the biblical patriarch and his son passed into the hands of this or that Arab tribe and finally into those of the Quraysh, Muhammad's own ancestors; and how that passage of power was accompanied by a lapse into polytheism and idol worship. That was the gist of the great historical triptych composed by Ibn Ishaq (d. 767) more than a century after Muhammad's death in 632. The work is lost, but it was later pared down to a simple biography of the Prophet that is available to us in the version of Ibn Hisham (d. 833), and it was later used with profit in its unabridged form by the historian al-Tabari (d. 923) and others. This is one strain of tradition, the political-historical one. The other is the repertory of information collected and topically arranged by Hisham ibn al-Kalbi (d. 819) in his sacred anthropology called *The Book of Idols*, the most substantial treatment we possess of the religious practices of pre-Islamic Arabia.

Finally, there is whatever we can glean from the Quran, which polemicizes against the still flourishing paganism of Muhammad's day and at the same time incorporates some aspects of Meccan ritual — notably the hajj, or pilgrimage — into the emerging picture of Islam. One can also always attempt to work back to pre-Islamic origins from the Quran's religious vocabulary, an undisputed reflection of the religious life of western Arabia, which was, on the evidence of the Quran's loanwords from the lexica of the Aramaic Syrians of the Fertile Crescent and the Ethiopians across the Red

Sea, already aglow with the spiritual goods of Middle Eastern monotheism.

This, then, is the evidence before us: what the Arabs, now all Muslims, thought, remembered, or imagined about the Mecca into which Muhammad was born and out of which the Quran emerged, this latter not as effect from cause but as a convinced monotheistic interlocutor in dialogue with a pagan milieu the Quran often echoes but whose own voices are no longer available. The Quran's remembered past may be biblical in the already explained sense of that word, but the Muslim Scripture was in the first instance addressed to the obdurate pagans of Muhammad's Mecca.

MECCA BEFORE THE PROPHET

Mecca, the town that no one had heard of, stands midway down the western side of the Arabian Peninsula, between the Jordanian border on the north and that of Yemen on the south, forty-five miles inland from its Red Sea port of Jidda. If it was unknown or ignored by contemporaries, later Muslim authors professed to know a great deal about the history of the place where the Prophet was born. They focused their attention on three areas. First was on what might be called institutional Mecca, where the reports in question describe the various municipal offices — far more than the size of the place would seem to require — whereby Mecca was governed. The offices were "municipal" only by courtesy, however, since they were chiefly connected with the supervision of Mecca's shrine complex rather than with the town as a whole. The exception was the *dar al-nadwa*, a kind of *hotel de ville* of pre-Islamic Mecca where events both political and ceremonial took place, including the meetings of the "council" of magnates who ran the town. How they actually governed the settlement, we have very little idea. More, for all their emphasis in the chroniclers, these alleged organs of government are nearly invisible in the biographies of Muhammad, where running the city occurs through informal gatherings of Mecca's most powerful clans. There can be no doubt, however, that the various rights and privileges connected with the shrine — its wardenship and the control of food and drink for pilgrims — are authentic and ancient; many of them persisted as coveted emoluments into Islamic times, which would explain their prominent place in the later historians.

More ubiquitous in our sources, though preserved in a far more diffuse and discursive fashion, are observations about the social (and deeply political) relationships that underlay the town's organization. "Town" may be somewhat overgenerous: Mecca was a tiny, haphazard collection of mud-brick dwellings around a water hole. It was, for all that, a permanent settlement and not a nomadic camp, yet it was tribal in its outlook and its manner of conducting its affairs. The tribal Quraysh were the masters of the place, but they suffered their own internal divisions from the outset, divisions that escalated into continuous power (or perhaps class) struggles between the principal clans of the Quraysh and came to a head in the formation of powerful though shifting alliances among them.

Finally, though organized as a tribal society, Mecca was also socially open. The rulers of Mecca welcomed individuals and small groups of immigrants from among its tribal neighbors. There were tribal outsiders as well, merchants and mercenaries, at least some of whom were Jews and Christians. Some among the population of Mecca appear to have been Abyssinians from across the Red Sea, Christians most likely, and they were possibly part of a merchant colony, or perhaps even a mercenary contingent that served as the Quraysh's military arm.

THE HOLY PLACE

Mecca the haram, the holy place, appears to antedate Mecca the city. The later Muslim authorities credit the latter to Qusayy, who, if he is a historical personage, must be dated in the late fourth or early fifth century of the common era. That there was a shrine before a settlement in that inhospitable valley we assume simply from the circumstances of the place: Mecca possessed none of the normal inducements to settlement, none, certainly, that would give the place a history, and even a long tradition of contested possession. A holy place, in contrast, requires little beyond the sanctity of the site, a sanctity connected with a spring, a tree, or a mountain. Only its sanctity, however obscure the origins of that holiness, explains the existence of Mecca, and only a shrine yoked to other considerations, social, economic, or political, explains the eventual presence of a city there.

It was the Zamzam, then, or perhaps the two high places called Safa and Marwa, that established Mecca's sanctity, although when that occurred we cannot say. Muslim sources trace the sanctity of the Meccan Haram exclusively to the Kaaba, the edifice built at God's express command by Abraham and Ishmael. In the face of this unyielding unanimity in the literary sources, there are two alternative ways of approaching the shrine at Mecca. One is to use evidence of ancient Semitic cult centers that seem similar to the arrangement in Mecca; the other is to examine more contemporary evidence in the expectation that some of the older practices have survived the advent of Islam. What we know of early practice is chiefly from literary sources like Ibn al-Kalbi. Archaeological evidence is sparse indeed, particularly from Arabia, where excavation is still in its very early stage, and what sparse results there are have been speculative in the extreme. Given the quality of the material evidence, we are left, then, at least for the time being, with the Muslim literary authorities. More promising than archaeology, however, are other examples of the shrine phenomenon, some from ancient sources and some reflecting more contemporary practice in Arabia, which can be used to understand and interpret the often random information supplied by the early Muslim authors.

Whenever or however it began, religion was unmistakably the business of Muhammad's Mecca, in the sense that without its shrine the prospects of what was a notoriously ill favored settlement (see Quran 14:37) would have been exiguous indeed. But with its ecumenical shrine — all gods were welcome in the Meccan Haram — the settlement served as a religious and commercial magnet. When the later Muslim sources speak of Mecca, they conjure up a vision of that seventh-century settlement as a thriving mercantile center that controlled a lucrative international trade in luxury goods flowing from east Asia to Roman consumers around the Mediterranean. There is not much evidence that this was the case, or even that such trade existed in that era, much less that the mud-brick-housed traders in Mecca either controlled or even profited from it. The nearer reality is that the Meccans used the annual truce-protected pilgrimage to do some trading with the Bedouin. The Quraysh seem to have enlisted the latter to supply transport and protection for a local trade network, perhaps in raisins and leather, that the Quraysh were building in the Hejaz. But also likely is that this Haram-generated commerce, however modest it may have been, determined Mecca's social and political evolution. The evidence for that is chiefly from later Muslim sources, but the Quran too seems to support such a construct. Its unmistakable commercial terminology showed a familiarity with trade; the condemnation of usury and of the "heaping up of gold and silver" seems addressed to a greedy mercantilism (9:34); and finally, one sura of the Quran seems actually to describe that mercantilism (2:275–276).

THE KAABA

In the midst of Mecca rises an unusual building called simply *al-Kaaba*, or "the Cube." The flat-roofed building sits on a narrow marble base on mortared courses of a blue-gray local stone, and its dimensions are not exactly cubical: it is fifty feet high, and although its northeast wall—the corners rather than the walls are oriented toward the compass points—and its southwest mate are forty feet long, the two "side" walls are five feet shorter. The northeastern face is a facade only in that it holds the one building's door, about seven feet above ground level. Inside there is an empty room, with a marble floor, and three wooden pillars supporting the roof. There are some inscriptions on the walls, hanging votive lamps, and a ladder leading up to the roof. Built into the eastern corner of the Kaaba, about four feet above the ground, is a black-ish stone of either lava or basalt, which is fractured and now held

together by a silver band. The building is draped with a black bro-
cade cloth embroidered in gold with quranic texts; the bottom
edge can be raised or lowered by a series of cords and rings.

The Kaaba stands in the midst of an open space enclosed by
porticoes. This is the Haram, the "sanctuary," and there are some
other constructions in it. Facing the northeastern facade wall of
the Kaaba is a small domed building called the Station of Abraham, a title that applies equally to another stone it enshrines and in
which human footprints are impressed. Behind this building is a
colonnaded wellhead called Zamzam and next to that a pulpit.

For hundreds of millions of Muslims the Kaaba is the holiest
building in the world, and its holiness — like that of the Zamzam
and the Station, and, indeed, of the entire sequence of pilgrimage
rituals that surround them and the environs of Mecca — derives, as
we have already seen, from their connection with Abraham, the
biblical patriarch. But it is the shrine in Muhammad's day that
interests us here, before its conversion, or, as Muslims would contend, its reconversion, to Islam.

Not much history can be concluded from the present Kaaba in
Mecca, which substantially dates from a ground-up rebuilding in
1629. But from the many literary descriptions we possess, the sev-
enteenth-century reconstruction seems to have differed little from
the building that stood there all through the medieval era and back
to the late seventh century. In 683 C.E., however, the Kaaba had
been rebuilt on ideological grounds. The rebel Ibn al-Zubayr (d.
692), who then held Mecca against the reigning caliph in Damascus, reconstructed it, we are informed, as it was in Abraham's day.
The original building was joined to the shoulder-high semicircular
wall, the *hijr*, at the northwest face — how or to what purpose we
are not told, though there is plentiful evidence that this, and the
space between it and the Kaaba, was a taboo area. Hagar and
Ishmael were purported to have been buried there and there too
Muhammad was sleeping when he was carried off on his famous
"Night Journey" (see chapter 3). The Kaaba had two ground-level
doors, "one toward the east for people to enter and one toward
the west for people to exit." This tradition goes back to Muhammad, on the authority of his wife Aisha. The Prophet was recalling

the rebuilding of the Kaaba in his own day, sometime about 605 C.E., a project in which he cooperated but did not approve, since it distorted Abraham's original building. The reason the Quraysh closed one door and lifted the other well above ground level was, according to the same tradition from Muhammad, "to make sure that no one but whom they [that is, the Quraysh] wished would enter it." The clear implication was that the Kaaba was intended to be open to all but that access was, in Muhammad's time, controlled, not by any notions of purity or holiness, but by the will of the Quraysh, who had "guardianship" of the building.

THE RITUALS OF THE KAABA

In most ancient temples, and the Kaaba seems to be just that, in obvious contrast to later synagogues, churches, and mosques, whatever ritual was required was practiced outside the building, generally in the form of sacrifice on an altar. The inner parts of the building might be entered, but since they were regarded as the domicile of the god, entry was denied to the profane, those who stood "before the shrine." Indeed, at that other Semitic temple in Jerusalem, access to the cube-shaped Holy of Holies was severely limited to the high priest, and then under strictly controlled circumstances. Although it is true that the primary liturgy connected with the Mecca building, the ritual circumambulation, was performed outside, there is almost no trace, either before or under Islam, of the notion that the interior of the Kaaba was in any way more sacred than the surrounding Haram. Indeed, the most primitive cult traditions associated with the building have the Meccans and their pilgrim guests behaving much like the perfidious biblical Ephraimites who "mumbled their prayers" and kissed their calf-idols, as other idolaters kissed the image of Baal (Hos. 13:2; 1 Kings 19:18). Before Islam, and even after, the devotees at Mecca were not kept away from the Kaaba, as the Israelites were from Sinai or the inner temple precincts; rather they attempted to establish as close contact as possible. They clung to the building's drapes pressed themselves against its walls, and touched and kissed the Black Stone embedded in one of its corners. The Israelites feared impurity by contagion; the pre-Islamic Arabs of Mecca, like many others, early and late, were more interested in the contagion of holiness.

Access to the interior was controlled, as it is today, but exclusively, it would appear, on the grounds of political privilege. People, including Muhammad himself, prayed both inside and outside the Kaaba, and visited it whenever the privilege was granted to them. There was, then, nothing taboo about "Allah's House" in Mecca. Even after Muhammad had effected his "high god" revolution there, and created an analogy whereby the Kaaba should have exactly corresponded to the Holy of Holies in temple Jerusalem—an analogy strongly urged by Muhammad's changing his direction of prayer from Jerusalem to the Meccan Kaaba during his early days at Medina—the old rituals continued to be followed. Muhammad's close associate, and the second caliph of Islam, Umar, apparently had a more perfectly formed Muslim conscience than Muhammad himself when he remarked, in what Muslims affirm as an authentic tradition, "If I had not seen the Prophet kissing it [that is, the Black Stone], I would never have kissed it again." The Islamic revolution was one of concept, not of cult.

THE MECCAN HARAM

Mecca was not simply the Kaaba. There were, and are, three religiously defined and connected areas in Mecca and its environs. First is the just noted Bayt Allah, the *templum Domini*, that still stands at the center of the modern city. The second is the area immediately surrounding the shrine building. This was not properly a *temenos* or sacred enclosure in that in early times it was not defined in any sense other than as an open space: the walls of the surrounding dwellings provided its only definition. Under Islamic auspices it was enlarged and eventually enclosed by a columned and gated arcade, which effectively converted it from an open into an enclosed and constructed space, and today, a monumentally and massively constructed space. Finally, there is the larger district of Mecca. In this instance there were markers, sacred stones that, like the Greek *hermes*, were both boundary signs and objects of veneration; from very early times they defined the sacred territory of Mecca.

There are indications that the entire territory of Mecca constituted a haram, the "secure sanctuary" of the Quran (28:57). The sacred stones at its limits have already been remarked; and within it no trees or shrubs were to be cut down, no wild animals hunted, no blood spilled in violence. Indeed, no profane soil should be mixed with that of the haram. As for access, the city-territory of Mecca, which today is marked by large signs in Arabic and English on the Saudi thruways banning entry to all non-Muslims, shows no evidence of having been so restricted in late paganism or early Islam.

MECCAN PAGANISM

The Muslim Arab authorities were not at all certain who was first or chiefly responsible for turning Ishmael's holy place into a pagan city. More, their version of the degradation of the Meccan cultus has to do primarily with the cult of idols, though we are assured by somewhat wider evidence that who was being worshiped in Arabia, how, and why, were much broader questions than our eighth- and ninth century sources were willing to allow. The inhabitants of Arabia assuredly had a religious tradition before Islam, and although we are not particularly well informed about it, it appears to have been quite complex, as we would expect to discover in societies that were splintered into tribes and clans of widely varying sizes, some sedentary and some nomadic, with a number of the latter ranging seasonally over enormously broad terrains.

The inhabitants of the Hejaz worshiped the way they lived: the small settled population visited fixed shrines in oases, whereas the Bedouin carried their gods with them. The objects worshiped were principally stones, trees, and heavenly bodies, or rather, the gods thought to reside in them, or possibly — and here we begin to enter a world we do not fully understand — represented by them. Reasonably clear is that in the more recent Arabian past sacred stones were increasingly being shaped into human likenesses, rough or fine, perhaps, it has been surmised, because of the extension of Hellenistic styles into the peninsula.

However the devotees thought of it, Arabian cultus was highly volatile, the deities often sharing characteristics, being harmonized into families, or passing now into the possession of this tribe and now of that. There is a distinctly tribal notion to the Arabs' worship of the gods. On the basis of the South Arabian evidence, with which the more meager Arab tradition concurs, each tribe or tribal confederation had a divine patron whose cult gave the group a focus for its solidarity. In a practice that points directly to what was occurring at Mecca, each of these "federal deities" was the "lord" of a shrine that served as the federation's cult center.

The Bedouin, who normally lived on the grazing steppe in well-established (though at times contested) transhumance zones, came into the towns to worship at the fixed shrines of the gods there. The incentive may have been principally commercial—fairs are a consistent feature of such urban shrines—and there was undoubt-edly conscious policy at work. The movement of the effigy of a popular god into a town shrine meant that its worshipers would eventually follow—cult followed cult objects—if certain condi-tions could be guaranteed. The chief of those was security. Like highly territorial animals, Bedouin were ill at ease in very close quarters. A vividly remembered network of tribal vendettas and blood feuds incurred from collisions on the steppe made any tribal encounter potentially dangerous. The solution was the usual one of the "truce of God," sacred months when hands and weapons were restrained by divine injunction. Under such security tribes came together, worshiped and traded, and then returned to their other, more routine ways. Sacred shrine, sacred truce, worship, and trade is a combination with a venerable history. Small wonder since it worked to everyone's advantage, and not least to that of the guardians of the shrine, the Quraysh at Mecca, for example.

We can approach the religious beliefs and practices of Muham-mad's Mecca only through a series of approximations that con-verge on, but do not yet adequately describe, the exact religious

milieu of the Prophet. We can work backward, as has been remarked, through the Quran's own portrait of pre-Islamic religion
at Mecca, or we can come at it laterally, by analyzing what we
know of the religious life of the Bedouin or the South Arabians,
though the milieus that produced them are by no means identical
with Muhammad's own by reason of being "Arabian." The religious beliefs and practices of the nomadic Bedouin are not likely to
be the same as those of the sedentary and agricultural societies in
South Arabia, and neither group promises to tell us exactly what
we might wish to know about the gods and cult at Mecca, which
was neither a Bedouin society nor yet an agricultural one.

The principal ethical ideal of the Bedouin, who were notorious
among later observers for the lightness with which religion sat on
them, was not in fact religious at all, but was rather constituted of
"virility" or "manliness." It was almost inevitable that it should
appear so: the chief source for this analysis is the body of pre-
Islamic poetry whose rigid, highly stereotyped and relentlessly "literary" sensibility does not much encourage us to consider it a
broad tapestry of the Bedouin culture. The poetry only rarely
touches on religious themes, and although it is possible to recon-
struct a moral and social value system from the poems, that system
is almost never grounded in religious beliefs and practices.

THE QURANIC EVIDENCE

The Quran is our most certain testimony to the religious life in
Mecca before the appearance of Islam since at least in the beginning of his career Muhammad's concern was not, as it was later in
Medina, with regulating the life of a community of believers but
rather with reforming the beliefs and practices of his fellow Meccans. "Reforming" is a more appropriate term than "converting"
since the Quran also reveals, as we have seen, that the worship of
Allah was already well established there before Muhammad. At
question, then, was not simply belief in or worship of Allah, which
the Quraysh certainly did, but the Meccans' "association," as the
Quran calls it, of other deities with Allah — an issue that seemed to

accept the existence of other gods in the "exalted assembly," while at the same time denying that they had any autonomous power, though perhaps they could help humans if God so willed.

If we turn from the Muslims' much later impressions of pre-Islamic Mecca to the contemporary, though far more oblique, evidence of the Quran, we can get an impressionistic overview of how the gods of pagan Mecca were worshiped in the days before Islam. The chief liturgy was doubtless sacrifice, of both animals and cereals, and the rites — a common one was divination — were performed not in but outside the Kaaba and several other places in the vicinity, notably at Zamzam. Pilgrimage to Mecca by the surrounding tribes was a popular — and seasonal — practice, and included ritual processions or circumambulation (*tawaf*) around the Kaaba and a similar rite between the two hills of Safa and Marwa just next to the Kaaba sanctuary. The rite called the hajj took place at sites outside Mecca. There was sacrifice at a place called Mina and "standings" and "runnings" at Muzdalifa and Arafat, the latter a high place eleven miles from Mecca. These are only fragments of ritual; the larger religious contexts in which they originally occurred have been removed or forgotten, and in their place we have transparently artificial connections with Abraham and Ishmael. What is most curious, however, is that these exurban rites had little or nothing to do with Mecca or the Quraysh and yet became the centerpiece of Muslim ritual, whereas the Quraysh-directed and Mecca-centered festival called the *umra* was relegated to the status of the "lesser pilgrimage," which might or might not be made at the pilgrim's pleasure.

Many of the pilgrimages of pre-Islamic Arabia had fairs attached to them. There does not appear to have been such connected with Mecca, however. The close confines of the town may have been too dangerous for the hostilely jostling nomads since all the fair sites associated with the hajj were deserted places where the Bedouin could camp at a safe distance from one another. It is somewhere in this complex of not always coherent evidence that we must locate the prosperity of the Quraysh, as verse 4 of sura 106 invites us to think, and possibly their later opposition to Muhammad's preaching.

There was prayer in the pagan era, but it is characterized in the Quran as "whistling and clapping of hands" (8:35). One form of prayer has been preserved. When Muslim pilgrims approached the sanctuary on pilgrimage, they cried out again and again a formulaic salutation beginning "We are here, O Allah, we are here." This is the so-called *talbiya*, which, like most else connected with the pilgrimage, antedated Islam and survived into it.

Allah was worshiped at Mecca before Islam, as the Quran, which calls him "the Lord of this house" (i.e., the Kaba) makes clear (106:3). So too was a male deity named Hubal, whose idol in human form — Allah had no idol — seems to have been placed inside the Kaaba. The Quran curiously makes no mention of Hubal, but it does speak of three other deities of the many worshiped at Mecca in pre-Islamic days: Manat, al-Uzza, and al-Lat, called collectively by the Quraysh the "daughters of Allah." We do not know their stories since one of the characteristics of Arab paganism as it has come down to us is the absence of a mythology, narratives that might serve to explain the origin or history of the gods. These Meccan deities were manifestly cult objects and we have only the cult descriptions, and an occasional appellative, to instruct us about them. Thus we have no idea why the Quraysh should have assigned them their filial roles, save perhaps simply to introduce some order into the large and somewhat chaotic Meccan pantheon. Nothing we know suggests that Allah was otherwise thought to have had daughters, or that the three goddesses possessed any family relationship. They often swapped characteristics and shared shrines, but Manat, al-Uzza, and al-Lat were quite discrete divinities, and the best examples, by all accounts, of the personified worship of heavenly bodies.

Muhammad no more invented Allah than he did al-Lat, al-Uzza, and Manat. The cult of the deity termed simply "the god" (*al-ilah*) was known throughout southern Syria and northern Arabia, and was obviously of central importance in Mecca, where the building called the Kaaba was indisputably his house. Indeed, the Muslim profession of faith, "There is no god (*ilah*) but The God (*al-ilah*)," attests to precisely that point: the Quraysh are being called on to repudiate the very existence of all other gods save this one. It seems equally certain that Allah was not merely a god in Mecca but was widely regarded as the "high god," the chief and head of the Meccan pantheon, whether this was the result, as has been argued, of a natural progression toward henotheism or of the growing influence of Jews and Christians in the peninsula. The most convincing evidence that it was the latter at work is the fact that of all the gods of Mecca, Allah alone was not represented by an idol.

THE CULT PRACTICES OF THE ARABS

If the myths, and, to use a wildly anachronistic word, the theology behind the worship of these Arabian gods and goddesses have disappeared, we are left with many details about the rituals practiced by the pre-Islamic Arabs of Mecca and its environs. Like their Semitic and Arab fellows elsewhere in the Near East, the Arabs of the Hejaz used sacrifice as a primary way of forging and maintaining a relationship with the realm of the divine. "To every people," the Quran says, "did We appoint rites of sacrifice that they might celebrate the name of God over the sustenance He gave them from animals" (22:34). Then follow (22:36) more precise directions on the benediction and the consuming of the animal sacrifice, again reflecting on what seems to have been the current practice.

Though the sacrifice of animals, the staple of the Jewish temple cult in Jerusalem, was banished from the Haram in Islamic times, it continued to be practiced at Mina during the hajj; indeed, it was and is an essential part of fulfilling the pilgrimage obligation. Each devotee offered his own victim, and whereas animals sacrificed in the desert in pre-Islamic times might sometimes simply be left behind, as they often were at Mina during the hajj, if the sacrifice took place in town, the animal was usually cooked and eaten as part of a common meal—a practice that created problems for the first Muslims as it had earlier for Christians. But this was only one form of sacrifice known to the pre-Islamic Arabs. The later Muslim authorities tell us of animals simply dedicated to the gods and kept within their sacred precincts without being sacrificed, and the

Quran seems to refer to the practice of such animal offerings in 5:106, as part of a repertoire of pagan ritual practices.

Among the things forbidden to the believer by the Quran is "that which has been sacrificed upon a stone" (5:4). Such sacrificial stones are described as "abominations," and the "work of Satan" (5:93). These are familiar objects indeed, already known from the story of Jacob's stone pillar in Genesis (35:14). Stones on which one poured out the blood of animal sacrifice were widely used among the ancient Arabs, not only as here in the vicinity of the Kaaba, but even as tombstones and boundary markers for sacred enclosures. After the coming of Islam their use constituted a form of idolatry, and the believer might not share in the food sacrificed thereon.

Besides animal sacrifice, grain and milk were offered to the gods, as well as the captured arms of enemies, and precious objects like the golden gazelles kept in the treasure pit of the Kaaba. Such pits or hollow places were generally near altars, and sacrificial blood or other offerings were collected in them. As often seems to have occurred in such circumstances, the pit and the altar stone began to participate in the same sacred quality as the sacrifice itself, a characteristic they then shared with, or borrowed from, the god who was the object of the cultus.

There is little or no reference to the practice of formal liturgical prayer in Meccan paganism, not in its later Islamic sense, at any rate. Whatever evidence there is emerges, somewhat indistinctly, from the Quran, which is, of course, derisive of the pagans' prayer. The Quraysh's prayers at the Holy House are described as "nothing but whistling and clapping" (8:35). The word used in this verse, *salat*, is the same as that employed for the Muslim's own canonical prayer and is almost certainly a loanword borrowed from Aramaic/Syriac and so taken over from contemporary Jewish or Christian usage. But there is a somewhat more authentic Arabic word, *dua*, a "calling" (on God), an "invoking," and one verse of the Quran (2:186) seems addressed to reassuring the Muslims' questions concerning the efficacy of their own practice of "calling": "When My servants ask you concerning Me, (say) then: I am

near, I answer the call of the caller when he calls. So let them respond to Me and believe in Me. O may they go straight!"

THE JEWS OF ARABIA

We know too little to speak of "Arabian Judaism" on the eve of
Islam. We know only that there was in the sixth century a considerable Jewish presence in the once prosperous land of the Yemen
and that there were other tribes, often the paramount tribes, who
were identifiably Jewish to their Arab contemporaries and who
dwelled in the oases strung like a necklace from Medina 275 miles
north-northeast of Mecca all the way north to the present border
between Jordan and Saudi Arabia. The Yemen was a settled land
with a literate people — South Arabian, with its linear script, is well
preserved and related to the Ethiopic of the peoples across the
narrow straits of the Red Sea — and so we are somewhat better
informed about them than we are of the northern oasis dwellers.

Two pieces of information are pertinent here. In the sixth century Jewish monotheism is on prominent display in the preserved
South Arabian inscriptions, and in the same era a Jewish royal
house, probably indigenous, came to rule in the Yemen. This rise
to prominence brought Jews into direct conflict with a growing
Christian presence that had originated with missionaries from
Christian Abyssinia and was supplemented and augmented by an
actual Abyssinian colonial force in the Yemen. By the early sixth
century Jews and Christians there were locked into a cycle of mu-
tual persecution that came to a head in a slaughter of Christians at
various towns in the Yemen, followed by an Abyssinian intervention and the death of the notorious Dhu Nuwas, the last Jewish
king of South Arabia. Most of the Abyssinian invaders eventually
went home, but they left behind one of their generals, Abraha,
who soon declared his independence and ruled the Yemen, a Chris-
tian-dominated Yemen, in his own name. The Jews there had lost
their political power but they were neither annihilated nor expelled. Not too long afterward Islam was drawing some of its most
illustrious converts, and the source of much of their later informa-

tion on the biblical background of the Quran, from among the Yemeni Jews, like the semilegendary Kab called "the Rabbi" (*al-Ahbar*), who was reportedly converted to Islam in 638 C.E. and who seems to stand behind so many of the Israelite tales that filled in the later Muslims' knowledge of the Bible.

Little of this rich background, which was known to the later (eighth- and ninth-century) biographers of Muhammad, appears in the Quran, which makes what does appear to be a single, oblique reference to an attack by Abraha (?) against Mecca (sura 105). The Quran does betray some Yemeni, possibly Jewish, influence in its early references to the god Rahman, "the Merciful One," who shows up often in the South Arabian inscriptions. Though at first the quranic Rahman does not seem to be identical with Allah, soon the two are harmonized (cf. sura 17:110), and rahman eventually took its place as a simple title or attribute of the High God of Islam.

Turning northward from Mecca, we encounter the other already noted Jewish communities in the oases of northwestern Arabia. Epigraphical evidence, the Quran and the Talmud, as well as the later Arab historical tradition, all attest to their existence, though not very certainly to their beliefs and practices. We cannot say how they got there, although likely it was by emigration from the north, nor precisely when. But if they were ethnic outsiders, the Jews of the Hejaz oases were fairly acculturated, though by no means assimilated, to the Arab ways of their neighbors. Muhammad encountered Jews in the oasis of Medina when he arrived in 622, but there is no evidence of a fixed or identifiable Jewish community at Mecca, which was not, like the other Jewish settlement sites, an oasis but a shrine center with closely linked trade and commercial ambitions. It is not unlikely, however, that before and during Muhammad's lifetime there were Jews in his native town as transient merchants perhaps, and the Meccans' obvious familiarity with the Quran's frequent biblical allusions promotes the likelihood of some kind of pre-Islamic Jewish presence at Mecca to a strong probability.

THE CHRISTIANS OF ARABIA

Although there is abundant material on a Christian presence in Arabia, our sources are principally literary ones from the high Hellenic tradition, both secular and ecclesiastical. The first dwell chiefly on the political relations between the empire and its federated Arab allies among the nomads, and it is clear that religion, more specifically conversion to Christianity from the indigenous polytheism, had a major role to play, as a condition for entering into a treaty relationship with the Roman state and then in the fierce sectarian strife that shook the Middle Eastern Churches of the fifth, sixth, and seventh centuries. But the ecclesiastical writers provide some sense of what, besides politics, attracted the Arab tribes to Christianity, to wit, the example of Christian holy men already living in remote outposts where they were accessible to the nomads, even at a great distance, and the miracles that they and others could still perform in the name of Christ.

Though we can chart certain events in its history, describing the substance and practice of Arab Christianity is far more difficult. That the Christian Arabs constituted a kind of "church" is evident from the fact that there were bishops consecrated for their use at the camps of the Arab federates who patrolled the frontiers. Monasticism was particularly cultivated among them, and many of its more popular reflexes such as the veneration of holy men and of relics are attested. We do not know much about the actual Christian Arab cultus, an ignorance hinged to substantial doubts as to whether there was even available an Arabic translation of the New Testament, and its inevitable corollary, that the language of worship and piety was not Arabic but Syriac or Christian Aramaic.

We are, in consequence, ill informed about the quality of the Christianity beyond the immediate borderlands of the great empires, or, to be more precise, of the milieu from which Islam emerged. That there were some Christians at Mecca can scarcely be doubted, and the Quran, and hence Muhammad, know about the Gospel, Jesus, Mary, churches, monks, and monasteries. Indeed, the Quran's version of Christianity is a notorious hybrid, as we have seen, and it ill conforms with any existing model.

3. *"And Muhammad Is His Messenger"*

FROM the Christian perspective, Jesus is God's final revelation, the fulfillment of what had earlier been promised in the Bible, and the meaning of that revelation unfolds in the events of his life as described in the Gospels. His followers accept only the four Gospels that the Church as a whole had received as authentic and believed were inspired: the four canonical Gospels are consequently regarded as veridical accounts of the great work of redemption. Muhammad's life bears no such theological weight for Muslims. The Quran is the revelation, not Muhammad, who was merely its messenger, the mortal who delivered God's warnings and promises to audiences in western Arabia early in the seventh century C.E. Events reflect the difference in the Muslim and Christian perspectives: it was the Quran that was collected and preserved from the outset, not the life of the man who delivered it. People recalled Muhammad, of course, but no one thought to compose those recollections into a formal *Life* until well after his death, and once done, no one version ever gained canonical standing or even remotely approached the status of revelation.

THE MUHAMMAD OF HISTORY

A *Life of the Prophet* was eventually composed. Not only do we possess various biographies of Muhammad that purport to go back to the recollection of his contemporaries; we also have an enormous mass of free-floating, discrete reports that are thought to contain his sayings on a wide variety of topics from prayer to table etiquette. The reasons for this proliferation of information are not too surprising. Throughout the Quran, Muhammad is made to insist that he is merely a man (18:10) — his critics expected something more considerable of a divine messenger (6:37) and were understandably surprised when he turned out to be someone they knew from the market — but for his followers he was indeed the best of men since he had been chosen to deliver God's message of salvation. But more importantly, Muhammad was in his own person the most perfect embodiment of that message: he was the Muslim paradigm, as the Quran itself announces (33:21). That fact alone would explain the growing Muslim interest in the Prophet's life, but there is more. People remembered, of course, some of the things this remarkable man had said and done during his lifetime, and those recollections were handed down from one generation to the next. Eventually the reports of these recollections became a determining precedent in Islamic law (see chapter 7), and so it became important for some to verify the many statements in circulation that purported to describe what soon was called generally "the customary behavior (*sunna*) of the Prophet." An important branch of Islamic historiography was born.

Other motives urged the Muslim to become a historian in the matter of Muhammad. The Quran is, in many instances, an opaque document. It has almost nothing direct to say of either Muhammad or Mecca, for example, or indeed of contemporary events generally, and its teachings are most often delivered without discernible context. Only very rarely are we told what particular circumstances provoked or the reason behind this or that prescription or prohibition, and so the believer is often hard-pressed to understand the practical application of that same divine command. Context is immeasurably important in moral matters, as is clear from the Gospels, and the Quran provides little or none with its prescriptions. Muslims turned for that context to the life of Muhammad, for there, if anywhere, were the settings for the revelations that issued from his mouth over twenty-two years and that are preserved in the Quran. These circumstances came to be called by Muslim exegetes and lawyers the "occasions of revelation," and they were another powerful incentive for assembling the known facts of Muhammad's life in the form of a biography. Not unexpectedly, then, the preserved biographies of the Prophet do note the historic occasion when this or that revelation was "sent down."

HAGIOGRAPHY AND HISTORY

We have before us, then, a life, or rather a number of relatively early lives of Muhammad. As time passed those lives not only multiplied but, as happened with the lives of Jesus, they also expanded to include more and more material as both piety and theology added their own glosses to what had once been substantially recollection. It is easy enough for the historian to dismiss these later, overblown treatments of the life of the Prophet as hagiography of the type that surrounds many Christian saints. More pertinent is to ask how much of the traditional and standard *Life* — as it will be referred to here — the one composed by Ibn Ishaq (d. 767) and known to us chiefly in the edition of Ibn Hisham (d. 833), is made of the same stuff of piety and legend. Muslims, in any event, accept it is history, just as they accept the larger, more generously enhanced stories and tales of the Prophet that followed as a proper matter for contemplation and imitation.

As in some of the Gospels, and even in the Quran's own account of Jesus' infancy and adolescence (19:29–35), Muhammad's birth and early years are marked by epiphanies or recognition scenes in which he is recognized, against all expectation, as the future Prophet of God. In Jesus' case, the acknowledgment is chiefly by his fellow Jews, but according to the *Life* of Muhammad, it was Jews and Christians, those earlier recipients of God's truth, who recognized this last of God's prophets. Muhammad had in fact been predicted in their own Scriptures (61:6). The similarity of this and other motifs found in Ibn Ishaq's *Life* to those in the Jesus story may not be entirely fortuitous. The standard *Life* of Muhammad was written not in Mecca or Medina but in eighth-century Baghdad, in a religiously cosmopolitan milieu where the Muslim dialogue with Christians and Jews was well under way. Ibn Ishaq's work, particularly in its abbreviated form, served rather precisely as a Muslim gospel, to bring the "good news" of Muhammad to a community that still possessed little beyond the Quran and to provide the Muslims with a biographical book to emulate and rival the Gospels and so lessen the polemical advantage these latter gave the Christians.

MUHAMMAD: A LIFE

The traditional accounts date Muhammad's birth in Mecca to 570 C.E., which seems somewhat too early, but, as in the case of Jesus, the exact year is of no great consequence. Of greater importance was that Muhammad was orphaned at a young age, to which the Quran itself seems to allude in one of its rare personal asides (93:6), and the Book more than once urges a merciful justice toward such bereaved children. Otherwise Muhammad seems to have had an unremarkable youth, this young man of the Banu Hashim, a not particularly notable clan of the paramount Meccan tribe of Quraysh. He was regarded as an "honest" or "reliable" (*amin*) young man, and although the Islamic tradition has kept Muhammad at a very safe distance from the polytheism of Mecca even before his prophetic call, it does credit him with a role in the Quraysh's rebuilding of the Kaaba after it had been destroyed in one of Mecca's frequent flash floods. Muhammad had a "hidden life" up until his public ministry, not, however, as a craftsman like Jesus, but as a commercial agent. Furthermore, he was married, with children.

Sometime in his adulthood—the traditional date is 610—Muhammad received his first revelation. This might be the two visions described somewhat obliquely in the Quran (53:1–18), but the biographical tradition thought otherwise. It describes a far more graphic scene in a cave near Mecca, a struggle with the angel Gabriel, and finally the revelation of Quran 96:1–5 or, according to others, the opening verses of sura 74. Either might well be the earliest revelation in the Quran, but neither could possibly be Muhammad's first public utterance. We really cannot say what happened when Muhammad initially took to the public ways as a prophet; all we are sure of is that there are no verses in the Quran that explain to the Meccans that what they were about to hear were the newly revealed words of God. Whatever that earliest revelation, Muhammad was apparently uncertain of the source of this voice in his head, or perhaps of what he was expected to do in consequence. Only after psychological support from his wife and help from one of her relatives who knew something about Judaism and Christianity did Muhammad have the courage to venture into the public places of Mecca and announce this message whose name was Islam.

Imagining Revelation

Scattered through the early suras, and echoed and amplified in the biographical tradition, are allegations that Muhammad was someone unusual but familiar to his fellow Meccans, a poet or a seer (21:5; 69:41–42), with a demonic jinn as his muse (7:184; 68:2; 81:22). Poets and seers were not always identical in ancient Arabia, but nothing in the Quran suggests that the Meccans cut the distinction very fine when it came to Muhammad. Something about the style of his utterances — the frequent oaths, the insistent rhyme or assonance, the emotive verse, the highly wrought language, the often enigmatic expressions — and perhaps something about his personal demeanor as well — "O you wrapped in a cloak!" (74:1) — reminded them of a well-known type, a public crier who was inspired, possessed by a higher force. Muhammad spent considerable time thereafter attempting to correct this impression, which he eventually did, but it was his reputation as a charismatic bard that first seized the Meccans' attention and got him his first hearing.

The early Meccan suras betray all the indices of oral composition: a notable, even insistent, rhyme scheme, intense rhythmic patterns, short verse units, and recurrent formulaic themes. More, the putative occasions of those suras correspond to the circumstances of oral composition: a society of mixed orality-literacy in which, although writing was known and practiced by a few, oral composition or performance was still the standard form of expression. The earliest setting of the Quran was preaching: the Meccan *suras* constituted a message for the society as a whole and delivered to a public audience that noted the resemblance to the compositions of oral bards and seers in that society.

The revelations of the Quran were memorized, the tradition assures us and which we have no reason to doubt. But under what circumstances were those inspired utterances committed to memory by their audience? Here we may invoke the word "Quran" itself. The Arabic derives from *qeryana*, "recitation," a Syriac word with distinct liturgical connotations, and it may safely be assumed, in the light of the Quran's own remarks (17:78; 75:16–18) that almost from the beginning parts of what had been revealed were memorized, doubtless under Muhammad's own direction, for purposes of liturgical recitation. This is the most plausible guess as to the trajectory of the Quran's transmission history: that Muhammad's followers — perhaps certain professional reciters, or *rawis*, as they were called in Arabia — memorized portions of his "oracles," which were then recited in private gatherings as a form of prayer.

At Medina the circumstances of the Quran were drastically changed. As we shall see, Muhammad was no longer simply a preacher in the style of Jesus or John the Baptist but the Solemn Pontiff of a religio-political community of believers whose chief needs were confirmation, regulation, instruction. It is near impossible to determine the exact sequence of the Medina suras, a fact that renders somewhat problematic any attempt to unfold the various quranic meanings of the oft used word for "book" (*kitab*) and its synonyms. One use is certainly that of "Scripture," that is, the Book of God. In one telling passage, God tells Muhammad to seek confirmation of the truth of this revelation by questioning "those who recite the Book before you" (10:95), that is, the Jews and Christians, and he is further instructed (13:43) to give that same advice to doubters. Closer contact with the Jews and their Scripture at Medina may have given birth to the conviction that Muhammad's community would have its own "Book," like the one Moses brought to the Jews. Indeed, there are signs, notably the opening verses of the Medina sura 2, that Muhammad may actually have begun to compose such, and to collect and revise his earlier utterances for inclusion in it.

At Medina, with the growing community's freedom from persecution, the Muslim liturgy became more public and formal. The Meccan suras continued to be recited, but now, with the emergence of the essentially theological notion that the revelations constituted a Book, the prescriptive and didactic material was also included in the emerging canon to constitute, at least in theory, a sacred book on the Moses-Jesus model, though there is no evidence that Muhammad had any direct knowledge of either the Bible or the Gospels, nor, indeed that either of these Books had yet been translated into Arabic. But the project was far from complete at the time of Muhammad's unexpected death. Early on, while Muhammad was still at Mecca, there was, quite inexplicably, some dispute about what constituted the quranic canon (13:36; 15:90–91), and efforts to collect from memory and manuscript what he had recited, preached, or pronounced continued for nearly a quarter century, and perhaps considerably longer, after his death.

THE MESSAGE OF ISLAM

We do have some notion, as we have seen, which might have been the earliest suras or chapters in the Quran, and from them we can form an idea of the shape and content of the first preaching of Islam. Originally, it must be recalled, Muhammad's mission was to turn the Meccans from their cultic polytheism to the worship of the One God and to reform their corrupt morality. Later in the Quran, after he was the head of a growing Muslim community in Medina, the point of the message is somewhat different: it is directed to believers, no longer to pagans, and its objective is to reinforce and instruct them in their faith.

What God required of the Meccans, the Quran instructed, was "submission" (Ar. *islam*; one who has so submitted is a *muslim*) to God, *the* God, who is none other than the High God Allah worshiped at Mecca; the "Lord of this house," the Quran calls him, referring to the Kaaba or central shrine of Mecca. Muhammad had no need to introduce the Meccans to Allah: they already worshiped him, and in moments of crisis, as we have seen, they even conceded that he was in fact *the* God. The trouble was, they worshiped other gods as well, and that is one of the central aims of the Meccan preaching: to make the Quraysh and the other Meccans surrender their attachment to other deities, the idols and empty names they associated with the One True God.

This was the theological or cultic point of the early preaching, but from the beginning Islam was far more than an acceptance of monotheism. The Quran called on the Meccans to change their moral ways. A look at the very earliest suras shows that the reformation was overwhelmingly social, and perhaps economic, in its emphases. The Quran would eventually go on to speak of many things, but the original form of the message was narrowly targeted: it is good to feed the poor and take care of the needy; it is evil to accumulate wealth solely for one's own behalf.

This message got scant hearing from the Quraysh, whether they thought that monotheism would lessen the appeal of Mecca as a pilgrimage center (surely one of the gravest miscalculations in the history of commerce) or because they did not relish Muhammad's brand of social and economic reform. The early suras reflect the criticism directed back at the messenger. The heat of the quranic preaching begins to rise in reaction. There are now fierce denunciations of the scoffers and unbelievers: for them is reserved a fiery hell, just as the believers would have reserved for them a true paradise of peace and pleasurable repose. At this point both the language and the imagery suddenly become familiar to the Jewish or the Christian reader. The promised paradise is called the "Garden of Eden" (*Jannat Adan*) and the threatened hell, "Gehenna" (*Jahannam*).

The Quran early on unveils, in bits and pieces, its eschatological vision, not to stress its absolute imminence, as in the New Testament, but to warn the unbeliever that the price of doubt is high and the rewards of submission great. Though it has its own particular details, the Quran's version of the End is obviously different from anything we encounter among the pre-Islamic Arabs, but it is noticeably similar to that current among the Jews and Christians. Moreover, in the face of that same opposition, the Quran begins to unfold its own elaborate history of prophecy. Muhammad, the Meccans were told, was not the first prophet sent to humankind, though assuredly he was the last.

THE OPPOSITION

The Quran is profoundly interested in history, not the history of Mecca, to be sure, or even of Arabia; not in politics or in the tribal skirmishes, the "days of the Arabs" so celebrated by Muhammad's contemporaries. The Quran's view of the past is a version of Sacred History, how the divine dispensation, which began at Creation, has unfolded from Adam down to the present. The story of the prophets is rehearsed at length in the Quran, never quite consecutively in the manner of a history, but rather to make a moral point, to wit, when humankind has refused to heed the bearers of God's message, the consequences have been terrible. The lesson is clear: those who reject Muhammad will pay a fearsome price at God's hands.

Thus Muhammad established his own pedigree in the essentially biblical line of the prophets (as a successor in particular of Moses and Jesus), and his Book, this "convincing Arabic Quran," as it calls itself (36:69), took its place as an equal beside the sacred books of the Jews and Christians. Later, when Islam exploded into the populous habitats of those other communities, that claim to parity would take on meaning, but for Muhammad's original audience in Mecca, the references to other prophets were chiefly intended as a warning to reform and not as a prediction that a third great branch of monotheism had arisen out of the other two.

The Quraysh were not moved by either the man or his message. They accused Muhammad of being jinn-possessed, a charge usually leveled at poets (52:29–31; 69:38–43). The tone if not the content of Muhammad's "recitations" reminded his audience of the local poets and seers, though no pre-Islamic poet we know of concerned himself with preaching monotheism, much less social reform. As for the message itself — and here the reference seems to be to the Quran's biblical-type stories — the Quraysh thought Muhammad had simply lifted it from "old yarns" someone had perhaps told him in private and he then repeated in public (16:103; 83:13). Muhammad was fierce in his denial of these charges, as steadfast as he was in his refusal to validate his message, as the very prophets he cited had, by producing a miracle. Did they doubt the divine origin of his revelations? Let them produce even a single similar piece. The Quran was its own miracle.

The accusations that Muhammad had lifted his teachings from other sources, more precisely the Bible, did not end with the Prophet's death or even the astonishing success of Islam, and the Muslim commentators felt constrained to construct their own line of defense against the charge by parsing the Arabic adjective *ummi*, which is applied to Muhammad in Quran 7:157, 158, to mean "illiterate." If he were illiterate, the thinking went, he could hardly have stolen the material from those other Books. The point is specious, of course. It is not entirely clear what *ummi* meant. "Gentile" or "pagan" seems probable, that is, someone who was neither a Jew nor a Christian. The word apart, it is highly unlikely that someone engaged in trade would be entirely illiterate, but it is even more improbable that anyone at Mecca was reading either the Bible or the Gospels in Muhammad's lifetime since neither was translated into Arabic until two centuries later. Yet, in that oral culture it was hardly necessary to be able to read to know what was in those other Books.

We know more about the Quraysh's reaction to Muhammad than we do about their reaction to Islam. The only clue we are given to the latter is that they found ludicrous the doctrine of the bodily resurrection of the dead (Quran 13:5; 19:66; 27:67; 32:10–11). That teaching might indeed have seemed bizarre to the hard-headed Meccans, but it does not itself explain the fierceness of their eventual response. More likely they feared for their polytheism, or perhaps the business of polytheism to which they were attached. Muhammad's message certainly threatened Mecca's eclectic shrines and the commerce that the annual pilgrimages generated. But it is too simple to dismiss the degree of personal devotion to the deities of polytheism, whose practices seem altogether too magical and mechanical to those reared in a monotheistic and highly spiritualized tradition.

THE "SATANIC VERSES"

Muhammad may have attempted to appease his fellow Quraysh. The account that follows is absent from the Quran as we now possess it; the story comes rather from quranic commentary, notably that of al-Tabari (d. 923), who has already been cited as a historian but who was also one of the premier exegetes of medieval Islam. In any event, the story is so unlikely to have been invented by Muslim piety that Muslims and non-Muslims alike have been strongly inclined to accept at face value the tale of the so-called satanic verses.

It begins with something that *is* in the Quran, the quite explicit statement in sura 22:52–53 that God has on occasion, with all the prophets and not merely Muhammad, allowed Satan to cast verses into the Revelation in order to test the believers, although God subsequently removed them, to be sure. There follow the commentators' attempts at sketching the particular occasion of revelation of those two quite extraordinary verses. Muhammad, the story went, was rapidly sliding into despair at the Quraysh's invincible resistance to his preaching; he was hoping, we are told, for a revelation that would somehow reconcile the Quraysh to Islam. And he apparently received it. Verses 19–20 of sura 53 were "sent down," as the process of revelation is usually described: "Have you considered al-Lat, al-Uzza, and Manat, the third, the other?" This was followed immediately by "They are the exalted cranes, and their intercession is to be hoped for." The cultic expression "exalted cranes"—the phrase may have been part of a pagan prayer—is difficult for us, but its main point was not lost on the Quraysh: if the divinity of the so-called daughters of Allah was not explicitly confirmed, they were certainly intermediaries, powerful intercessors with God. On hearing this revelation, the Quraysh prostrated themselves on the spot and worshiped at the side of Muhammad.

This happy solution disappeared as abruptly as it had appeared. Muhammad, the story continues, immediately began to doubt the provenance of the apparent revelation, and God responded with a new and authentic one to replace the old. After "the third, the other," the Quran says, "Do you have male (children) and He female? That indeed would be unfair. They [the goddesses in question] are but names that you have named, you and your fathers, for which God has revealed no warrant" (53:21–23). This was not the end of this curious business. The Quran felt some need to explain, hence Quran 22:52–53 about God's practice of permitting such a thing as a test of faith. Had not God himself done the same in the Bible's story of Abraham, where the Lord commanded the binding of Isaac for sacrifice and then canceled his own command? It was apparently a telling point, and one of the earliest Jewish scholars of the Islamic era, Saadya Gaon (d. 942), took some pains to make clear to his fellow Jews that God had not commanded the actual sacrifice of Isaac but merely that the child be "reserved" for such.

MUHAMMAD'S NIGHT JOURNEY AND ASCENSION

On the Quran's own testimony, Muhammad stoutly refused to perform—or have God perform—miracles on his behalf, despite the fact that the Quraysh demanded such as verification of the truth of his message. At one point he did relent, and in the face of charges of being misguided or misled, he did refer, very obliquely and enigmatically, to certain supernatural visions he had experienced (Quran 53:1–18). There is another verse, however—Quran 17:1—that suggested to later Muslims that some other, more circumstantial supernatural experience had been given the Prophet. The verse had him carried "by night" — the Muslim biographical tradition specified he had been sleeping near the Kaaba — to "the distant shrine." The event was eventually identified as a reference to a miraculous journey from Mecca to the Temple Mount in Jerusalem. Later this same journey was connected with the belief that after his stay in Jerusalem, Muhammad had been briefly taken up into heaven — although this is explicitly denied in the Quran (17:95). According to the fully developed tradition, Muhammad was carried up, past his various prophetic predecessors, to the seventh heaven, which was guarded by no less than Abraham himself. Finally, he returned to Mecca that same evening. Muhammad's association with the city through the Night Journey explains in part the Muslim attachment to Jerusalem, whereas his Ascension may very well mark the occasion when the totality of the Quran's contents were revealed to Muhammad, though in "real time" they were sent down to him piecemeal and as the occasion dictated (25:32).

MUHAMMAD CLEANSED, AND RAPT

The Christian mystics who passed from a careful cultivation of self-denial to a desire to stand before the divine throne, or even to look on the face of God, had ample precedents in their still meditated-on Jewish and Hellenic pasts. The early Sufis knew of no such transports to other realms. They had instead the example of their own master. After an initiatory ritual, the prophet Muhammad himself had once ascended to the highest heaven and communed with God. These two events, called respectively the Opening of Muhammad's Breast and the Ascension, are rich in subsequent Islamic associations but are touched on, in a typically oblique fashion, in the Quran. "Did We not open your breast, and take from you your burden which was breaking your back?" asks Quran 94:1–3. The biographical and exegetical tradition wove a story of an angel physically opening Muhammad's breast, either early in life or immediately before his vocation as a prophet, removing whatever imperfection existed there and pouring into its place plenteous faith and wisdom.

This cathartic initiatory procedure is followed immediately in the mystics' imaginings by Muhammad's being carried in his sleep first to Jerusalem — the famous Night Journey just described — and thence, from the temple site in the Holy City, to the highest heaven. This is the Prophet's Ascension (*miraj*), which is never quite described in the Quran but is often celebrated in literature and art. Some of its details seem extrapolated from what were almost certainly traces of the Prophet's actual visions, like the ones described almost in passing in Quran 53:1–18. The Quran's own annotation of these visions is minimal in the extreme, but the Sufi tradition, including the Prophetic reports (*hadith*) that purported to go back to Muhammad himself, placed the Ascension firmly and forever in the context of Muhammad's heavenly journey. The Prophet is borne aloft by a mythical steed through the seven heavens of the ancient and medieval cosmologies to stand in the presence of God.

As in the Jewish "Chariot" and "Palaces" literature of celestial ascent, each heaven of Muhammad's journey is entered only after a challenge and a response given to its prophetic guardian — Adam in the first heaven, then Jesus, Joseph, Idris (Enoch), Aaron, Moses, and finally, in the seventh heaven, Abraham. Beyond this patriarch is God himself, who, according to Muhammad's own account reported in the hadith, "inspired in me what He inspired." There then follows another altogether typical "bargaining" sequence (cf. Abraham's on behalf of the doomed Sodom in Gen. 18:20–32) in which God initially assigns fifty daily prayers to the Muslim community, which Muhammad gradually bargains down to the canonical five.

This prophetic paradigm proved infinitely fruitful for later Sufis of Islam. They too had their own "ascensions" over the same terrain, though often embellished with new details, to end in the same awesome place before the throne of God. Now in the sacred company of the prophets assembled there was Muhammad himself to greet his mystical fellow traveler.

BOYCOTT

It is hard to imagine that the success of Muhammad's movement — if that is not too generous a term — troubled the Quraysh. The new prophet won a few followers, but they were younger men by and large — his cousin Ali was little more than a child at the time — and they were neither wealthy nor powerful. Yet they were not so few as to be invisible, and everything we know about Mecca of that era speaks of shifting alliances constantly being made and remade. In coalition politics a little counts for a lot, and so this new faction of "Muslims," whose allegiance was not tribal and whose self-interest could not be appealed to, may have counted for far more than its numbers suggest.

The rulers among the Quraysh were alarmed in any event. Ill treatment of the Muslims yielded to more concerted and more serious action against the Prophet. No one had attacked Muhammad directly since he was under the protection of Abu Talib, the clan head of the Hashim and the uncle who had raised him (and was also the father of the much younger Ali). Since Abu Talib would not withdraw his protection of his nephew, the two leading clans of the Quraysh declared a public boycott against their old commercial rivals of the Hashim, Muhammad's own kin. The Prophet may have anticipated more serious troubles ahead. He arranged for some of his followers to migrate to the kingdom of Abyssinia across the Red Sea. The choice is interesting. Christian Abyssinia had long had commercial relations with Mecca, and Muhammad must surely have thought that his Muslims would receive a sympathetic hearing there, as apparently they did. Many stayed on in Africa but others rejoined Muhammad after he had resettled in Medina.

We cannot say how the boycott, which did not seem terribly effective, would have played out since events intervened, notably the death in 619 of Muhammad's wife Khadija, who was, by all accounts, one of his chief psychological supports. The same year also marked the death of Abu Talib, the uncle whose steadfast resolve in the face of the boycott was essential to his nephew's safety. Muhammad's days in Mecca were obviously numbered, as he himself recognized, since there was now little to restrain the Quraysh from violence. The Prophet began to search for another, safer venue for his preaching. The nearby town of Taif was one possibility, but the Quraysh were powerful there as well. He next turned to the Bedouin tribes who annually converged on Mecca and its environs. They came under the cover of a sacred truce to worship at the shrines and do the kind of business that their endless blood feuds made impossible at other times and in other places. They declined; the Bedouin had little interest in prophets.

THE HEGIRA

Eventually Muhammad's call for help fell on responsive ears. Pilgrims from Yathrib, an oasis 275 miles to the north of Mecca, heard Muhammad preaching at one of the market fairs connected with the annual pilgrimages in and around Mecca. He interested them and they him, because, we are told, they were allied to the Jews at Yathrib. Whatever the reason for the interest, Muhammad explained submission to them and recited parts of the Quran; they were sufficiently impressed to return the following year and seek him out again. On this occasion, twelve of the Yathribis concluded a kind of agreement in principle to cease their polytheism, not to steal or commit fornication, not to kill their (female?) offspring, not to plunder their neighbors, and, most important at this particular juncture, not to disobey Muhammad. There is no mention yet of formal prayer or almsgiving, probably because these had not yet been laid down as obligations in the hostile climate of Mecca, where any public display of the new faith would likely have been dangerous.

The following year, the Yathribis came back again, seventy-three this time — the numbers should not be taken too seriously in these accounts, particularly when they approach the numbers of Jesus' apostles (twelve) and disciples (seventy-two) — though not all of them were believers. They offered Muhammad a safe-conduct in Yathrib — getting there was his responsibility — but what they required in return, indeed, their motive in inviting him in the first place, becomes clear only in the sequel. Muhammad began to send his followers quietly and secretly in small groups to Yathrib. He himself followed in September 622. This "migration," or *hijra*, as it was called in Arabic—Anglicized, from the Latin, as "hegira"— though unmentioned in the Quran, was regarded by Muslims as a turning point in the fortunes of the Prophet and his movement.

Note: According to report, it was the caliph Umar (r. 634–644 C.E.) who chose the year 622 to mark the formal beginning of the Muslim era, and documents began to be dated from it, counting, of course, by lunar years of 354 days. The first year of the Muslim era—often denoted in English as A.H. (*Anno Hegirae*) on the analogy with A.D., *Anno Domini*—was moreover dated back from 24 September, when Muhammad actually migrated, to the first day of that lunar year, 16 July 622.

---

4. *The Prince of Medina*

MECCA was a parched and shadowless settlement collected around a single well—the Zamzam of Muslim
lore—and a shrine. Yathrib, or, as the Muslims soon
started calling it, Madinat al-Nabi, the "City of the
Prophet," and now in English simply Medina, was a
quite different place. It was an oasis whose underground water supply supported plantations of date
palms and a comfortable population of agriculturalists. Those agriculturalists were, for a couple of generations before Muhammad's arrival, Arabs, chiefly the
tribe called Khazraj, who had first approached Muhammad at Mecca, and another, the Aws. But there
were other people in Medina as well, various tribes of
Jews who had once controlled the oasis and were in
622 in a dependent alliance with either the Aws or the
Khazraj. We do not know when or how the Jews arrived in that remote outpost of the Diaspora, but a
Jewish population is attested in many of the oases that
stretched northward from Medina toward what is now
the Jordanian frontier, and there was a large and powerful Jewish presence in the southwestern tip of Arabia,
in the Yemen. Yet, we do not know in what precisely
the religious beliefs and practices of those Medina Jews
consisted.

Life was easier in Medina than in Mecca, or it
should have been, given its natural advantages. But
while the Quraysh held their fragile settlement in a
shifting but nonetheless tight political grip, the Arabs

of Medina had fallen to contesting ownership of the limited plantation land, and by the second decade of the seventh century social strife was beginning to pit the Aws and their Jewish clients against the Khazraj and theirs. The clans lived locked within their fortified farmsteads and awaited the inevitable showdown. These were the circumstances that brought Muhammad to the place that would one day bear his name. His audience at Mecca had said that he sounded like a possessed poet or, alternatively, a "seer" (*kahin*), both of which identifications he vehemently denied, but it was surely as some kind of *vates* or holy man that he was brought to Medina. Where today parties in conflict might bring in an impartial arbitrator with binding powers, the Medinese imported a charismatic holy man whose wisdom was not stipulated but God-given.

THE MEDINA ACCORDS

Several important events took place at Medina between Muhammad's arrival in September 622 and the defining military action at Badr Wells in 624. One of the first, begun while he was still at Mecca, was Muhammad's arrangement of fictive "brotherhoods" whereby his fellow "Migrants" (*muhajirun*) — whose name was a badge of honor and who soon became a somewhat privileged class — were attached, family by family, to counterparts in the still small group of Medina Muslims called "Helpers" (*ansar*) to ensure some degree of economic and social support for the penniless and resourceless Meccan Muslims. Muhammad himself lodged with some Medinese supporters until a house was built for him. Its courtyard soon became the Muslims' first public prayer house or mosque.

The biographical sources on the Prophet have preserved what may be the agreement drawn up between Muhammad and the folk of Medina. The so-called Medina Accords constitute a complex document with numerous later additions, but at its heart we can discern that the Medinese agreed to accept Muhammad as their leader in the sense that they would refer all disputes to him and accept his judgments. Though he is called the "Prophet of God" in the document as it is preserved, the terms themselves demonstrate that the Medinese by no means pledged to all become Muslims. The signatories formed, however, one community (*umma*); Medina polytheists and Jews preserved their tribal organization, while Migrants and Helpers slowly — and very imperfectly — merged into a religious community without regard to tribal or even family ties. There is no indication that Muhammad was intended to "run" the oasis in any sense. The arrangement simply made him the sole and final arbitrator in all disputes, and it seems likely that the settlement operated much as it had before, through a series of agreements among the various tribes and clans. What Muhammad's authority did was suspend sine die — it is difficult to believe that anyone there actually forgot or forgave — the annually compounded costs of blood feuds within the tight confines of an oasis settlement.

THE PRACTICE OF ISLAM

The chronology of the Quran's Meccan suras can be laid out with some reasonable degree of certainty, though there are notable soft spots as to which are early, middle, or late within that twelve-year span. There is no such conviction about the long suras that date from Medina. Pieces of suras can be connected with specific events like the battles at Badr or Uhud or later Hunayn, but no one has succeeded in arranging in sequence the whole or even a considerable part of them over Muhammad's ten years at Medina. We do not know, for example, when some of the primary ritual obligations of Islam began to be practiced. Ritual prayer (*salat*) would probably have been impossible in the hostile climate of Mecca; we can guess, however, that it began to be practiced soon after the Prophet arrived in Medina. Obligatory tithing (*zakat*) would likewise make sense in Medina, where early on there were Muslims of some substance, the Helpers, and others with little, the Migrants. The mention of tithing in Quran 2:177 in connection with the change in the *qibla*, or prayer direction, makes it seem an early act at Medina, but the Muslim tradition also connects its imposition with 9:11–12, which seems to reflect the tribes' capitulations of the year before Muhammad's death, and where it has the flavor of a tribute tax. The fast of Ramadan was likewise a Medina phenomenon (2:184–185); its specification as a religious obligation was almost certainly an outgrowth of the Prophet's early disputes with the Jews of the oasis between 622 and 624. Finally, we can be certain that no Muslim made the ritual pilgrimage until the very end of the Prophet's life: the sole hajj he himself performed was in February 632, four months before he died.

MUHAMMAD AND THE JEWS

Before his arrival at Medina Muhammad had often spoken of the Banu Israil, as the Quran names the Jews. He had used, as we have seen, the eschatological images and language current in the Jewish tradition in his attempt to convince the Quraysh of the seriousness of their predicament and had invoked the example of the biblical prophets both to explain his own mission and to illustrate what happened to those who resisted God's commands. The Bible was a religious terrain that Muhammad shared with the Jews and the Christians. He had sent his followers to Christian Abyssinia — in belief and practice the most "Jewish" of the area's Christian cultures — with some expectation that they would be favorably received, as they apparently were, and now, newly arrived in Medina, he may have anticipated that his own prophetic claims would be acknowledged by the Banu Israil whose God he too worshiped.

If this is what Muhammad in fact expected, he was sorely disappointed. The parts of the Quran revealed at Medina show a notable hardening of attitudes toward contemporary Jews, now straightforwardly referred to as Yahud. We know too that certain religious practices Muhammad had once observed — rituals that apparently derived from Jewish ones — were altered soon after his arrival in Medina. He no longer prayed facing Jerusalem, as the Jews did and as he had previously done; his qibla was now the Meccan Kaaba, the old Quraysh cult center in Mecca. Nor did he any longer fast the Ashura, the tenth day of the Jews' month of Tishri or Yom Kippur. This was the day, Muhammad discovered, on which the Torah had been sent down to Moses. We cannot be certain of the chronology, but at some point after this he no longer required his followers to fast on Yom Kippur but decreed instead the fast of Ramadan, the month during which the Quran, which Muhammad explicitly compared to the Torah (11:7, etc.), was sent down to the new Moses (2:185; 97:1–5).

On the evidence we can only conclude that something went wrong between Muhammad and the Jews of Medina. It seems fairly certain that they rejected his claims to prophethood — which many Jews in Arabia and elsewhere later accepted — but there may have been a great deal more. There is no indication that the Jews there had anything to do with the civil strife that brought Muhammad to Medina in 622, but we may at least suspect that their fall from proprietors of the oasis to clients within it left some scars on the local politics, and the political overtones of Muhammad's subsequent treatment of them suggests the same. The biographical tradition is more explicit; the "Jewish rabbis" — whatever that might mean in that time and place — "showed hostility to the Messenger in envy, hatred, and malice because God had chosen the Messenger from among the Arabs." Some version of that judgment we may well have surmised on our own, but the Jews of Medina were also allegedly joining forces with men from the Aws and Khazraj who had obstinately clung to their heathen practices and beliefs. The Jews, then, according to this and similar accounts, took religious exception to Muhammad — how loudly or publicly we cannot tell — and then made a political alliance with those Medina Arabs who, for whatever reason, were beginning to oppose the new ruler from Mecca.

THE RELIGION OF ABRAHAM

For the moment there was no political response from Muhammad; it is unlikely that he, newly arrived in Medina and on uncertain terrain, had the means or inclination to do so. But he did begin to fashion a religious retort, one that grew sharper, firmer, and more confident in its details over Muhammad's ten years in Medina. Muhammad was the successor of the other prophets, to be sure, and notably of Moses and Jesus. But he was not simply adding to Judaism or Christianity — why didn't he just become a Christian or a Jew, some were asking; rather he was chosen for something far more radical. Islam was a renewal of the pristine — and pre-Jewish — religion of Abraham (Quran 2:135). Abraham, the Quran pronounced triumphantly, came before both the Torah and the Gospel (3:55–58); Abraham was, in fact, the first *muslim*, the first submitter to God in absolute monotheism (2:127–134).

According to the standard *Life*, the first hundred verses of the second chapter of the Quran were sent down on the occasion of Muhammad's break with the Jews during his first years in Medina. We cannot say if that was really the case, but that sura is in fact the Quran's most extended meditation on the Jewish past and the newly revealed Muslim present in God's plan of salvation — the Muslim scriptural parallel, though with very different rhetorical techniques, to Paul's letter to the Romans. Among its more startling declarations was the already noted claim that Abraham and his son Ishmael built the Kaaba in Mecca (2:125–127; 22:26) and instituted the rituals of the hajj in Mecca and its environs (22:27–30).

If it is true that Muhammad changed his qibla, or prayer direction, from Jerusalem to Mecca during his first months in Medina, linking Abraham with the shrine and rituals of his hometown reflects an even more radical theological reorientation toward Mecca. From the beginning Muhammad had identified the God he worshiped with the "Lord of the Kaaba" (106:3), but behind the pronouncements of the Medinan sura 2 lies the largely unarticulated assumption that Mecca had once, in Abraham's and Ishmael's day, been a settlement of monotheists whose rituals were directed toward the worship of the One True God, and that in the intervening centuries it had lapsed into the polytheism that Muslims learned to called *al-jahiliyya*, or "the era of barbarism. We do not know the extent to which these assumptions were shared by the audience of the Quran, which never averts or explains them, but a later generation of Muslim historians and storytellers put robust flesh on the bare bones of Abraham's stay in Mecca and the subsequent lapse of Muhammad's town into the heathenism into which the Prophet himself was born.

Muhammad's career at Medina falls into two main phases. The first, as we have just seen, covered the two years immediately following the Hegira, when Islam underwent a new shaping, first and chiefly by reason of Muhammad's contact with the Jews of the oasis. Previously his preaching had taken place in the form of a simple antagonistic antiphony: the monotheist trying to convert the polytheists, whose refusals, denials, and accusations fly out from between the lines of the Meccan suras. At Medina a third voice is heard, that of the Jews. It was a voice that Muhammad had likely expected to harmonize with his own but it proved to be a grating discord. He did not change his tune; he simply refined and enriched it. The earliest definition of Islam was figured against the totally "other" of the polytheists: "Say," God commands Muhammad in an early sura, "you disbelievers, I do not worship what you worship and you do not worship what I worship. . . . You have your religion and I have mine" (109). At Medina it assumed a more complex identity as Muhammad, somewhat like the early Christians, had to define his faith and practice against a "parent" group, which in both instances rejected its putative offspring.

This process of religious identification continued throughout Muhammad's stay in Medina, but early in his second year there he began a course of action that would eventually make him the true master of a Muslim Medina. In 628, he embarked on a more expansive thrust that made him, before his death in 632, the lord of Arabia.

THE MASTER OF MEDINA (624–628)

If Muhammad's mandate was to bring peace and stability to Medina, he went about it in a curious but, as it turned out, extremely effective fashion. He had problems at Medina: there was trouble with the Jews, and some Medinese resistance to the religious

preaching of this self-styled "Messenger of God" with a disturbing
set of attitudes. The Medinese opposition to Muhammad is not
given a very high profile, but it glimmers nonetheless from the
Quran. And finally, there were economic difficulties. Muhammad
had already begun to address these with his creation of brotherhood arrangements between the Meccan Migrants and the Medinese Helpers. But the landless refugees from Mecca, who could
neither sow nor reap nor do any other kind of productive work in
that closed oasis society — whose normal hospitality expired after
three days — must have continued to be a burden to the Medinese
Muslims and a source of concern to Muhammad.

It may have been anger that initially prompted Muhammad and
his followers to engage in skirmishes with the Quraysh in the
wastelands between Mecca and Medina, or it may have been the
hope of stealing some sustenance from their enemies — and their
relatives. One of the most remarkable elements Islam introduced
into the hostilities of Arabia was internecine strife within families.
In Arabia tribe battled tribe; kin fought alongside kin. But Islam's
claims were supertribal; they transcended blood and family, much
as Jesus' own, who said he had come "not to bring peace but a
sword, to set a man against his father" (Matt. 10:34–35). But
Jesus' followers had never had to resort to the sword, whereas
Muhammad's had it thrust into their hands. While still at Mecca, if
we have the chronology right, during Muhammad's last days
there, a revelation had come to him for the first time permitting
Muslims to resort to force, or rather, to meet Quraysh violence
with violence (Quran 22:39–41).

Nothing came of these early episodes as far as we know, but at
Medina Muhammad grew more aggressive. He seems to have led
attacks on isolated Quraysh bands without any apparent provocation. Economics suggests itself as a motive: when Muhammad
heard of a rich Meccan caravan returning home from the north in
624, he ordered his followers to attack it, since "perhaps God will
give it to us as prey." Not all the Muslims were keen on the project, which seemed imprudent — probably even more so when the
Quraysh got wind of the plan and sent reinforcements to escort the
caravan home. There was a major confrontation between the two

forces to the west of Medina at Badr Wells. It was an astonishing success for the outmanned Muslims, so astonishing that the Quran later cited it as an example of divine intervention on behalf of Islam (3:13). The spoils were rich enough for the Muslims to quarrel about their disposition and a good part of sura 8, "The Spoils," is given over to the topic. The non-Muslims at Medina must have taken note of both the military success of the venture and the new-found wealth of the Muslims among them.

The battle at Badr Wells was a *casus belli* not between the Quraysh and the Muslims but between Mecca and Medina. Most of what we know about violence in pre-Islamic times has to do with Bedouin trials of honor, whereas the celebrated "battle days of the Arabs" were mostly about tribal fracases over watering holes and pasturage grounds. We know nothing of one town making war on another as was the case here. The Quraysh made two attacks on the unwalled oasis of Medina. The first, in March 625, is enshrined in Muslim mythology as the Battle of Uhud—there is a small hill of that name north of the town—when three thousand Meccans marched on the town. By all rights it should have been a Quraysh victory. The casualty figures were the reverse of what happened at Badr. Many Muslims were killed, but not Muhammad. He was wounded—struck by a thrown stone—but survived unrepentant and undeterred. The Quran apparently offers a lengthy explanation (3:120–199) of what happened and why, including the assurance that God had once again sent his angels into battle, three thousand of them, with many more in reserve if necessary (3:124–125).

The Quraysh lay relatively quiet for two years; enthusiasm for an anti-Muslim crusade must have been waning at Mecca. Then in March 627 they made one final attempt on Medina. According to our sources, the attack was prompted by the Medina Jews, who were suffering growing ills at Muslim hands. Whatever the case, this was no pitched battle like Uhud, where the Muslims came out of the oasis and fought, but rather a siege. The Muslims stayed within their Medina oasis forts and apparently covered some of the open ways into the town by digging a trench or ditch. Not all were keen for the project, if Quran 24: 62 refers to it, but the effort was successful. What later came to be called the Battle of the Ditch was in fact no battle at all: the Quraysh could not enter the town and the Muslims did not come out to confront them. Predictably — with our hindsight — the besiegers soon lost interest in a war of attrition far from home and began to drift off. This was pure fiasco. It was also the last serious attempt by the Quraysh to rid themselves of their homegrown prophet or, as it turned out, even seriously to oppose him.

These engagements brought most of the Medinese to the Prophet's side. They had little choice perhaps. They had offered Muhammad protection. But his aggressive actions toward the Quraysh moved the hostilities of one tribe against some of its own troublesome clansmen into a war between two settlements with no prior history of enmity between them. We hear of no mass conversions among the Medinese; there is merely the gradual disappearance of the issue of polytheism. Muhammad had indeed settled the civil unrest in the oasis but only by creating a common enemy for all parties, his own, the Quraysh. If Islam now began to seem inevitable to the Medinese, shortly it would appear profitable as well.

MUHAMMAD AND THE JEWS (CONTINUED)

Not merely modern political sensibilities make the Jews of Medina loom large in Muhammad's later career. The issue sprawls across the oldest biographies of the Prophet and runs, sometimes explicitly, sometimes implicitly, throughout the Medina suras. References to the Jews grow darker and more truculent as the Quran progresses, and the judgments are indeed more in anger than in sorrow. The Arab historians and biographers profess to explain why. Their explanations are not all of a piece, however. Some treat the theme theologically: the punishment of the Medina Jews, who were invited to convert and refused, perfectly exemplify the Quran's tales of what happened to those who rejected the prophets of old. Other early historians prefer a more political explanation, to which we now turn.

There were three principle Jewish tribes in Medina: the Qaynuqa, the Nadir, and the Qurayza. The first overt action against
them took place in the wake of the military success at Badr. Muhammad, possibly emboldened by his unexpected triumph, decided to push his advantage. The Qaynuqa were invited to convert
or face the dire consequences. "Don't be deceived," they answered. "The Quraysh knew nothing about war. *We* will fight!" So
they fought. It was that simple. The Jews' Arab patrons at Medina,
who had solemn obligations to the Qaynuqa, attempted to support
them, though not apparently with unanimity or enthusiasm. The
Qaynuqa locked themselves in their plantation fortresses, but to
no avail. Whoever among the Qaynuqa managed to survive were
driven from the oasis and the Muslims took over their properties.

A similar fate overtook the Nadir after Uhud. Here the accusation had to do with a plot to assassinate Muhammad. The Nadir
took to their forts and Muhammad flushed them out. Once again
the tribe was deported, men, women, and children, with whatever
property they could carry. Their lands, we are told, became the
Prophet's to dispose of as he would. He divided them among the
Migrants, to the exclusion of the Helpers, presumably because the
latter already had land of their own. Following the failed Quraysh
raid on Medina in 627 it was the turn on the Qurayza, the last of
Medina's major Jewish tribes. According to the *Life*, the Qurayza
had urged the Quraysh to attack the oasis and then failed to help
when they did. This restraint, or prudence, did not save them from
the Prophet's wrath. Indeed, Muhammad received a special revelation — it is not recorded in the Quran, but only as a story in the
Life — commanding him to attack the Qurayza. He did, and after
nearly a month of determined resistance, they saw the end was
near. The *Life* tells another oddly heroic story about the Jews —
already it had portrayed the Nadir marching off into exile with
flags flying and heads held high. In this instance, the Qurayza rejected the suggestion that they convert to save themselves and likewise refused to attack the Muslims because it was the Sabbath.
Finally, they appealed to their Arab patrons of the Aws. Once
again, the response was unenthusiastic: no one was willing to cross
Muhammad at this stage. Muhammad was conciliatory only to the

extent that he allowed one of the Aws to determine their sentence. His judgment was that the males of the Qurayza deserved death and that the women and children should be sold into slavery. It was done: between six hundred and eight hundred males of the Qurayza were publicly beheaded in the main market of Medina, and, if we are to credit the *Life*, Muhammad himself was the chief executioner. The tribe's real property was again divided among the Muslims.

That was the end of the Jews of Medina, a not inconsiderable part of the population, we can guess, though they had recently been reduced to clientage to the paramount Arab tribes of Aws and Khazraj. There is some evidence that they were the most literate Medinese and in many cases the craftsmen of the settlement. The Muslim newcomers appropriated the Jews' property — their lands and inventories — but not their skills. Yet they had little need for the latter; an even more profitable windfall had come upon them.

THE LORD OF ARABIA (628–632)

Later in 628, with Medina apparently in his control, Muhammad conceived the notion of participating in the umra, the Meccans' annual springtime religious festival. (The hajj was more "international" in character and took place in the autumn outside Mecca). He took with him the Migrants and Helpers, and in an effort to swell their ranks, whatever nearby Bedouin might be persuaded to go to Mecca. Though his intentions were said to be peaceful and he brought livestock to sacrifice at the Kaaba (a practice discontinued in Islamic times), we cannot know Muhammad's actual intent in this rather curious move. The Quraysh were not, in any event, inclined to allow their implacable enemy and his followers into the town. He got as far as a place called Hudaybiyya, where he was forced to halt. Envoys were exchanged with the Quraysh, and after a homely exchange of insults on both sides and a false rumor that his close follower Uthman had been killed by the Quraysh, an odd sort of agreement was worked out. Muhammad had to agree to withdraw so that "none of the Arabs [that is, the Bedouin tribes thereabouts] could say that he had made a forceful entry," and to postpone his umra until the following year. Whatever loss of face occurred was more than made up for by the main clause: hostilities between the two sides were suspended for a period of ten years during which people were free to join Muhammad or the Quraysh as they pleased. To discount what many may have suspected was a compromising show of weakness on Muhammad's part, a revelation was sent down declaring the Hudaybiyya agreement a "signal victory" (Quran 48:1).

The armistice, far from caving in to the Quraysh, may in fact have been a brilliant piece of strategy by Muhammad. Freed from any fear of attack from Mecca, Muhammad embarked on a series of increasingly daring raids at ever greater distances from his Medina base, all directed against the oases to the north and northeast of Medina. We do not know how the Bedouin had read the events at Hudaybiyya, but they were surely impressed by the new successes of the Muslim troops — townsmen turned raiders might be a more accurate description; these date growers and town dwellers were not born to the saddle — who, under the command of the man who called himself the Messenger of God, were imposing their will, and exacting tribute, from the richest settlements in western Arabia. Perhaps more to the point, these successful military ventures conducted in the name of religion brought a new and unexpected prosperity to the Muslims of Medina, and to whoever else they permitted to join the enterprise. The latter included the Bedouin who, ever the opportunists, began to join the colors of the Prophet in growing numbers.

MUHAMMAD AND THE JEWS (CONCLUDED)

Out of these successful raids a policy began to emerge. The settlements under attack were offered terms by the Prophet. If they acquiesced and surrendered, they agreed to pay an annual tax-tribute to Muhammad and the Muslim community. They retained the use of their property, but only on the understanding that it belonged to the now sovereign Muslims, who might claim it whenever they chose, which they rarely if ever did. Those who refused the terms and resisted forfeited all prospects if they were defeated, as they invariably were. The lesson was not lost on the next settlement up the trail.

These arrangements were part of Muhammad's political and military strategy and their consequences eventually disappeared within the larger political reality of the rapidly expanding "Abode of Islam." What persisted far longer—down to the present day since they became part of an unchanging religious law—were the religious demands and concessions made of and to the inhabitants of these same conquered oases. Khaibar, the first of them, was largely inhabited by Jews, whose numbers were swollen by Nadir refugees from Medina. But the Jews of these oases settlements were no longer treasonous members of the Medina umma. Politically, they were surrendered foes, and their submission won them concessions; religiously, they were People of the Book, Scripturaries like the Muslims, and that theological status won them tolerance.

The tolerance granted the Jews of Khaibur was formalized in the *dhimma*, the contract between the Muslim community and their subjects from among the People of the Book. This concordat guaranteed the latter the privilege—it is not a question of rights here; the victors are dictating terms to the vanquished—to continue to practice their religious rituals, a privilege not granted to the polytheists among the conquered peoples; they had to submit or face death, convert or perish. "Fight against those who do not believe in God or in the Last Day," the Quran forthrightly says (9:29). But the dhimma also imposed certain obligations on the vanquished Scripturaries. The full list of privileges and restrictions later appears in a document called the Covenant of Umar. It was supposedly granted by the second caliph, Umar ibn al-Khattab (r. 634–644), to the Christian inhabitants of Jerusalem on the occasion of the city's surrender in 635. Although the document itself is a later forgery and often brandished by Eastern Christians in their disputes with their Muslim sovereign—in that sense it is the Muslim counterpart of the forged Donation of Constantine—the Covenant of Umar does embody some of the basic conditions that bind the *dhimmi*s from that day to the present.

We can be certain that not all the later specifications were present in the dhimma dictated by the Prophet to the Jews of Khaibar — there were far more complicated, sophisticated, and aggressive People of the Book ahead for the Muslims — but it sets down the principles and conditions of all that follow. The Banu Israil of the Quran were monotheistic paradigms from a remote, unthreatening, but still educational past; the Yahud of Medina were treacherous allies who defaulted on a political contract. A third cohort was now added, the Jews who would come tumbling under the sovereignty of Islam, along with countless Christians. Many of them converted to Islam, as did many, many Christians, but others lived for well over a millennium under the universal and perpetual dhimma.

In the midst of this military activity, Muhammad in 629 did what he failed to do the previous year. He led a delegation of Muslims to Mecca to perform the umra there. It was his first visit to his birthplace since his dangerous escape seven years earlier, but he received a cold reception. After three days he was told his time was up and that he should leave. It must have been an unpleasant episode, though Muhammad's influential uncle Abbas appears to have embraced Islam on this occasion.

THE WIVES AND CHILDREN OF THE PROPHET

While briefly in Mecca for the umra, Muhammad married Maymuna, the widowed sister-in-law of Abbas. She was, by one count, his eleventh wife, and possibly his last, though early in 627 he received as a gift-concubine the Egyptian Christian Miryam. As might be imagined, Christian polemicists, who shared the assumption that prophets should be ascetic, if not celibate, had merry sport with the Prophet's many wives, and modern Muslim biographers of Muhammad have had to address the issue at every turn. His marriages did, however, cause some problems for his contemporaries as well, not because they suggested unbridled sexuality, which could be comfortably parsed as virility, but for other reasons. Arabian society was, no less than the biblical to which it was cousin, a polygamous one. The Quran addressed this custom and, for reasons that are not clear to us, though the context is one of equitable treatment of orphans, it limited the number of wives a Muslim might have to four (4:3). It is not a commandment, at any rate; it is a permission, and the very next line of the Quran warns that unless a husband can be equitable toward his wives, then it is better to be monogamous. But Muhammad had more than four, and we can sense something in the wonder this may have caused in Quran 33:50, which explicitly states that Muhammad— "and only you, and not the Believers"—may have as many as he and the women in question may wish. The other issue that perplexed Muslims—and provided additional ammunition for the later Christian enemies of Islam—was the fact that he married Zaynab, the wife of Zayd ibn Haritha, the Prophet's own former freedman and much favored adopted son. Adoption created consanguinity among the Arabs, and custom frowned on such near-kin marriages; there may also have been talk about the unseemliness of the divorce. It is clear from Quran 33:37–38 that Muhammad feared public opinion about this marriage, and not until he received an exculpatory revelation did he dare go through with it.

Muhammad was first married to the already twice widowed Khadija, and to her alone, for perhaps fourteen years, and she bore him all his children save one. There was first the boy Qasim, who died in infancy, and then the girls Zaynab (whose husband never converted to Islam), Ruqayya (who was married to the third caliph, Uthman—she accompanied him to Abyssinia with that early group of émigrés—until her death in Medina in 624), Umm Kulthum (first married to a son of Abu Lahab, Muhammad's archenemy at Mecca—Quran 111 deals with him—and then, after Ruqayya's death, to Uthman), and Fatima (who married Muhammad's cousin, and the fourth caliph, Ali). Khadija died in 619 and soon afterward, while still in Mecca, Muhammad married Sawda, the widow of one of his fellow Muslims. Also at Mecca, he became betrothed to Aisha, the then six-year-old daughter of his close associate Abu Bakr. The marriage was not consummated, however, until after the Hegira, presumably when Aisha reached puberty.

Note: Aisha, by all reports Muhammad's favorite wife, had an interesting history. She is the eyewitness who stands, despite her gender and age — she was only about eighteen when Muhammad died — behind many of the reports of the sayings and deeds (hadith) that form the core not only of the Prophet's biography but of the very substance of Islamic law. Her life with Muhammad is embroidered with a great deal of fancy, but there is a strong consensus that Quran 24:11–20, which reprimands the Muslims for believing in a scandalous libel, was about her and an incident that was thought — falsely, as the Quran itself makes clear — to have compromised her reputation. Among those alleged to have thought her guilty was Ali, Muhammad's cousin and confidant. If true, it would go far toward explaining Aisha's later antipathy toward Ali — she actually accompanied troops into battle against him — in the great political skirmishes for the leadership of the umma between 556 and 661.

It is difficult to make generalizations about Muhammad's eleven-odd wives and perhaps two concubines. Many of the relationships seem to have been political, some compassionate, some, perhaps Aisha and Zaynab, affairs of the heart. At Medina, after Aisha, Muhammad married Hafsa (his companion Umar's widowed daughter); Zaynab bint Khuzayma (already twice a widow); Umm Salama (another Muslim widow); Zaynab (his adopted son Zayd's divorced wife); Juwayriyya (daughter of a defeated Bedouin chieftain; perhaps a hostage or a spoil of war, or both); Umm Habiba (widow of an Abyssinian émigré and daughter of the powerful Quraysh leader Abu Sufyan); Safiyya (widow of the Jewish ruler of Khaibar, killed by the Muslims in 628; she converted to Islam); and Maymuna (sister-in-law of Abbas, another powerful Quraysh leader). In addition, we know of two concubines: the Jewess Rayhana of the Qurayza, who became Muhammad's property when the tribe surrendered in 627, and Miryam, the Coptic "gift" who bore him a son, Ibrahim, who died in infancy.

THE OPENING OF MECCA

The Quraysh, who had treated Muhammad coldly, even shabbily, on the occasion of his umra to Mecca in 629, received their harsh comeuppance soon enough. The ten-year armistice of Hudaybiyya was of course still in effect, but there were, almost inevitably in those fluidly moving tribal zones, violations of the truce between the Bedouin allies of the Quraysh and those of Muhammad. They were not likely fatal since the dispirited Quraysh appeared willing to negotiate, but Muhammad would have none of it. The moment was at hand, he decided, to deal with the Quraysh once and for all.

An expedition was prepared. That fact could not be concealed, but its destination was, at least till the raiders were already on their way, this time, unusually, toward the south, toward Mecca. Luck was with them. Abu Sufyan, the leader of the Quraysh, was surprised and captured outside Mecca and was persuaded to save himself by embracing Islam.

> *Note*: Two late Meccan converts, Abu Sufyan and Abbas, turned out to be the progenitors of the two great Arab houses to rule Islam as an empire: Abu Sufyan of the Umayyads (661–750 in Damascus) and Abbas of the Abbasids (750–1258 in Baghdad). We have no preserved Umayyad historians so the figure of Abu Sufyan lies largely unredeemed in the debris of early Islamic history, but the many historians who wrote under the Abbasids did their best to rehabilitate the memory of Abbas. As we have seen, Muslim tradition has Muhammad marrying, Umm Habiba, Abu Sufyan's daughter, in 628, and Maymuna, Abbas' sister-in-law, the following year.

The Muslim troops entered the city with orders to act with restraint. Little was necessary since resistance seems to have been negligible. There followed a scene of quiet triumph. Muhammad entered the Haram and proclaimed, "The truth has come and falsehood has passed away." He ordered the numerous idols burned or smashed to pieces. Pictures were removed from inside the Kaaba, all save one of Jesus and Mary that the Prophet allowed to remain.

> *Note*: The Kaaba had been rebuilt during Muhammad's youth—he had assisted in the project, as we have seen—out of timbers from a recent shipwreck on the Red Sea coast. The project was under the direction of one of the survivors, named Baqum (Pachomius), since the Meccans, whose dwellings were of mud brick, had little idea how to construct a timber roof. The pictures may have come from the wreck, or perhaps they were the work of that same shipwrecked Christian. Whatever the case, they disappeared in later reconstructions of the building.

The Quraysh were treated with what appears to be remarkable leniency. "Go," Muhammad said, "You are freed." And he left the town. Muhammad had little to fear. Mecca had fallen to the Prophet long before he actually entered it.

The Bedouin, the camel and sheep steppe nomads among the Arabs, were opportunists, but they were not blind to oasis politics. Some among the tribes scented danger in the rise of the new master of Medina. We cannot follow all the workings of what followed— the internal history of the Bedouin is written in sand—but there was enough fear of where Muhammad was heading to generate a coalition of tribes that made one final attempt at taking him down. The Bedouin collected their forces at a place called Hunayn, and Muhammad led his Muslims out of Medina to meet them. The Muslims were superior in numbers, but the circumstances of this kind of "display" battle may have been new to them, and initially there was some panic in the Muslim ranks. They rallied, however, and in the end it was the Bedouin who broke and ran. Once again the Quran makes one of its few contemporary allusions. "On the day of Hunayn," it instructed the Muslims, "God sent hosts you could not see and punished those who did not believe" (9:25–26). As on the fields of Badr (8:9) and Uhud (3:121–125), God had intervened through his angels on behalf of his Prophet.

Problems before and after Tabuk

The raiding continued. Earlier in 629, between his umra of that year and his conquest of Mecca, Muhammad had launched his most ambitious and perhaps most ill conceived expedition deep into distant Roman-Byzantine Syria. The alleged reason was the murder of one of the Prophet's emissaries to someone said to be the Arab governor of Bostra (today Busra). The truth of that does not concern us here, but the raid, which was met by government troops at a village called Muta east of what is now the city of Kerak in Jordan, is well attested — indeed, it is the first event of Muslim history mentioned by a non-Muslim source, in this case the Byzantine historian Theophanes (d. 818) — as is the fact that it was a disastrous defeat for the Muslims. Muhammad did not accompany the raiders, but he was there to console them on their return. In his weekly sermon he assured his fellow Muslims that he had had a vision of the "martyrs of Muta" at their ease in Paradise.

In March 630, after his triumph at Hunayn, Muhammad made the umra to Mecca, though not the hajj, which, according to the standard *Life*, "The people made . . . that year in the way the (pagan) Arabs used to do." Then he planned yet another raid far into the north, not as foolhardy as the expedition to Muta perhaps, but dangerous enough for some Muslims to balk at it. The situation was sufficiently critical that a revelation addressed it, lashing out at those who preferred to "sit at home" and "preferred to be with the women who remain behind" (Quran 9:81–86). God's advice is strong and straightforward:

> It was not fitting for the people of Medina and for the Bedouin in the vicinity to refuse to follow God's Apostle, nor to prefer their own lives to his, because everything that they would suffer or do would be accounted to their credit as a deed of righteousness — whether they suffered thirst or fatigue or hunger in the cause of God or trod paths to anger the unbelievers or received any injury. (9:120)

We are not well informed on either the motives for this expedition or the motives of the disinclined. The Helpers may have been disappointed at the almost total absence of booty from the conquest of Mecca, or the obvious leniency Muhammad showed his fellow Meccans in its sequel. The need for funds may have been growing and the obvious expedient was another raid, this time not into Roman territory as such—the Byzantines had recently driven their enemies the Persians from Syria and were reestablishing their authority—but only as far as the northernmost limits of what was now emerging as the "Medina Empire." The Prophet may have been probing. Or he may have been fishing.

On the available evidence, the malingerers had little to fear. This particular raid, which was led by the Prophet in person, halted at the town of Tabuk close to the present Jordan-Saudi border and seems to have been marked by little or no fighting. As soon as the Muslims showed the flag, a number of settlements sent their delegates to Muhammad at his camp at Tabuk to signal their capitulation. Notable among them was the "ruler" of Ayla, later Aqaba/Elath, at the head of the Aelanatic Gulf. He seems in fact to have been the bishop of the city, an example of how thoroughly Roman civil authority had already deserted its own provincial towns. This was also, significantly, the first Christian community to submit to Islam and be accorded the dhimma.

When he returned to Medina, Muhammad discovered that what had been malingering at the beginning of the campaign had turned into something far more serious. The Quran tells us:

> And those who have taken a mosque in opposition and unbelief, and to divide the believers, and as a place of ambush for those who fought God and His Messenger aforetime—they will swear "We desired nothing but good"; and God testifies they are truly liars. (9:107)

This is really quite mysterious, and the Muslim historians and commentators on the Quran have no single explanation of the events lying behind it. They all agree that the Prophet himself had approved the building of this mosque before leaving for Tabuk and that when the revelation just cited was sent down, he ordered it to be destroyed. A strong suspicion points to certain Medina Helpers as the builders, perhaps the same people who are referred from

Uhud onward by a word commonly translated as "hypocrites" (*munafiqun*), which is also the title of sura 63. What they actually were is more complex; perhaps "disaffected nominal Muslims in Medina" comes closest to describing them. But here they begin to take on the aspect of a schismatic community, a group of believers who wished to worship on their own (without the Prophet's supervision?) and in a place of their own. Whatever their motives, they were judged by God himself to be in "opposition and unbelief" and the mosque was destroyed at Muhammad's own command.

THE LAST YEARS (631–632)

In the ninth year of the new Muslim era, Muhammad made his final break with the polytheism into which he had been born and against which he had been preaching for more than two decades. It is announced in the opening verses of sura 9, called "The Immunity," a grave notice to the polytheists of the Hejaz that God's patience was at an end. The biographical sources attempt to fill in the details. This "proclamation" announced in the Quran was not delivered by the Prophet himself but by Abu Bakr or Ali—there was, as often, later disagreement on these points—on the occasion of the hajj of 631. It was the last pilgrimage in which the pagans would be allowed to participate, which may explain Muhammad's own absence. All treaty obligations contracted with them would be unilaterally dissolved. It was the formal end of the original Medina umma, the one initiated by the agreement signed by Muhammad and the Medinese, Muslims, pagans, and Jews shortly after his arrival in the oasis, and the beginning of a new umma, this one composed of Muslims alone, a theocracy that would be at the same time a church and a state.

The pagans were granted a four-month grace period during which all the treaty obligations would be scrupulously observed. But once that time was over, the consequences would be terrible: "When the sanctuary months are over, fight and slay the polytheists wherever you find them, and seize them and confine them and lie in wait for them in every kind of ambush. But if they repent and establish prayers and give the tithe, then open the way for them. Indeed, God is forgiving, merciful" (Quran 9:4–5)

Thus in the beginning of 632 Muhammad made his first hajj as a Muslim, and, as it turned out, his last. It was also in a sense the first Muslim hajj. Previously, at least in 631, Muslims and polytheists had side by side participated in the ritual as it had always existed, without any obvious modifications either in the liturgy itself or in the Muslims' participation in it. In 632 only Muslims were present, according to the proclamation at the previous pilgrimage, and they were led by Muhammad himself, who seems to have carefully picked his way through the elaborate ritual, changing here and there as he went along. The umra and the hajj were, after a fashion, combined; the practice of intercalation was forbidden. All this occurred in connection with this famous "Farewell Pilgrimage" and it became a template for all that were to follow: the Prophet's acts and instructions were recollected at length in the biographical sources.

Muhammad returned from the hajj in March 632; three months later he was dead. Yet his death was not sudden, though it was unexpected. To all appearances he was still a vigorous man, hardly the sixty-two-year-old of the traditional dating, which at that time and place would have made him an old man. Indeed, he had led a dangerous military operation over a long distance less than two years earlier. We are not told precisely what his ailment was. He simply grew ill and died. He had time to make certain dispositions — he appointed Abu Bakr to lead the prayer during his illness — but not the most crucial of all: he appointed no successor to head the umma. Muhammad died in bed, at his own residence, in June 632, the tenth year of the new Muslim era, as it would soon be called, surrounded by his wives and family. He lies buried in a rich tomb within the now extraordinarily grandiose Mosque of the Prophet at Medina. Next to him is an empty tomb that awaits Jesus.

COLLECTING THE QURAN

The Prophet of God was dead and the revelations had ceased. The Quran, as it existed at that moment, was in the hearts, memories, and, to an extent, records of the Muslims who survived Muhammad. *Our* Quran, the finished book, though its content authentically represents the revelations given to Muhammad, is surely not the work of the Prophet himself: other hands collected the suras. If Muhammad himself was not responsible, these same hands may even have joined some of the suras together since many of them, as we have just seen, appear to be composite, that is, made up of more than a single revelation. What those near-anonymous editors certainly did was arrange the suras in their present order, which is generally in descending order of length, longest to shortest, and assign them the names — "The Opening," "The Cow," "The Abundance," and so on — by which they are generally cited by Muslims.

Systematic study of the Quran as a canonical document began in Islam in the late eighth or early ninth century, and Western scholarship has been working on it for somewhat more than a century, trying to restore the original order and understand the editorial process that began at Muhammad's death and led to the Quran that is before us. The task has not been easy. The Quran as it stands is a very complex and often opaque text and we know remarkably little about what was happening in the Muslim community in the crucial first century of its existence. Almost all the sources of our information about the earliest community of Muslims, their concerns and accomplishments, date from after 750, or even later, better than a century after Muhammad's death.

The Bible and the Gospels are filled with many of the same themes and images as the Quran, but in the former books they are surrounded by a body of narrative that provides a context that smoothes the way to comprehension. The Quran, in contrast, has no narrative framework. It is not that God's utterances are totally disassociated from contemporary events; it is simply that we do not always, or even often, know what he is talking about, though Muhammad and his audience apparently did. Where the revelation does take the form of a story, in the "Joseph" sura (Quran 12), for example, the narrative is so allusive and disjointed that one can only assume that the Meccan and Medinan listeners were already somewhat familiar with the matter.

The Quran's literary style has been characterized as "referential rather than expository." The audience, we must assume, caught the references, but there is somewhat more to it than the listeners' privileged position. The ellipses and repetition of themes in the text, the abrupt shifts in the narrative point of view from first to second to third person, the great number of hanging pronouns whose antecedents are uncertain, also point to a text that was orally composed — or, to be more theologically correct, orally recollected and orally delivered. Seventh-century western Arabia was an overwhelmingly oral society, and whatever knowledge of writing existed was surely limited to a very few practitioners and to a few occasions. Nobody suggests that Muhammad himself wrote down the Quran, though there is strong evidence that he edited it. What the Muslim sources do insist on is that, while many were memorizing the Quran as it was delivered, parts at least were written down by others during Muhammad's lifetime. We know not what to make of this. The overwhelming orality of the culture and the deficiencies of Arab script at that time and place — its signs could only very imperfectly distinguish one letter from another: *b, t, th, n, i,* and *y* would all appear identical, for example — make it seem highly unlikely that such was the case. But the Muslim tradition says it was so, and Muslims accept this.

According to Muslim tradition, there were at Muhammad's death some believers who had memorized the Quran, while others, like his wife Hafsa, the daughter of the later caliph Umar, had in their possession written "copies." The tradition goes on to assert that under the early caliphs there were three separate attempts to collect and codify these various testimonies to the Quran. The first was under Abu Bakr (r. 632–634) immediately after the Prophet's death; the second, under Umar (r. 634–644); and a final, definitive effort under Uthman (r. 644–656). All three attempts seem very similar, with respect to motive — the fear of the multiplication of different versions and the death of "reciters" who knew the full text by heart — and even procedure. To accomplish their task, a committee was assembled, generally under the direction of the Prophet's "secretary," Zayd ibn Thabit, to collect all the available evidence, to "debrief" the reciters, and to assemble and collate the various written versions of the Quran. So it was done, and a standard edition was produced. Copies were sent to all the Muslim centers, with the order that older versions be destroyed. The latter might seem like an impossible task in an early medieval society, and so it evidently was since modern scholars have discovered in very old manuscripts and the remains of ancient commentaries various slightly different readings of quranic lines and verses. None of these variants challenges the basic meaning of the received text, but there are enough of them to cause us to believe that somewhat differing versions of the Quran were in circulation long after 650, and to suggest to others the even more radical position that the Quran as we know it, at least in the form we know it, did not come into existence until well into the eighth century.

THE ARRANGEMENT OF THE SURAS

Though the collection of God's revelations to Muhammad is self-described as *al-Quran*, or "The Recitation," it also calls itself a "Book," though that word is to be understood in its symbolic sense, in much the same way we use "Scripture." These revelations, the Quran asserts, are a Book in the same sense that the Jews and Christians possess a Book, a Scripture. That Book came from God, it is made clear, was delivered to Muhammad and pronounced by him, but the actual physical book in the sense of pages within covers came later and was produced by human beings. So too was the order of the suras, which, as we now have them are arranged, after a short introductory prayer (the *Fatiha*, or "Opening") that is reckoned as the Quran's first sura, roughly in descending length. This arrangement, whose original purpose we cannot fathom, obviously tells us nothing about the order in which they were actually revealed to Muhammad, but it is possible, based on their changing style and differing content, among other things, to discern somewhat generally their original chronological sequence.

From the point of view of prayer, ritual, or meditation, the chronological order of the suras is of no concern whatsoever to Muslims, who recite the work in its present nonchronological order, either by selecting passages deemed suitable for special occasions or in a monthly cycle. For this latter purpose, the standard edition of the Quran is divided, just as the Hebrew Bible is for an annual reading cycle, into thirty sequential "portions" of roughly equal length—they are generally marked in the printed text—to be recited as an act of piety, half a portion at the morning, half at the evening prayer, over the course of a month. But some Muslims *were* interested in the historical order of the revelation—even the original editors had affixed "Mecca" or "Medina" at the head of the suras. These were chiefly lawyers and exegetes for whom it was important to establish the context of each revelation, the so-called "occasions of revelation," so that the exact legal implications of each enactment might be understood. As we shall also see, there was the doctrine of "abrogation" that held that a later verse of the Quran might nullify an earlier one, a view that obviously puts the historical order of the suras, and even their verses, in play. Finally, later historians desired to provide a biography of Muhammad, for which the Quran was an important if elusive source.

The Muslims had, then, good reason to attempt to arrange the suras in their chronological order—though never to publish the Quran in that form, as is sometimes done in the West. The standard edition of the Quran, the present version of the book, has become in effect almost as canonical as the Book itself. Non-Muslims embarked on the enterprise of rearranging the suras only in the mid–nineteenth century as part of the general Enlightenment project to treat even sacred books, whether Bible, Gospels, or Quran, as documents rather than as Holy Writ. The results were not very different from what medieval Muslim scholars themselves arrived at: the Meccan suras can be divided into "early," "middle," and "late," whereas the long suras dating from the Medina period of the Prophet's activity, many of which are composite, defy much further categorization.

With these admittedly tentative results in hand, we can begin to trace the trajectory of Muhammad's ministry. Many of the suras that appear to be early show a manner and an elevation of style not unlike that of the Jewish prophets, as they admonish men to reform, or warn of the judgment of eternity. The later suras are longer and contain detailed regulations for the conduct of the already converted. Little wonder. At Mecca Muhammad was chiefly engaged in converting pagans, persuading their submission to the One True God. At that early stage submission meant primarily daily prayer, almsgiving and a strict commitment to worship only Allah, a deity well known to the Meccans, who nonetheless associated other gods, his so-called daughters, with him. Muhammad warned his fellow Meccans that in the past God had visited terrible punishments on those who ignored the prophets—many of the examples are drawn, as has been noted, from Bible history— whom God had sent to them. To no avail. Driven from Mecca to Medina in 622, Muhammad began to gain a more favorable hearing, and the Medina suras show him addressing a Muslim rather than a pagan audience. Both the background of his revelations and what is implied by submission are now spelled out in greater detail. Muhammad, we discover, stands at the end—there will be no other after him—of a line of prophets that began with Adam. Three of these prophets were notably entrusted with a public revelation in the form of sacred books—Moses the Torah, Jesus the Gospel, and Muhammad the Quran—illustrating God's continuing mercy toward a wayward humanity. The present revelation is, in a sense, the most fundamental of the three since it goes back to, and revives, the religion of Abraham, something that had managed to survive at Mecca in a disfigured form for centuries. That is why Islam still venerates the Kaaba built by Abraham and Ishmael— and toward which Muslims now pray—and must continue to practice the ritual of the hajj begun in Abraham's day.

MUHAMMAD AND JESUS:

AN ESSAY IN COMPARISON

Muhammad and Jesus, who figures by name more prominently in the Quran than Muhammad, are both recognized as in some sense the founders of the two religious communities that claim more adherents than any others. Both men are deeply revered among their followers and both have served as role models for countless believers, but beyond that, they have little in common. At the outset, it has already been remarked that it was Jesus' life, and particularly his death and resurrection, that founded Christianity, whereas it was Muhammad's message that founded Islam. Muhammad reported a revelation from God; Jesus *was* God's revelation. As his contemporaries remarked with amazement, Jesus spoke on his own authority.

Placed side by side, the two lives show remarkable differences. Jesus was born into a sophisticated religious and social milieu that already had nearly two millennia of development behind it. He read Hebrew and spoke Aramaic and likely some Greek. Though not a bookman in what was already becoming a bookish society, he had something of a local reputation as a scholar. Jesus is to us and was to his Jewish contemporaries a rather familiar figure in a very familiar landscape. Muhammad was not born and raised in a vacuum, of course, but as far as our knowledge is concerned, he might just as well have been. We know pitifully little of seventh-century Arabia, even less about the Hejaz, the region that nurtured him and where his life unfolded, and almost nothing about Mecca, his native town, save what is almost accidentally uncovered in the Quran. Muhammad was barely literate, we guess—a minor merchant we never see buying or selling. Jesus, whom we never see doing carpentry either, functioned nonetheless in front of what is for us a rich tapestry of context; Muhammad, against an almost blank screen.

In his ministry Jesus was speaking and acting before an audience of fellow Jews whom he was trying to convince that a new era, "the Kingdom," had dawned — or was about to explode in their day, an apocalyptic or eschatological notion with which they were all to some extent acquainted. Muhammad had more radically to convince polytheists to monotheism, and without benefit of sign or miracle, which Jesus had in abundance. Their lifestyles differed. Jesus was an itinerant preacher, a celibate, from all the evidence. Muhammad had a home, whether in Mecca or Medina, a wife — indeed many wives — and a large family that grew even more extended through marriage. Jesus had a specially selected and carefully trained inner circle, the Twelve. Muhammad had followers, some of them close, but he did not select apostles, nor did he even have disciples in the ordinary sense of the word. Jesus' active career lasted one year at the minimum, three at the maximum; Muhammad's, for twenty-two, during which he had the opportunity, which he manifestly took, to edit and emend the body of revelations he received. The suras of the Quran show many signs of having been rearranged and added to, and by the Prophet himself. Although he was the subject of the Gospels, Jesus obviously had no say as to what went into them, which of his sayings were reported and which not, or how accurately.

At the end of his brief career Jesus was publicly executed as a criminal, deserted by most of his followers. Muhammad was close to suffering the same fate. After twelve years of preaching at Mecca he had made relatively few converts and was himself in danger of being assassinated by enemies from among his own people. The apparent failure of Jesus' mission at Passover in 30 C.E. was "redeemed" by his resurrection, which gave his followers a new vision and a new hope. Muhammad was saved from a similar failure by his migration to Medina, where, in a new setting and under new circumstances, he began to make converts in such increasing numbers that by his death in 632 there were Muslims throughout western Arabia and the prospect of others beyond.

At Medina Muhammad became the head of a functioning community, at first an apparently civil one, but soon, with the conversion of the Medinese and the expulsion of first the Jews and then, at the end, of all non-Muslims from the umma, a community that was at the same time, and inextricably, religious and political. Muhammad was, in short, both prophet and statesman, pope and emperor, during the last ten years of his life. Jesus, in contrast, showed no interest in politics — "My Kingdom is not of this world." For someone to show no interest in politics in first-century Palestine was no simple matter, and the Gospels seem to go out of their way to show how Jesus avoided the political traps that his hostile questioners often set for him. Yet, for all that, Jesus was executed by a political authority on what appear to be political charges. "Kingdom," it is clear, was a term that could cut many ways in Roman Palestine, some of them dangerous.

If we cannot always come to terms with Jesus' political views, it is clear he wielded no political power. Although he was undoubtedly regarded as a leader by his inner circle of followers — Muhammad had no "apostles" in the same sense — it is difficult to recognize in that band of itinerants a society, or even a movement, in any ordinary sense. In any event, it was effectively ended by Jesus' death and had to be reconstituted by his followers afterward. Jesus had no personal role in the shaping of his *ekklesia*. This was the work of his heirs, including some, like Paul, who had never even known him in the flesh. Muhammad, in contrast, was stoutly, convincingly, and unmistakably in charge of his community from the beginning of his mission to the end of his life. He led its armies, collected its taxes, comforted, cajoled, and guided the umma from the time it had ten members till the day it had ten thousand, and counting.

5. *The Muslim Scripture: The Quran*

THE QURAN is the Scripture of the Muslims and comprises the series of revelations "sent down" — the Quran's own preferred expression — to Muhammad between 610 and his death in 632. The revelations were delivered orally, in a variety of circumstances, and, as it was explained, through the medium of the angel Gabriel. These God-sent communications were repeated verbatim and publicly by Muhammad over the twenty-two years of his ministry, first at Mecca between 610 and 622, and then at Medina from 622 to 632, and were finally collected into the Book as we have it. Thus the Quran is literally the Words of God, repeated, without error, by his "envoy" or "messenger" (*rasul*), as he is called in the Quran, and as every Muslim must and does affirm.

In its book form roughly the size of the New Testament, the Quran is presently divided into 114 units. In translations these suras are numbered in the manner of chapters, in the Arabic original of the Book they possess only titles — "The Opening," "The Spoils," "Noah" — which suggests that their sequence is not terribly important, though they also bear the rubric "Mecca" or "Medina," which indicates their point of origin and, by implication, that their order does in some way matter. The suras seem to be arranged roughly in descending length, and are themselves subdivided into verses (*aya*; pl. *ayat*), which are numbered in the text, so here at least the sequence does make a difference. Like the suras themselves, the verses vary in length, but in many instances they appear to be more natural units than the suras since numerous verses are end-rhymed and conform to a rhythmical pattern, whereas many suras seem to be composite, with different elements simply assembled into a whole.

SCRIPTURE: A HISTORY

Islam is reckoned, along with Judaism and Christianity, as a scriptural religion, that is, all three affirm the existence and their possession of a divine revelation in written form. "The Sacred Writings," "The Scripture," or "The Book" are practically interchangeable terms among the three communities, and their adherents can all be identified in some sense as "People of the Book," as the Muslims do in fact call them. The history of the three Scriptures in question shows marked differences, however. In the Jewish — and Christian and Muslim — view, God gave, and Moses wrote down, a distinct and discrete multipart book, the Law or Torah. But though the Torah holds pride of place in Jewish revelational history, God's direct interventions were in one manner or another continuous between Moses at the beginning and Daniel at the end of the Bible. Thus the Jewish Scripture is a collective work that includes, under the three headings of "Law," "Prophets," and the miscellany called "Writings," all of God's revelations to his people.

This was certainly the Jewish view in Jesus' day, when the community was coming to consensus on what was the Bible and what was not, and there is no reason to think that Jesus regarded Scripture any differently. He produced no new Writings or Book of his own, and so Christian Scripture is formally quite different from what the Jews thought of as such. The Gospels are accounts of Jesus' words and deeds set down, in approximately a biographical framework, by his followers. In the eyes of Christians, Jesus did not bring a Scripture; he was himself, in his person and message, a revelation, the "Good News." His life and sacrificial death sealed a

"New Covenant" that God concluded with his people, and so the Gospels, the account of the deeds and thoughts of the early Christian community recorded in the Acts of the Apostles, and the letters of various of Jesus' followers all came to be regarded by Christians as a New Covenant or Testament to be set down next to the Old — that recorded and commemorated in the Jewish Bible.

Muhammad may have had a somewhat different understanding of this complex process. Though he commonly refers to the Jewish revelation as *Tawrat*, the Prophet of Islam was certainly aware that there were other Jewish prophets, and so possibly other revelations, after Moses. But he never mentions a New Testament; his sole references are to a singular "Gospel," in Arabic *Injil*, and he seems to have thought of it as a sacred book that Jesus had brought or written, much as Moses had the Torah.

Muhammad had a strong sense of the prophetic calling and the line of prophets that had created the Judeo-Christian tradition; after some brief initial hesitation, he placed himself firmly within that line. He too was a prophet, and when God's earlier revelations had become distorted at the willful and perverse hands of the Jews and Christians, God had given to him, no less than to Moses and Jesus, a revealed Book. What God himself had instructed Muhammad to "recite" was in fact a series of messages delivered to Muhammad by the angel Gabriel over twenty-two years. Each part was already identified as Scripture during the Prophet's lifetime, and the Book was finally closed only with Muhammad's death.

The Quran, then, differs from the Bible and the New Testament, neither of which began, as the Quran did, with the assurance that it was Scripture. Indeed, the other two became Scripture only after a long and, to us, largely invisible process — at the end of which the community conferred scriptural status. What came forth from Muhammad's, mouth, in contrast, was self-described first as "The Recitation" (*al-Quran*), almost certainly in the liturgical sense reserved for God's words, and then unmistakably as Scripture (*al-Kitab*) and unhesitatingly located within the Judeo-Christian Holy Writ tradition.

THREE SACRED BOOKS, THREE PEOPLES OF THE BOOK

When the Peoples of the Book, the Muslim designation for Scripturalists, are said to "possess" a revelation in written form, it does not mean merely that they have access to it or follow it or venerate it, all of which they do; it also signifies that they were its designated recipients and that they remain its privileged guardians and interpreters. The Scripturalists are, each of them, also a Chosen People, and the Scripture they possess both records and validates that choice. Chosen People is a unique claim—there are no Chosen Peoples in the eyes of any of them—and so there is an obvious tension between the plural Peoples of the Book and the very singular Chosen People. There are three sacred books and three Peoples of the Book but only one of them, one of those Scriptures and one of those peoples who possess it, is truly authentic.

The Books in question—the Bible, the New Testament, and the Quran—though looked on as emanating from the same source, are very different works. The Bible is a complex and composite blend of religious myth, historical narrative, legal enactments, prophetic admonitions, cautionary tales, and poetry composed over a long period and edited at some point into a single Book. The time span for the composition of the New Testament is considerably shorter, a half-century perhaps, but it too has a very mixed content of quasi biography, community history, letters, and, in some versions, an apocalyptic Book of Revelation. The Quran, as we have seen, is also composed of parts, not books but shorter, more chapterlike units called suras. Though they are formally identical to the words sent down by God and inerrantly reported by Muhammad, the suras differ materially among themselves in length, style, and content. Finally, as we have seen, they all date from a twenty-two-year span in Muhammad's life.

Thus there came into being three sacred books, each in some sense the Word of God. Each collection has traditionally been regarded by its faith community as a complete, authoritative, and universal statement regulating the role and conduct of humankind vis-a-vis its Creator. Each Scripture was, in addition, the birthright and charter for a community that had not existed before. Each community lived in the profound conviction that God had spoken to it for the last time: the Jews, for the first and final time; the Christians, for the second and final time; the Muslims, for the third and final time. And each had a highly ambivalent view of the Books in the hands of the others.

The phrase "People of the Book" first occurs in the Quran. When it is used there, or by Muslims generally, it refers to those communities — Jews, Christians, Muslims, and latterly some others, like the Zoroastrians, more out of political pragmatism than theological courtesy — that came into being by way of a prophet's bringing them a revelation in the form of a sacred book sent down by God. Although the source of the Books, the unique God worshiped by the monotheists, and so their truth, is the same, the Scriptures themselves differed — witness their different names — not only in their prophetic messenger and the occasion of their revelation, but far more substantially, as we shall see, after the Jews and Christians began tampering with their Books, as the Muslims allege.

On Tampering with Scripture

At one point the Quran regarded what it calls the *Tawrat* as confirmatory evidence for the truth of its own message (4:47; 6:92). It must not long have served as such, however, not at least at Medina where the Jews had access to a Torah, though in what form we do not know, whether textually or through a Targum paraphrase or as an oral transmission, or some combination of such. In any event, there was religious and political trouble between the Jews and the new Muslim master of the oasis, which is reflected in the Medina suras of the Quran. Questions were raised about the Jews' reliability as transmitters of the Torah and so too of the authenticity of the "text" in their possession. "Woe to those," sura 2:79 intones, "who write Scripture by their own hand and then say, 'This is from God'" Again, in 3:78: "And truly there are some among them who twist Scripture with their tongues so that you suppose that it is Scripture and it is not; and they say, 'This is from God,' and it is not from God. They lie against God and they know it."

These are the grounds for what soon developed into the Muslim doctrine of *tahrif*, or "falsification," the charge that the Jews (and latterly, the Christians) altered their Scriptures. The Quran's instance of that charge may have had to do with the Medina Jews' failure to acknowledge Muhammad's prophethood, or even, as the standard *Life* of Muhammad later suggested, of differing interpretations of a biblical passage. The way the story unfolds in the *Life*, it was a question of an actual text (Deut. 22:24) that an unnamed Medina rabbi attempted to conceal by placing a hand over it in order to belie Muhammad's judgment that the punishment for adultery was stoning (suggested, without detail, in Quran 5:42–49). The case may indeed have been, as Quran 5:42 suggests, that some Jews called on Muhammad, now the Grand Arbiter of Medina, to judge a case of adultery between two Jews of the oasis and that the Prophet attempted to render a judgment on what he understood to be scriptural grounds. What is highly improbable, however, is that there followed an argument about a *text*, which the local rabbis possessed and whose reading they attempted to conceal and which Muhammad then demonstrated *ex litteris* was the correct one.

Muslims recognize that both the Torah and the Gospel originally represented true and authentic revelations from genuine and esteemed prophets, Moses (Musa) and Jesus (Isa), but subsequently Jews and Christians tampered with the texts—they removed predictions of Muhammad, for one—and so their present versions are generally unreliable. They are not, in any event, either required or even recommended reading for Muslims. Christians argued with Jews throughout the Middle Ages on what the Bible, which they both accepted, meant. Muslims devoted their polemic energies rather to demonstrating that that same Bible, and the Gospels as well, had been tampered with to the extent that they were unusable.

Who Wrote Scripture?

The Bible is not merely God's direct speech — indeed, examples of such direct discourse form only a small percentage of the whole — but is a composed narrative framework within which actions as well as speech unfold, and most often it is the speech of mortals. The Jews understood that the biblical books had authors — Moses, for example, and David, and Ezra — and to that extent they were linguistically conditioned, though nonetheless inspired. The Quran, in contrast, seems to present itself as the *ipsissima verba* of God, and in "manifest" or "convincing" Arabic (Quran 16:103, etc.). It has no framing narrative, however, no authorial signature or presence. In the Muslim view, Muhammad is not even a transmitter; he merely announced with absolute accuracy what he himself had heard. The consequence, then, is that the Quran contains the precise words of God, without human intervention or conditioning of any sort; that God had spoken, and Muhammad had heard and reported, Arabic speech. Finally, both Jews and Muslims use the text of Scripture as the essential base for their liturgical prayers. Though the Mishnah explicitly allows the use of the vernacular ("any language") for the central liturgical prayers, the pull of the original tongue is strong among Jews, whereas among Muslims the practice of using Arabic in liturgical prayer is practically universal.

Islam did not have, then, or did not recognize, an author or a multiple-author problem. God had spoken in this instance to one sole messenger, Muhammad, and the Quran is, in effect, his Torah; it is, in its entirety, God's Word, without the addition of either the Books of Kings or Job. Muslims, moreover, will distinguish rather sharply the "inspired" Muhammad, whose word was Torah, from the man of Mecca and Medina who offered explanation, advice, and wise counsel. These latter were not in the Quran but were collected in a kind of deutero-canonical form in the "Prophetic reports," or hadith (see chapter 7). Some non-Muslims have argued that the hadith are a kind of Muslim apocrypha, the sayings pool out of which the Quran was selected and anointed as revelation, but the vocabulary, style, and content of the great body of hadith are so different from what we have in the Quran as to make that possibility highly unlikely. The hadith belong to another world. They had their origin in Muhammad's own inspired, but decidedly human, head and heart, according to the Muslims, or in the fertile but tendentious imaginations of eighth- or ninth-century lawyers, according to most non-Muslims.

A DIFFERENT BOOK

If we turn to the earliest of the monotheist traditions, we do not know how Judaism, if that is the right word in this context, began. In the Bible, whence the entire tale hangs, God, *the* God who created them, seems to be on intimate terms with Adam and Noah and any number of other mortals, offering advice and admonition as seems required. Then later — the generations are told off with great specificity — he speaks to Abraham, a "Hebrew" of "Ur of the Chaldees" who had migrated with his family to Palestine, and suddenly everything becomes more focused and more consequential. We have entered the master narrative of the entire Bible through the portal called "The Covenant," the treaty or pact that was broached and concluded by God with Abraham. Its sequel, which unfolds through the twenty-odd books of the Bible, may be titled "The Chosen People" and it traces the ups and, remarkably, the considerable downs of the Covenant among its recipients, the Israelites. The narrative winds down in the sad dark days after the Israelite return from Exile in Babylonia but the story itself goes on, now told by contract writers, historians, poets, aphorists, and lawyers who understood the story line but brought somewhat less inspiration to their work.

It is no Bible before us in the Quran or Recitation, however. There is no master narrative, no reassuring "In the beginning . . ." to signal the commencement of anything resembling a "story." There is, in fact, no beginning, middle, or end to the book save in the most literal physical sense that the Quran has a first page and a last. The Recitation is a quilt of stitched-together discrete pieces, which are indeed units but whose sequence leads from nowhere to nowhere. The longest and most circumstantial of them stand at the beginning and the brief, and most emotive — some little more than an exclamation — at the end. They might be reshuffled in quite random fashion, and though the result would be a profound affront to nearly a millennium and a half of tradition, the rearrangement would not materially affect the Quran's message or our understanding of it.

The absence, then, of a narrative line is part of what renders the highly recognizable biblical figures in the Quran somewhat unfamiliar as well. The biblical prophets do have a purpose and a context in the Quran; it is just that they are not the Bible's own. They are put forward, with some few exceptions, as "warnings" — Muhammad himself is qualified as a "warner" — as exemplifications of what happens when people ignore the warnings of those same prophets. They are cited rather than described by the "speaker" in the Quran, whether that be God or Muhammad on God's behalf, for the benefit of the audience of the Recitation, the plural "you" who are sometimes unbelievers and at other times those who have already "submitted" to the One True God. They speak only in indirect discourse: God quotes them — "They say . . ." — only to refute them — "You say (to them) . . ."

THE OTHER SCRIPTURES

There can be no doubt that the Quran "used" the earlier Scriptures of what had been up to that point the Judeo-Christian tradition and henceforward might be characterized as the Judeo-Christian-Islamic tradition. Behind this usage lurks another question, though it is not one entertained by Muslims since it implicitly assumes that Muhammad is the author of the Quran and explicitly asks where he got his obvious acquaintance with the Bible and the New Testament. The Quran, as we have just seen, has a great deal to say about the Bible, though somewhat less about the New Testament. Little wonder, the Muslim says, since all three revelations are from the One True God, who, in this, the latest of his revelations, reflects on and interprets his earlier messages. But the non-Muslim is, of course, asking the question not of God but of Muhammad: where and when did this apparently illiterate Arab of a remote settlement in western Arabia get his information about the Books of the Jews and the Christians?

There are a great many (speculative) answers to the non-Muslim's question about Muhammad's sources, but they will not be discussed here since they deny the essential premise shared by all Muslims. It should be remarked, however, that the question was asked (and answered) in a highly leading manner of Muhammad himself: somebody had supplied him with this material (Quran 16:103), which was nothing but "old yarns" (25:5), of which more will be said later. Muslims and non-Muslims alike might raise a parallel question not with respect to the Quran but concerning its audience. Where did *they* derive their knowledge of what they were hearing? How was it that those largely illiterate villagers of Mecca knew more about the biblical Jesus and Mary than later literate and far more cosmopolitan Muslims who had to have the Quran's often opaque scriptural allusions explained to them by Jewish and Christian converts to Islam? Muhammad's Mecca and the Meccans who first heard the message of Islam remain a profound mystery. We have the Quran before us, but we can scarcely imagine its original audience.

One thing seems safe to say about those early seventh-century Meccans. Whatever knowledge they possessed of things biblical was not *textual*. The Quran's audience was not literate. If Muhammad was unlettered, as Muslims claim and he almost certainly was, so too were the Meccans who heard his pronouncements. Nor was there a text available even if he or they had been able to read. No version of either the Bible or the Gospels was available in Arabic in the seventh century, and none would be for perhaps two centuries after the Prophet. The religious culture of Muhammad's Arabia was overwhelmingly, if not exclusively, oral, and, at least among Arab speakers, midrashic rather than textual. Except for certain liturgical uses, the Bible had been replaced by Bible history, stories derived from the Scriptures but then enlarged, enhanced, and illumined in the manner of haggadic midrashim. And it was precisely those midrashic tales of the prophets and Jesus and Mary that had passed through Jewish and Christian hands and finally come to rest in the Quran, some, undoubtedly, with one final homiletic turn from the Prophet himself.

The Quran's citation, and understanding, of selected passages from the Bible and the New Testament became, for a very long time, the Muslims' only access to those earlier revelations: first, because the Quran had superseded them, and second, because the Jews and Christians had either concealed part of their sacred books or else tampered with them, rendering them useless not only to those other communities but to the Muslims as well. This essentially theological point of view, which the Quran invokes to explain why the Jews in particular had not accepted Muhammad's prophethood, long narrowed the field of discourse between Muslims and the other monotheists. The polemic from these latter was often directed at the Muslims' misunderstanding of their Scriptures, and the Muslims, if they chose to address the accusation directly, were hampered by their unfamiliarity with the full texts of either the Bible or the New Testament in Arabic. Even when such translations were finally in circulation among Jews and Christians in the ninth and tenth centuries, Muslims seem not to have used them. As late as the fourteenth century learned Muslim authors still apparently preferred using oral (and often inaccurate) accounts of the scriptural texts from converts among the People of the Book.

IN THE SILENCE AFTER THE SEAL

All who believe in a purposeful God are assured that the divine purpose is manifest in the world. God's providential care and purpose are visible in various signs of nature, and the Creator is thought to have occasionally intervened directly in the affairs of his creatures for the benefit of his favorites among them. What sets the three monotheistic communities apart, and unites them as Peoples of the Book, is their shared conviction that there has also been a direct and verbal revelation of God's will to his Chosen People, and thus, through them, to all humankind. That revelation has been, moreover, successive: across the books of the Bible; for Christians, from the Old to the New Testament; and for Muslims, from *Tawrat* to *Injil* to *Quran*. For Christians and Muslims at least, those revelations have also been progressive, one following another toward a foreseen end. The divine plan in this serial revelation was more apparent to Christians than to Muslims perhaps. For Christians, the biblical revelations were preordained to end with Jesus, the promised Messiah who was in his own person the revelation of a New Covenant. Although Muhammad and the revelation entrusted to him are the climax of what had been sent down before, he is merely asserted to be the end or "seal" (Quran 33:40) of a series of prophets speaking for God. Even less determined was the earlier end of the prophetic (and so the revelational) tradition in Israel: though there was considerable speculation on the subject, the Jews were unsure why God had fallen silent after Haggai, Malachi, and Zechariah.

When God fell silent, the believers began to read and speak and the great age of scriptural scholasticism began. The Word was now text—not until the nineteenth century did it become for some merely a document—and the process of unpacking its infinitely rich contents was under way. What is now figured as unpacking was once more soberly known as exegesis (Gk. *exegesis*, a "drawing" or "leading out")—in Hebrew *midrash*, "inquiry" and in Arabic *tafsir*, a "disclosure" or "explanation"—a name for the general process of extracting the meaning from a text, which in this case happened to be the transcribed Word of God.

All scriptural exegesis, Jewish, Christian, or Muslim, is, of course, committed to discerning both what the text means in its literal intelligibility and, more specifically, what its behavioral imperatives are for us, the community of believers, and for me and thee, the individual believers. But how the text is approached, with what methods and with what assumptions, differs considerably within the faith communities. The earliest scribal tradition in Israel, and the first to address the study of the Torah in a systematic fashion, appears to have been motivated chiefly by lawyerly and didactic concerns, the same that led to the collection and canonization of Scripture by those same professionals. The objective was to keep a people in the rapidly changing post-Exilic world—even Hebrew, the very language of revelation was disappearing—in touch with and observant of the community's foundation traditions. There may have been a mimetic element at work as well: the Israelites' was not the only scribal tradition in the ancient Near East, nor was the Torah the only holy book. Both Egypt and Babylonia provided exemplary modes of how to read a sacred text.

There was a larger dose of mimesis ahead. This systematic and chiefly legal approach to the Bible on the part of post-Exilic Jews was confronted from the third century B.C.E. onward by quite another exegetical tradition that read its texts as both literature and theology; that is, it passed them through filters that focused on either their aesthetic value or their underlying sense, a procedure the Greeks called *allegoria*, or "another reading." This allegorical reading was at once more figured, more spiritual, and more profound than the literal sense with which Israel's lawyers had chiefly concerned themselves. The Hellenic ideologues behind this "New Criticism" were chiefly Stoics, who were much concerned with semantics, and the later Platonists, whose visions of the distinction between the present material appearances and spiritual realities that lay behind them powered the search for allegoria.

It was chiefly in the academic environment of Alexandria that Jewish exegesis, and later its Christian counterpart, began to apply Hellenic New Criticism to Scripture. The Jew Philo (d. ca. 25 C.E.) was the absolute pioneer in reading the Torah through the filters of Hellenic exegesis, and he already shows the anxieties that would thereafter haunt allegoria, whether its practitioners were Jews, Christians, or Muslims. The texts that lay under the hands of the pagan Hellenic exegetes were neither guaranteed nor normative, while those of the Scripturalists were God's and not humans' words, and they served, moreover, as the basis of each community's behavioral code. That normative function of revelation lay principally in its literal sense—"Thou shalt not kill"—and so any movement away from the letter in the direction of allegory threatened at worst a kind of antinomianism and at best a degradation of the importance of the plain sense of what God was saying. Philo at the outset and many after him clung tenaciously to the literal sense of Scripture even as they explored the riches of allegoria.

UNPACKING THE WORD OF GOD

If we turn to the Quran and its early exegesis, we are in a very different landscape. The Quran is not history; its initial intent was to convert—the Quran's original audience were idolaters and polytheists—and its literary form is kerygma, "proclamation," or preaching. Hence, its "exegetic truth" was never the same as that of the Bible and the Gospels. The Gospels too are "preaching" — the Gospels and the Quran share the title "The Good News" (Quran 17:9)—though in the Gospels the proclamation is embedded in a historical narrative wherein Jesus' reported words and deeds constitute the kerygma. All three revealed texts were "true," of course, in the sense that they came from God, but the issue here is the exegetic point of approach to the text, the extraction of God's intended meaning from God's words.

The literal sense of Scripture was certainly the primary concern of both Jewish and Muslim exegetes. There were, however, times when the literal meaning did not make any sense, or contradicted something else in Scripture, or was simply unacceptable, usually on moral grounds. Indeed, the very first book of the Bible reads like a textbook of such instances and produced a score of scriptural conundra to test the exegetical skills of Jews and Christians alike. If that latter seems like an odd notion in connection with the Word of God, consider how many Jews and Christians are now incapable of understanding Genesis in its literal sense, that the world and all in it were created in six days, or that God required "rest" on the primitive beginnings of what turned out to be a weekend. In addition, many Jews of the Greco-Roman era, and many Christians and Muslims after them, were unwilling to accept the anthropomorphisms of Scripture, where God is portrayed in human terms ("He stretched out His hand," "He spoke thus to Moses," "His throne is eternal," etc.). The Septuagint softened many of these Hebrew anthropomorphic expressions in their passage into Greek, but other students of the Bible still had to resort to an "other reading" (allegoria), a sense residing behind or under the literal meaning, in order truly to explain Scripture.

The earliest Muslim concern about the "reading" of Scripture was along a crucial fault line to which the Quran itself had drawn attention, that between the "categorical" (mukhamat) and the "ambiguous" (mutashabihat) verses in the Quran (3:7). The Arabic words describing the verses are themselves somewhat ambiguous, as was the possibility of understanding these latter, whether by God alone or also by "those firmly rooted in knowledge," that is, the experts. They pointed, in any event, to some type of distinction within the verses of the Quran, and exegesis was bound to follow where the arrow pointed.

The Quran thus openly warns of its own ambiguities, and so Muslims have not hesitated to attempt to unravel the obscurities of the sacred text; indeed, they have devoted enormous energy to the task of tafsir in all the same types practiced by the Jews and Christians. These exegetical efforts eventually ranged from detailed and sophisticated study of the lexicographical and syntactical problems posed by the Quran to driving the meaning into the sometimes remote regions where sectarian preferences or mystical longings wished it to go. But not perhaps from the very beginning. Since the Quran was not a historically conditioned revelation, but rather was thought to reflect an eternal heavenly archetype composed of the very same words, the so-called Mother of the Book, the Muslim approach to its exegesis was initially quite different from that pursued by the other Peoples of the Book. The Quran did not easily suffer either translation or paraphrase. On the Christian premise, Jesus was his own revelation: he could teach its significance with authority and pass on that teaching to his disciples in a formal and imperative fashion. Muhammad, in contrast, was the conduit of God's revelation, much as Moses was, and during his own lifetime there was no question that he and only he was the authoritative interpreter of that revelation for the Muslim community.

THE QURAN READS ITSELF:
ABROGATION, EMENDATION, ELABORATION?

It is a commonplace belief in the three monotheistic communities that Scripture interprets itself, that later verses sometimes elucidate and explain earlier ones. The latter books of the Bible often revert to the Torah, and the New Testament constantly reflects on the Old. Paul's later letters revisit earlier ones to enlarge and clarify matters. Matthew and Luke "read" and edited Mark, and Mark himself, it has been argued, was revising the earlier Pauline "gospel" by supplying it with a narrative framework. The Quran too is its own primary exegete, though it represents a somewhat different case from the other Scriptures. It has been suggested, for example, that the Medina suras, which differ markedly in style and manner from what preceded them, are already a kind of "reading" of the "primary" revelation contained in the suras sent down during Muhammad's twelve years at Mecca.

To divide the Quran into a "primary" and a "secondary" stratum, even if both are called revelation, does violence to the Muslim tradition, but no one would deny that the work is the output of a single individual over some twenty-two years. There was no lack of opportunity, then, for that same individual, to offer revisions, emendations, or elaborations to what had already been promulgated. There is internal evidence that this is indeed what happened. In some early suras — 74:31 is a good example — the internal rhythm and assonance scheme of the prose-poetry is abruptly interrupted by an intrusive prose passage that appears to be a later interpolation to explain a problematic word or concept in the preceding line, after which the original rhyme and rhythm resume.

The Quran introduces, however, a radical form of scriptural reinterpretation. The notion of inspiration, coupled with the conviction that God is both omniscient and unchanging, strongly argues that God's Words are totally and simultaneously true, and the three monotheistic communities have generally regarded them as such. But where there were apparent contradictions or inconsistencies between two passages, these could be ironed out by careful application of a harmonizing exegesis. But at two points in the

Quran (2:106 and 16:101), God allows that on occasion he himself has substituted one verse for another, which had the effect of
abrogating or canceling the earlier revelation. Besides serving as a
powerful inducement for Muslims to attempt to discover the actual chronological order of the suras — the later verse would presumably abrogate the earlier one — the notion led to considerable
speculation about whether any of the abrogated verses were still in
our Quran and why such an action was necessary in the first place.

THE MIRACLE OF THE QURAN

The early Muslims, most of whom lived in an environment very
different from the Arabian backwater in which the Quran first appeared, had to serve as their own exegetes, with little help, it
would appear, from ancient Alexandria. They contrived their own
homegrown *ars rhetorica*, which drew its confirming *testimonia*
(*shawahid*) from the old Arab poetry and which evolved contem-
porarily and in parallel with the spread of Islam and the diffusion
of the Quran (and its very gradual passage from "recitation" to
"book"). The primary function of this new endeavor was to illustrate the (theological) proposition announced by the Quran itself,
that the Recitation was beyond human competence: Challenge
them, God instructed his Prophet, to produce suras like these
(Quran 10:38; 11:13; 28:49). The challenge was never met by Muhammad's contemporaries; what was proceeding from Muhammad's mouth was, in short, inimitable. Later Muslims weighed and
assessed this quranic quality of "inimitability" (*ijaz*) and judged it
a miracle, not in the sense of the "wonders" (*karamat*) that God
allowed his "friends" (including Muhammad) to perform on occasion, but as a unique display of divine omnipotence inimitable by
mortals, no matter how favored. Thus the inimitability of the
Quran was a probative miracle (*mujiza*), absolute proof of the
Quran's divine origins and, simultaneously, and perhaps more
pointedly in the circumstances, of Muhammad's genuine prophethood. The inimitability of the Quran thus plays the same authen-
ticating role in Islam as the resurrection does in Christianity, and

the Muslim might well echo Paul's assertion to his fellow Christians that "without it, your faith is futile" (cf. 1 Cor. 15:17).

How earnestly the Quran's challenge to produce its like was uttered or understood by Muhammad's listeners we cannot know, but later Muslims took it seriously indeed. The Prophet's opponents had criticized both the manner — Muhammad was a familiar poet, a jinn-addled versifier — as well as the content — old stories, cribbed from someone else — of what they were hearing. We might be excused for thinking that the challenge/defense of the Quran was about the content of the revelation since all the preserved pre-Islamic poetry has to do with quite different matters — love and war, manliness, honor, and nostalgia — but there were early arguments among Muslim scholars on whether the Quran's ijaz rested primarily on God's rendering humankind incapable of imitating the Holy Book or whether the Quran's inimitability was intrinsic, that it was quite simply superior to anything mortals could produce. The latter view eventually prevailed, though without fully driving out the notion of God's miraculous "incapacitation" of would-be competitors in quranic composition.

The Quran nonpareil? It does not seem so to us. We are, of course, nonbelievers, the Muslim would quickly point out. But so was that first audience who were asked to believe that there was nothing to equal this Recitation. It may simply be a matter of a different aesthetic, that the criteria for literary admiration were different for seventh-century Arabians and us. Although that much is self-evident, the Quran does not in fact conform very closely to our best preserved examples of seventh-century Arabian literary artifacts, the poetry of the pre-Islamic Arabs, which had presumably shaped the tastes of Muhammad's audience but whose strict metrics and prosody and even stricter conventions of form and content find no parallel in the Quran.

The cause of this misprision of the Quran's literary merits, why one group of people judges them miraculous while another finds the book at best difficult and at worst obscure and ambiguous, may be quite other. It is entirely possible that the beauty of the Recitation lies precisely and primarily in its *recitation*. As we have seen, the Quran, or at least its Meccan suras, were surely sung or, perhaps better, cantilated, somewhat in the manner of Gregorian chant. "Poetry," that audience cried when they heard it, and they were correct: what they were hearing was a performance of an art-song cycle in "clear Arabic," an ongoing concert — not a "reading." The Book in our hands — which calls itself "The Book" (*al-Kitab*) as well as "The Recitation" (*al-Quran*) but only in its later stages, when it begins to aspire to be not only revelation but Scripture on the Judeo-Christian model — contains only the lyrics to those songs. The music is gone, at least for those of us who are condemned to reading the Quran and wondering why anyone should have thought it music. The Muslim, particularly the Muslim living in a deep Islamic environment, still hears the music, though assuredly not the same way it sounded in Mecca in the early decades of the seventh century.

Even if we grant this hypothesis, serious questions remain. We can imagine, even if we cannot hear the music, that the Meccan suras were first chanted or sung in performance by Muhammad and then, once again, by the believers in a liturgical reperformance of what they had heard, either in imitation of the Prophet or at his urging or instruction. What we cannot imagine is how or why the long prose instructions issued at Medina, the Leviticus to the Meccan Psalms, should have been "set to music" in the same sense, as they assuredly were. We can only guess that they were reckoned "Recitation" because they proceeded from the same source, God via Muhammad, albeit not in the same manner. It seems obvious that Muhammad was no longer "singing" at Medina, but by then the liturgical convention of the cantilation of revelation may well have carried those suras too into plain chant.

The early Muslims did not speak about the music, however. As early as the essayist al-Jahiz (d. 869), it was the Quran's eloquence that was thought to have defeated the attempts of Muhammad's poet contemporaries, some of them quite accomplished, to duplicate the style of God's revelation. This was a literate scholar's choice (or guess), that it was the quranic style, and quite specifically its literary style, that was inimitable — the probative miracle of Islam was aesthetic — and the theme of quranic "eloquence," or, as it later came to be called, its "rhetoric" (*balagha*), or aesthetic effectiveness, became commonplace in both literary and theological circles in Islam. The Quran was thought to represent the pinnacle of literary achievement, a compliment never lavished on the New Testament, which has the initial handicap of being written in the *koine dialektike,* the "common speech" of the Hellenized Mediterranean and not the pure Attic of an older, more elegant age. Christian apologists had to struggle with this issue in the face of fastidiously Hellenic pagans of the second and third centuries, but there was little opposition from either inside or outside Islam — both Jewish and Christian dhimmis had learned their Arabic at the Quran's knee, so to speak — to the Muslim Book's aesthetic preeminence.

HISTORY AND SCRIPTURE

Many books of the Bible and the four canonical Gospels of the New Testament present themselves as history, as a narrative of human events that have actually occurred. History was not, however, the primary concern of the professionals who studied and explained those books. Though moral edification, the so-called homiletic midrashim, was given its proper place, Jewish exegetes of the Bible functioned more as lawyers than as historians, and the Christian exegete was essentially a theologian; his reading of the historical texts that constituted Scripture was determined by his theology. The Muslim exegete, in contrast, paradoxically acted like a historian: his work was primarily to determine how to arrange the individual traditions that lay before him.

There is history in the Quran, of course, but it is used as a trope and is not the very substance of the text as it is in much of the Torah and the Gospels. But trope or substance, such historical allusions beckoned the exegete, and these exemplary references to the prophets of old produced a florid growth of *biblica,* back stories, front stories, and expansive internal details on everyone from Abraham to Jesus. This material appears sometimes in quranic exegesis proper and sometimes in an independent genre that grew out of it, the "Tales of the Prophets" that enlightened and entertained early generations of Muslims.

There is another kind of history in the Quran, though it is spread thinly and obliquely through the text. These are the rare allusions to contemporary events, the famous battle at Badr Wells, for example, in Quran 3:123. They had some claim to explanation, but there was another historical motive at work, or rather, a legal motive with historical implication. The revelations were received by Muhammad and proclaimed, it was understood, on this occasion or that over the course of twenty-two years. At times the "occasional" quality of the revelation is underlined in the text. Some are precise replies to very specific criticisms of or allegations against the Prophet (e.g., 33:37) or, on one famous occasion, his wife (24:11–20). But where, when, and under what circumstances were the allegations made or the responses sent down?

The historical net may be spread even wider. Many of the quranic revelations are prescriptive, whereby Muhammad or the community of believers as a whole is bidden to perform one act (like ritual prayer) or avoid another (like swearing oaths). Fulfillment of these commands and prohibitions, at least in their particulars, required knowledge of the circumstances that prompted such a revelation. This had raised biographical and historical questions that were answered in precisely a historical manner by Muslim exegetes and that, like the biblical material, produced its own freestanding literary genre, the "Occasions of Revelation."

THE "OCCASIONS OF REVELATION"

The extant early biographies of Muhammad, which are arranged in traditional chronological order, often gloss events in his life by reference to specific verses in the Quran, most notably 93:6–8 on his preprophetic days and 53:1–18 on his visions. The connection is of course equally effective in the opposite direction: the biographical event inevitably illuminates the quranic verse by providing the sorely needed context—the Quran provides none of its own—in which the verse was sent down. These latter stories, taken discretely, constituted an entire genre of Arabic literature. The "Occasions of Revelation"—its most famous example is a work of that same name by al-Wahidi (d. 1075)—find themselves midway between biography and exegesis. Standing separately, as they did in the "Occasions" collections, they are clearly intended to explain scattered, though by no means all or even most, verses in the Quran. Arranged chronologically with a linking narration, they become the stuff of a "Life" of the Prophet.

As exegetical devices, the anecdotes dubbed "Occasions of Revelation" served both halakic and haggadic ends, that is, to illumine behavioral prescriptions and prohibitions or to enlarge, for any of various reasons, a quranic pointer into what remains in the sacred text a dark corner. In the first instance, the Quran's various injunctions against drinking wine are explained in the "Occasions" through a series of anecdotes in which one or a number of Muhammad's followers come drunk to prayers or commit other improprieties, which then provokes the sending down of the verse. Thus, it becomes clear that wine is forbidden not because it is impure or unclean, like the prohibited flesh of swine or carrion, but because it causes intoxication, which in turn leads to impropriety.

The haggadic occasions are more diverse since their end is not so much practical as informational or devotional. Many of the verses of sura 2, for example, are explained in terms of Muhammad's confrontation with the Jews of Medina in 622–624. In another approach, Quran 2:116 notes (with disapproval) that "They say, 'God has taken a son. Glory be to Him!'" without, as often, bothering to identify "they." Al-Wahidi, in his *Occasions*, explains, not entirely helpfully, that the "they" of this verse refers to "the Jews when they said Uzayr [Ezra?] is the son of God and the Christians of Najran when they said the Messiah [that is, Jesus] is the son of God, and the polytheists among the Arabs who said the angels are the daughters of God." The verse, then, is expanded either from an independent source or, far more likely, from what seems plausible to either Al-Wahidi or other practitioners of the genre.

PLAIN AND ALLEGORICAL EXEGESIS IN ISLAM

After Muhammad, it fell to his followers to puzzle out what the revelation meant. Many of the developments in Islamic exegesis are traditionally attributed to the second-generation Muslim Ibn Abbas (d. 687), but like many other such attributions in early Islamic history, its object may have been to confer antiquity on something that occurred a century or more later. What we know for certain is that most of what was done in the earliest Islamic attempts at explaining the Quran was assimilated into the *Collection of Explanations for the Exegesis of the Quran*, simply called *The Exegesis*, composed in the 880s or 890s by al-Tabari, and which from his day to this has held pride of place in Muslim exegesis. Al-Tabari's enormous commentary—in its original form it had thirty parts and its early printed edition ran to fifteen volumes—proceeds majestically through the Quran sura by sura, indeed, word by word, combining legal, historical, and philological explanation of great density. Each word is taken and turned over in his hand, this way and that, and its every lexicographical and grammatical feature noted and often explained, as already noted, by reference to the pre-Islamic poetry of the Arabs, which was used continuously by Muslim exegetes, somewhat in the manner of an etymological dictionary of Arabic with which to unpack the text of the Quran.

Since he occasionally addressed himself to the question, it appears from Al-Tabari's commentary that in his day there was already understood to be another distinction in exegetical approach that cut across the categories just discussed: that between *tafsir*, or "plain" exegesis, and *tawil*, which is often understood as allegorical exegesis. The distinction may go back to the Quran itself, which, as we have seen, seems to suggest that there are two kinds of verses in Scripture, those whose meaning is clear and those others that require some kind of explanation. The explanations that followed have been no more than the application of personal reasoning (*ijtihad*) or some mildly critical research to the text, as opposed to the acceptance on authority of the plain meaning—a distinction that was current, and debated, in legal circles. Most of the commentators and commentaries discussed to this point operated within a tradition that regarded the body of prophetic hadith as the primary exegetical instrument for understanding the Quran, particularly on legal matters, much the way the Talmud served the rabbinic exegetes in Judaism. On that understanding, the difference between tafsir and tawil was not, then, between exoteric and esoteric passages but rather between clear and ambiguous ones. Where tawil took on its allegorical association was when exegetical principles began to be used to elicit from Scripture dogmatic and mystical understandings of which both Muhammad and the Quran were apparently totally innocent.

The Quran was not a historical document in Muslims' eyes, nor was Muhammad a historian. Since the Enlightenment secular critics have looked on the Bible, the New Testament, and the Quran as revelations not of God's will but of the desires and anxieties of their times. The believers, however, see in those Scriptures a point of contact with God himself. Each of the three communities continues to take its Scripture seriously as history, of course, first in the sense that it was revealed at a fixed moment of human history, and then, that its behavioral prescriptions refer to ongoing human life, in all times and places, and that they have historical relevance. But Philo, as we have seen, attempted to peer beneath the historical surface of the Bible into the timeless riches beneath. He thought he could discern there the truths of which the Greek philosophers also had some presentiment, or may even have borrowed from Israel. The Christians peered through the same aperture that Philo had opened, and then the Muslims after them, and all saw in their Scriptures the same perennial truths. But there were some who looked even more deeply, into the profound heart of Scripture where God himself dwelled. This is the Scripture of the mystics, the Torah of the Kabbalists, the New Testament of Bernard of Clairvaux, and the Quran of Ibn al-Arabi, a presence contained not only in the whole of Scripture but also, without distinction of importance, in each verse and even in every word and letter.

THE MUSLIMS STRUGGLE WITH REVELATION AND REASON

Early Islam witnessed a profound struggle for its soul and its identity. On one side were the "partisans of tradition" who longed for a Quran- and prophet-oriented society whose image was slowly emerging, in a highly idealized version, in the enormous collection of hadith, the Prophetic reports that purported to define and describe the community's earliest days. The Quran was viewed in those circles as an object as holy as God himself, and their reading of the text, as is common among religious conservatives, remained reverentially close to the plain meaning. Opposition to these "traditionists" came from the "partisans of dialectic," particularly from the group known as the Mutazilites. It is not known whether these latter rejected the hadith or, as seems more likely, merely took a more hypercritical view of them than was common in most Muslim circles. What is certain is that they preferred to ground their Muslim sensibilities in the Quran. But they read the Book like rationalists: the gross anthropomorphisms of the simple-minded pietists were not for them. But the Mutazilite dispute with the traditionists went deeper than this. The latter's veneration for the *ipsissima verba* of the Quran and the Mutazilite insistence on using dialectical methods of analysis came to term in the profound and profoundly disruptive debate on whether the Quran was created, and so, by implication, conditioned, as the Mutazilites held, or whether it was eternal, coeval and coequal with God.

For the Mutazilites, an uncreated Quran was a theological affront to a unique God as well as a manacle that chained human reason and conscience to a text, however revered that latter might be. In traditionist eyes the uncreated Quran was a mysterious embodiment of the sacred, an almost sacramental link between a transcendent God and his earthly creation. In a verbal struggle in which all the weapons belonged to the dialecticians, it is difficult to piece together the nuances of the traditionist position, but from their circles came two Islamic "schools," those of Ahmad ibn Hanbal (d. 855) and Dawud ibn Kalaf (d. 884), from which a coherent stance can be derived. Both groups insisted on the evident (*zahir*; Dawud's followers were called Zahiris) sense of both the Quran and the hadith — on pious, conservative grounds, to be sure, but almost as surely as a reaction to a Mutazilite exegesis of the sacred text that was based on somewhat free-wheeling analogy (*qiyas*) and critical investigation of its meaning.

Exegesis lay at the heart of the debate over the conflicting claims of faith and reason in the domain of revealed religion. The rationalizing theologians wrested some of the rights of exegesis away from the lawyers because they were more skillful in allegorical exegesis. Traditionists were tied by their own legal premises to literal interpretation of Scripture, a connection that committed them in nonlegal passages to certain gross anthropomorphisms that the dialecticians could devour with arguments. More, the theologians permitted themselves a far wider exegetical range, and could apply both learning and imagination to the text of Scripture, whereas the traditionists were largely limited to rhetoric and philology. Just how attractive a carefully wrought theological tafsir might be is demonstrated by the position won among all segments of the Islamic community by the monumental quranic commentary *The Unveiler of the Realities of the Secrets of Revelation* by the Mutazilite Zamakhshari (d. 1144).

Later the philosophers of Islam would make even bolder claims than the early partisans of tradition. For the dialectical theologians who came after the Mutazilites, rational discourse, whether in exegesis or elsewhere, was complementary to and defensive of the higher truths of revelation, but the philosophers, the Muslim Avicenna or the Jewish Maimonides, regarded philosophy's claim as the higher one. Scripture figured truth for the unphilosophical masses; philosophy uttered its very name. There can be no conflict, however. Where Scripture appears to conflict with the conclusions of demonstrative reasoning, it is a clear sign that the literal meaning of Scripture must be interpreted allegorically, not by the lawyer or the theologian, whose powers of reasoning are undermined by faulty premises, but by the philosopher, who alone possesses truly rigorous scientific knowledge.

SHIITE TAFSIR

If the philosophers imagined they had a privileged understanding of the Quran, they were not the only Muslims to make such claims. As already noted, the Quran makes quite explicit that Muhammad is but one of a line of prophets that stretches back to Adam. But that line closes with Muhammad, and however hard some sectarians like the Bahais and Ahmadis attempted to pry it open once again, the main body of Muslims has resisted: Muhammad was indeed the "seal of the prophets" (Quran 33:40). But if prophethood was a closed way, there was another route that led, almost as effectively, through exegesis. The Shiite Muslims believe that Muhammad was followed by a series of divinely appointed Imams who are God's vicars and infallibly guide the community. One of their powers is understanding the "hidden" sense of the Quran.

> Note: *Imam* is a generic Arabic term for leader. Besides its technical use by Shiites, the word is also often employed, generally uncapitalized, for either the leader at mosque prayer or the head of a Muslim congregation.

All the varieties of Shiites share a belief in the Imam as the head of the umma, but the group called the Ismailis, who possessed actual Imams longer than any of the other groups, (see chapter 6) developed an elaborate theory of prophecy and of exegesis. According to them, each of the prophets — or "speakers," as the Ismailis preferred to call the traditional prophets of the Quran — was entrusted with the "outer" or "obvious" (*zahir*) sense of the sacred texts. But each was followed in turn by a "deputy" (*wasi*) — Aaron for Moses, for example, Peter for Jesus, and, of course Ali for Muhammad — who was privy to the inner (*batin*) and so more profound meaning of revelation. Ordinary Muslims practice their tafsir on the literal sense of the Quran, which produces the standard practices and beliefs of what we call Islam. But Ismaili exegesis is not reading but interpretation (*tawil*). It fits within the broad category of what we have called the allegorical interpretation of the sacred text. Its specific differences are, first, that it is hidden — that is, from the mass of Muslims — and thus esoteric; and, second, that it is guaranteed, in this instance by the authority of the infallible Imams.

6. *The Umma, Allah's Commonwealth*

THE HEBREWS were a "polity" from the outset, albeit on the modest scale of an extended family or clan that led an apparently autonomous existence among the scattered tribes on the margins of the Middle Eastern agrarian societies of the Stone Age. Eventually they grew into something more substantial — as God himself had promised — and the kingdom of Israel survived politically in its exposed Palestinian home for more than three hundred years. In the end, however, there were too few Israelites for their "state" to be politically viable in the Fertile Crescent of the seventh century B.C.E., and in Babylonia in the opening decades of the sixth century the Jews began their millennia-long experiment in maintaining their identity and some degree of integrity as a people under the political sovereignty of others. For long periods those "others" were not the Babylonians but their own monotheistic offspring, and rivals, the Christians and Muslims.

Christians were born into the same politically subordinate status as the contemporary Jews of the first century, though they soon had to deal with their Roman masters from a far more exposed position than had the Jews. But the Christians, like Jesus himself, seem to have developed no distinct policy toward the Roman Empire in particular or toward worldly political power in general. The Christian churches had, in effect, a three-century period between Jesus and Constantine before they had seriously to think about the secular state and its place in the scheme of both Sacred History and their own lives. Islam's experience was profoundly different. From its inception, the Muslim community, the umma, was both a religious and a political association, a "church" as well as a "state"; Muhammad was his own Constantine.

THE CREATION OF THE UMMA

In 622 Muhammad accepted an invitation to leave his native Mecca, where he was the charismatic leader of a small conventicle of believers, and to emigrate to Medina as the arbitrator-ruler of a faction-ridden community of Arabs and Jews. This was a crucial period in Muhammad's life, and the years following his migration were spent trying to forge some kind of community in accordance with his religious principles and the political realities of the situation. As described in the Medina Accords, Muhammad's original "community" (umma) at Medina included not only his fellow Migrants from Mecca and the newly converted Helpers at Medina, but Jews and Medinese pagans as well. The Jews were soon purged from both the umma and the town, and the pagans were dragged willy-nilly into it; the umma finally became exclusively a community of believers who accepted the dominion of the One True God and both the prophethood and the leadership of Muhammad.

These were not artificial associations. Muhammad's role as a prophet within a community that he himself had summoned into being necessarily included the functions of legislator, executive, and military commander. God's revelations continued to spill from his lips. Now, however, they were not only threats and warnings to nonbelievers, but more often legislative enactments regulating community life, and particularly the relations of one Muslim with another. Thus was constituted an exclusively Muslim umma, and its institutionalization can be charted in the Medina suras of the Quran, which are devoted not merely to shaping the Muslim sensibilities of the believers but to laying out some of the basic ritual requirements, notably daily liturgical prayer and the annual payment of zakat, the alms-tithe incumbent on all Muslims.

After Mecca's submission to Muhammad in 629, the tribes of Arabia read the omens and decided that their future lay with the rising new power in Medina. There was no longer any need to pursue or to proselytize. Delegations came of their own accord to the Prophet in Medina and announced their submission. Most of them were Bedouin, though there may also have been representatives of some of the Christian settlements in the Yemen. Religion sat lightly on the Bedouin, as the Quran itself remarks (9:97), and for some or perhaps most of them acceptance of Islam may have meant little more than recognizing the sovereignty of Medina and paying what is set down in Islamic law as a religious tithe (Quran 9:98), but what must surely have appeared to the camel nomads as a tax or tribute. This conclusion is reasonably drawn from the fact that immediately after the Prophet's death, many of the Arab tribes abruptly stopped paying the alms-tithe and Muhammad's successor had to dispatch armed troops to enforce its collection. Muslim officials could not guarantee that everyone would say his prayers, but they surely knew whether the zakat arrived in Medina.

A Successor to the Prophet

Muhammad no more appointed a successor than Jesus had. The Christians' immediate eschatological expectations made that absence of concern seem natural, but there is little trace of such urgently imminent End Time expectations in Islam, either before or after the Prophet's death. Muhammad's illness and death in Medina in 632, if unexpected, was by no means sudden. There was ample opportunity to make provision for the succession, and though some Muslims maintain that he did, the majority agree that he did not. As the story is commonly told, at Muhammad's death the Migrants, those who had originally come with him from Mecca ten years earlier, and the Helpers, the inner cadre of the Medina converts, met separately to plan what to do next. When they learned of the other caucus, the Migrants led by Abu Bakr hurried to join the Medinese group, presumably to head off a preemptive choice of successor by the men who had, after all, once ruled the oasis. There was what appears to have been a rather secular and political debate on the relative merits of the two groups. We do not know what settled the matter, though expedience suggests itself, but in the end it was agreed that the senior Migrant Abu Bakr should assume leadership of the umma. All present took an oath of allegiance, Bedouin fashion, to the new caliph.

If we are unsure how or precisely why Abu Bakr was chosen, we are equally uncertain about how the succession was viewed. The title chosen for Abu Bakr comes from *khalifa*, used in the Quran of Adam and David as God's "deputies." But Abu Bakr, far from deputizing for God, seems not even to have acted in that capacity for the departed Muhammad, at least in any prophetic or charismatic sense. From what we can gather from his acts—he decided to send an army out against the Arabian Bedouin who at Muhammad's death signaled their opportunistic withdrawal from the umma—he seems to have succeeded Muhammad merely as head of the umma. Thus Muhammad's charismatic leadership possessing both spiritual and executive powers was routinized in the form of a chief operating officer. As one of the subsequent early caliphs, Umar II (r. 717–720), put it: "There is no Prophet after ours and no Holy Book after ours. What God has ordered or forbidden through our Prophet remains so forever. I am not one who decides but only one who carries out, not an innovator but a follower."

Clearly the caliph was not above the law—in the umma's case, God's Law—nor its maker. Indeed, Abu Bakr and his successors were closer in function to another title used of the early caliphs, Commander of the Faithful (*amir al-muminin*). They appointed and removed political subordinates. They decided military strategy and served as commander (*amir*) of the armies of Islam. The caliph was the chief judge and chief fiscal officer of the new regime. Most of the caliph's military, judicial, and fiscal responsibilities were soon delegated to others, however; the community was actually a number of armies on the march far from the centers of power, and though decisions might be made in the name of the caliph, they were increasingly made by others.

If the caliph and his delegates could decide, they could not or did not legislate. For their guidance, they now had the closed and completed Quran, and they could not add to that text, which, like Jewish law, addressed itself in great detail to matters of personal status but was mute on the political governance of what was rapidly becoming an immense empire. The caliph and his delegates resorted instead to many other devices to shape their purpose: tribal practices, local customs, pragmatic necessities, and, to some extent, whatever precedents the Prophet's practice suggested to them. There is no suggestion that the caliph regarded himself or was regarded by others as possessing special spiritual powers. He was the head of the umma, and though the umma was based entirely on a shared acceptance of Islam, the caliph was not a religious leader but the leader of a religion.

TENSIONS IN THE COMMUNITY

The caliphs, the earliest ones at any rate, had to face a problem Muhammad himself had forestalled with great difficulty during his lifetime. There was a tension in the community from the beginning between the notion of Islam as a universal religion that claimed the allegiance of all men, and that of the Arabs as a final version of the Chosen People. The latter phrase is Judaism's own, of course, and speaks to God's election of Israel as a fellow in his covenant. Muhammad's own perspective was perhaps somewhat different. He knew, from his own understanding of history, that previous revelations had constituted their recipients a community, an umma. It had been true of the Jews and Christians and now, in the final act of the drama of revelation, it would be so with the Arabs.

If this revelation of a "clear Arabic Quran" through an Arab prophet to Arabs of western Arabia was calculated to create a sense of unity among those peoples, the project cannot be judged entirely a success. Muhammad had problems with tribal rivalries in his own day, between the mighty and the low in the complex hierarchy of tribes and clans that dominated not only his native Mecca but most of the peninsula's Bedouin population. Boasting and vilification were common pre-Islamic instruments for establishing and maintaining that order, and though Muhammad decreed that the only aristocracy in Islam was that constituted by piety and merit, the tribal divisions of Arab society long outlived his efforts to suppress them in the name of either a single Arab umma or a universal religion for all humankind.

With the Prophet's death, the umma rapidly began to disintegrate. Only through the strenuous military efforts of his first successor, Abu Bakr (r. 632–634), was Islam successfully reimposed on the tribes across Arabia who had read Muhammad's death as the death knell of Islam and declared their secession from the community by refusing to pay the alms-tithe. What followed was more subtle and perhaps more insidious in the long run. The enormous wealth that came to the community as booty and tribute was distributed according to a system devised by the second caliph, Umar (r. 634–644). It recognized and rewarded the merit of early conversion and a concomitant willingness to bear arms against the enemies of Islam, but in institutionalizing this system of rewards and pensions, Umar restored the distribution rights to tribal chieftains, permitted this to be done along tribal lines, and allowed it to be effected in the new Islamic garrison towns whose social organization was precisely tribal.

The consequences of these purely administrative decisions were twofold, and each was far-reaching in its social impact. They preserved and perhaps reinforced the old pre-Islamic tribal rivalries, which continued to disturb the equilibrium of the Islamic body politic for at least a century afterward; and they conspired to create a distinction between Arab and non-Arab within the bosom of Islam. It is not certain that Muhammad intended an egalitarian community. What actually emerged was a society where both tribal and ethnic rivalries died a lingering death.

Ali ibn Abi Talib (601–661)

The caliphate, though an obvious pragmatic success, did not exhaust the possibilities of leadership in early Islam. There was

among some Muslims the concept of the head of the community as
a prayer leader (*imam*) or an eschatological chief or Mahdi, literally "Guided One." The latter has been invoked from time to time
in Islamic history as a challenge to the caliph or a magnet around
which to energize Muslim political action, but its successes have
been short-lived, and the figure of the Mahdi receded, like that of
the Messiah in rabbinic Judaism, into an indefinite future. That
was the majority view of the caliphate. But there were some who
saw, and continued to see, the office and role of the head of the
umma in a quite different light. This is the *Shiat Ali*, or "Party of
Ali," who trace their origins back to the person and history of Ali
ibn Abi Talib.

Ali ibn Abi Talib was Muhammad's much younger cousin —
thirty-one years younger by the traditional chronology — and it
was his father who raised Muhammad when the latter's grandfather and guardian died. Although Ali was only nine at the time,
tradition has remembered him as the first after Khadija to submit
and accept Islam. Ali, then twenty-one, migrated with his cousin to
Medina in 622 and thereafter he began to play an increasingly
important role in the life of Muhammad and the consolidation of
Islam. How important depends on whether one reads the standard
Sunni biographies of the Prophet, which certainly do not down-
grade Ali's importance, or the Shiite hagiographies, which not only
exalt him to the heavens — Ali's military prowess is equaled only
by his eloquence — but in their reading of some otherwise opaque
passages of the Quran (e.g., 5:55; 13:7) and in their remembrance
of other events in Muhammad's life, understand the Prophet to
have explicitly promised the succession to Ali and his family. On
his deathbed, Muhammad is said to have called for pen and ink,
"So I may write for you something after which you will not be led
into error." But death came before anything could be recorded.
According to the Shiites, as the *Shiat Ali* are called in English, what
Muhammad intended to put into writing was God's appointment
of Ali as his successor. Sunnis also remember the occasion, but
have different explanations of what was intended by Muhammad's
cryptic remark.

A DISPUTED SUCCESSION

Not all Muslims assented to the choice of Abu Bakr or even agreed that the succession to the leadership of the umma could or should have occurred in that fashion. The Shiites remember it somewhat differently. By all accounts Ali, who was then thirty-one, was not present at the meeting of the Migrants and Helpers after Muhammad's death. All further agree that once the choice of Abu Bakr was made, Umar and others went to Ali's house to ask — apparently to demand — that he too take the oath of allegiance. Ali may have resisted, though on what precise grounds we do not know. What the Shiites do recall, however, is that there were some who urged him to assume the leadership himself, and he declined. These included his uncle Abbas, the eponym of the later Sunni dynasty of caliphs, the Abbasids, and even Abu Sufyan, the head of the house of Umayya, another Sunni dynasty that some twenty-odd years later attempted to exterminate the house of Ali.

Where Sunni and Shiite historians totally disagree is on what followed between Abu Bakr's accession to the caliphate in 632 and Ali's own in 656. The Sunnis maintain that Ali accepted the legitimacy of his three predecessors, Abu Bakr, Umar, and Uthman; the Shiites vociferously deny it. Ali certainly had his enemies — Muhammad's favorite wife, and Abu Bakr's daughter, Aisha, prominent among them — but they seem not to have included the first three caliphs. When Abu Bakr died in 634 he secured the succession for Umar ibn al-Khattab. The latter attempted to regularize the succession process by appointing a council of six men, including Ali, to settle the caliphate at his death. When Umar was assassinated in 644, the choice once again passed over Ali for another early and devoted follower of the Prophet, Uthman, of the rich and influential house of Umayya. Uthman's caliphate (r. 644–656) is best remembered for his promoting the first standard edition of the Quran as well as his appointment of his relatives to important posts in the rapidly expanding Muslim empire. His reign was in any event a troubled one, and he was murdered in 656 by a conspiracy of pretenders to his office. Ali was not himself directly involved in Uthman's death, and in its wake he was named caliph to succeed him. Ali was then fifty-five, married to the Prophet's daughter Fatima (among others) with two sons (among others) who had been Muhammad's favorites, Hasan and Husayn.

Ali's caliphate (r. 656–661) was as trouble-plagued as his predecessor's. Important posts were still held by Uthman's appointees, who were often his own Umayyad relations, chief among them Muawiya, the governor of Syria, who orchestrated and maintained a steady drumbeat of criticism against the new caliph on the grounds that he, if not complicitous in the deed, was doing nothing to bring to justice, and may even have been sheltering, Uthman's murderers. Others, like Talha and Zubayr, abetted by Aisha, who had been slighted — perhaps even slandered — by Ali during the Prophet's lifetime, saw their own chances for the succession dashed by Ali's appointment and were resolved to unseat him.

Ali, who had been forced to move from Medina across the steppe to Iraq, disposed of Talha and Zubayr at the Battle of the Camel near Basra in 656 and Aisha was sent into permanent retirement. But Muawiya's campaign was more persistent and his power in the end more effective. He had the troops of Syria under his command and support in the other provinces as well. Ali moved his own army to oppose him and then, after an inconclusive battle at a place called Siffin in Syria in 657, he made what proved to be a fatal error: he agreed to submit his dispute with Muawiya to arbitration. Immediately he lost a considerable contingent of his followers who "seceded" from his cause — they came to be called Kharijis, "Seceders" — and turned against their leader. Ali had first to deal with these troublesome rebels, which he did at Nahrwan in Iraq. He won the battle but lost his life: while the dispute with Muawiya dragged on, the fourth caliph of Islam was struck down by a disgruntled Kharijite in January 661. He was buried, as the story goes, at Najaf in Iraq, which has become a major Shi'ite pilgrimage center.

THE UMAYYADS (661–750)

Muawiya acceded to the caliphate, moved the capital of the Abode of Islam out of the still rebellious Holy Cities to Damascus, where his own troops and power lay. He and his successors ruled not as the tribal shaeikhs that the first four caliphs still seem to have been, but closer to the style of kings on the Byzantine or Iranian model. The rule of Islam now belonged to a family, the Banu Umayya, or Umayyads, and the crown passed dynastically from head to head until it was wrenched away in turn by another family, the Banu Abbas, or Abbasids, in 750.

The Umayyads were widely condemned by later generations for introducing "kingship" (*mulk*) into the Islamic community — they were in fact proud of the title of king — and of showing more concern for the secular pleasures of the world than for the spirit and practices of Islam. Their style was indeed imperial, and Muawiya upset tribal if not Islamic precedent by appointing his son as his caliphal heir. But the Umayyads did have discernible Islamic sensibilities. They made a clear-cut theological claim to the caliphate. The monument of the Dome of the Rock in Jerusalem is an Islamic building with an Islamic function, and the same Umayyad caliph who conceived that building was also the first to devise an Islamic coinage for the new regime. He too began the Arabization, and thus indirectly the Islamization, of the still nascent apparatus of Islamic government.

At Ali's death, the Muslim community had already begun to display signs of serious schismatic disruption. The secession of the Kharijites from support of Ali ibn Abi Talib's uncontestably legitimate caliphate has already been noted; it is clear they held a far different view of the nature of the umma and, consequently, of who should stand at its head. Puritan-egalitarians who thought that the grave sinner ipso facto became an unbeliever and, in effect an apostate, the Kharijites, held that any Muslim might head the umma. They did not enjoy any great success among Muslims and their point of view did not survive long. The Shiites, in contrast, were more tenacious and in the end more successful, as we shall see.

THE SHIITE IMAMATE

That leadership should belong by right to a family rather than rest on the choice of the community or society has struck some as a rather non-Arab notion. But it has characterized the support of Ali from the beginning. Where simple loyalty to the house of Ali (Alidism) became Shiism was the point at which it began to acquire, besides a memory of Ali's importance in the earliest days of Islam, an ideology to explain the transfer of Muhammad's spiritual charisma, if not of his prophetic gift, to Ali and thence to certain members of his house. When or how that happened is not easy to explain since there are no Shiite documents earlier than the tenth century, when that ideology was already fully developed.

The historical footing grows firmer in the events of 680, when Ali's second son Husayn was lured from Medina by promises of support for his family's cause across the steppe toward Kufa. Husayn was intercepted by Umayyad forces at a place called Karbala, where he and most of his followers were slaughtered. It was the end, for the moment, of Alid political aspirations, but the massacre at Karbala was also, as it turned out, one of the foundation stones of religious Shiism.

There was no single Shiite view of the Imamate or leadership of the community and no greater degree of agreement among various Shiite factions than among the Sunnis, save on the principle that rule over the umma belonged by right and by designation to the descendants of Ali ibn Abi Talib, Muhammad's cousin and son-in-law and the actual fourth caliph, and that that ruler should possess religious as well as secular powers. Which descendant and which powers were much debated questions. The Umayyads never succeeded in destroying a strong sense of loyalty to Ali, his sons (notably the martyred Husayn), and their offspring. For their part, the claims to power of the Alid loyalists generally came to naught. One group, the followers of Muhammad ibn al-Hanifiyya, a son of Ali, found a zealous propagandist in a certain al-Mukhtar who proclaimed him Imam and Mahdi. The claim was taken seriously enough by the first Abbasids, who had seized power from the Umayyads in 750 and attempted to eradicate their rivals, for them to have put out the story that the Imamate had been transferred to them, the descendants of Abbas, by the son of Muhammad ibn al-Hanifiyya. The movement around Muhammad ibn al-Hanifiyya was one of the earliest signs of what was later branded "extremist" (*ghulat*) Shiism and the initial stage of a movement from loyalty to Ali's family to the clearly defined ideology that we call simply Shiism. The other stages toward the final formulation of this latter remain obscure since, with the accession of the Abbasids, the Shiites appear to have abandoned any real claim to the caliphate and to have contented themselves with wielding considerable political, though not doctrinal, influence on the Abbasid caliphs.

Although our clearest view of the formative process of Shiism comes in the earliest years of the tenth century, the roots of the movement go back to the circle around Jafar al-Sadiq in the eighth (see below). By the tenth century, however, most of the basic tenets of what is called Imami Shiism were in place: Ali was the designated Imam in succession to Muhammad, and after him had come, likewise by designation (*nass*), and likewise from among Ali's descendants and heirs, consecutive Imams, all of whom had been gifted with infallible spiritual powers for guidance of the community. This line came to a temporary end with the "concealment" (*ghayba*) in 878 of the twelfth Imam. This "Hidden Imam" would return one day, but only at the end of time as the Mahdi.

Thus, in the late ninth century, the Shiite Imamate apparently vacated history and politics for the safer ground of eschatology. By trading in their political claims for spiritual vindication, the Shiites ceased posing a threat to the current, strongly Turkish-buttressed Abbasid regime, and indeed there are signs that in the late ninth and early tenth centuries the caliphs began to take a more relaxed view of Shiism and Shiites. It was in this climate that the Shiite theologians constructed their new doctrinal synthesis on the Imamate. In summary, the Imami or "Twelver" Shiites regarded the Imamate not as an evolutionary consequence of the religion of Islam but as one of its basic and necessary ingredients, as fundamental as belief in the One God or in the Prophet's mission. The Imamate had been established by God as part of the primordial nature of things. There was a cycle of transcendental Imams in the *pleroma*, and in their historical manifestation they are the intermediaries between that transcendental world and the universe of humanity. Each Imam is God's "Proof" (*hujja*), and as such they are all impeccable and infallible. Moreover, they are the sole repositories of the understanding of the true, albeit hidden (*batin*) sense of Scripture. This divine knowledge was transmitted to Ali, the first Imam, by the Prophet himself and by Ali to his successors in each generation.

According to most Shiites, the Imamate passed from generation to generation by designation at the hands of the previous Imam. Where there are major differences of opinion is on the designated heir of the sixth Imam, Jafar al-Sadiq (d. 765). The question arose whether the Imamate passed to his eldest son Ismail (d. 760), whom he had formally designated his successor but who predeceased his own father, or to his younger son, Musa al-Kazim (d. 799), whom Jafar had designated Imam after Ismail's death despite the fact that Ismail had a surviving son, Muhammad. Could the designation be taken back, in effect, or did it necessarily descend on the dead Ismail's infant son? The different answers to this question set in train the division between the so-called Ismaili Shiites who regarded Ismail's son Muhammad as the only genuine Imam, and Imami Shiites who recognized Musa al-Kazim and his descendants as Imams.

This was the distinction in the eighth century, but by the tenth the two groups had taken an additional and significant step apart: the Imamis embraced, as we have seen, the notion of the concealment of the twelfth Imam in their line. This reportedly occurred sometime about 878, and though the direction of the community rested for a spell in the hands of deputies, by the mid–tenth century the Imamites had accepted the fact that there was no longer an Imam in the flesh and that until his return as the Mahdi, they were solely a spiritual community, a concession which, for all its attractiveness for the intelligentsia, had surrendered the Imamis' claim to the highest political power in Islam.

SUNNIS AND SHIITES

The Party of Ali thus maintained that (1) the umma was primarily a spiritual community, a "church" that runs a "state," so to speak; (2) that its leader or Imam—a term they preferred to "caliph"—

should likewise be a spiritual leader; if not a prophet like Muhammad, then a charismatic governing and teaching authority; and
finally (3) that God in the Quran—Shiites eventually dropped their
accusations that the actual text had been tampered with—and
Muhammad in his public pronouncement (since suppressed) had
announced that Ali was rightfully that Imam and that his family
would hold the office after him. They never really did so; the actual
power remained in the hands of the majority Sunnis, shorthand for
"partisans of custom (sunna) and the unity of the umma," who
were content to accept the "facts" created by history in all its
worldly imperfection.

The point at issue thus is who shall rule the umma. The Sunnis
were willing to accept the verdict of history as reflected in the
choices of that "whole first generation" of Muhammad's contemporaries and their immediate successors. The Shiites argued
against history in asserting Ali's preeminence, but in so doing they
were forced, to one degree or another, to attack the consensual
wisdom of the Companions of the Prophet from whom all the
Prophetic sunna ultimately derived. Disappointed by history, the
Shiites turned where some Jewish groups may also have resorted,
to a Gnostic wisdom, a kind of particularist and underground
sunna transmitted, generation after generation, by infallible Imams of the Alid house or by their delegates. In fully developed Shiism, which found its most lasting base by connecting itself with
Persian nationalism, the entire range of Gnostic ideas is on display:
the exaltation of wisdom (*hikma*) over science (*ilm*); a view of historical events as reflection of cosmic reality; and a concealed (*batin*) as opposed to an open (*zahir*) interpretation of Scripture. It
was simply a matter of time before Shiite Gnosticism found its
siblings within Sufism and philosophy.

When Westerners returned to the Middle East at the beginning
of modern times as travelers, traders, missionaries, and merchants,
some thought they could best understand the Sunnis and Shiites
as, respectively, a version of Catholics and Protestants. Or so it
seemed to some Catholic adventurers who saw the Sunnis as the
"orthodox" Muslims and the minority Shiites as some species of
heterodoxy, an attiitude that has not entirely disappeared. Func-

tionally speaking, the opposite seems closer to the truth. The Christian bishop and the Shiite Imam show the same charismatically transmitted powers and may speak definitively, if not infallibly, on behalf of God. The Roman Catholic view of the papal magisterium is in fact very close to that of the Shiites toward the Imam. One difference, however, is that whereas in Islam the transmission of that magisterium is by both designation and descent from the Holy Family, the Christian episcopate is an office held by a clergy that is celibate and so, by definition, without issue: the bishop receives his teaching powers by designation alone.

THE HIDDEN IMAM

The eleventh Imam in the sequence followed by the so-called Twelver Shiites was Hasan al-Askari, whose tenure began in 873. He died the following year, but had was a son, it was reported, born in 868 or thereabouts, bearing the Prophet's own name of Abu Qasim Muhammad. There were problems: some Shiites had apparently not heard of this son and turned instead to Hasan's brother Jafar, who denied there had been any son. Most were convinced that young Muhammad was the true Imam. He was nowhere to be found, however, and thus there began to circulate the same story of a concealment or an "occultation" that had earlier been broached in extremist and Ismaili circles.

> *Note*: The place of Muhammad's final concealment was later identified as a cave near the tombs of earlier Imams at Samarra in Iraq. Within it was a well down which Muhammad was said to have disappeared. The caliph al-Nasir had the place walled off in 1209, but Shiites continue to visit and pray for the return of the Hidden Imam.

The new phenomenon of a Hidden Imam must then have seemed little different from the prevailing custom of an Imam who had little or no public presence. Thus the system continued to function through the medium of a spokesman or delegate who, one after another, appeared to speak for the "concealed" Muhammad. They brought him the monies paid by the Shiites as their alms-tithe and carried back answers to questions posed to the Imams. There may have been doubts about this arrangement from the beginning, and there were problems with the four "delegates" — they called themselves "gates" or "ambassadors" of the now long-departed Abu Qasim Muhammad. There was a rather abrupt solution. In 941 the last of these deputies produced a document from the Hidden Imam announcing that the period of the Lesser Concealment was over and that henceforward there would be no delegates or spokesmen, no direct communication. The Lord of the Ages, who was still alive, though in another, spiritual dimension, had gone into a permanent Greater Concealment, not to return until the events preceding the Day of Judgment.

The concealment of the Imam, the infallible guide and head of the community, had repercussions on the entire structure of Shiite Islam. It was first thought that at the Great Concealment in 941, the Imams' functions were in fact in abeyance, that everything from the conduct of a holy war, to the enforcement of the *sharia* (Islamic law), to the collection of the zakat had effectively lapsed. No law-based community could survive, however, without an executive or judicial authority of some sort, and soon Shiite lawyers were exploring the possibility of the delegation of at least some of the Imam's powers. By the fifteenth century it was fairly generally established among Shiites that their *ulama* (legal scholars) exercised what they called a "general representation" of the Hidden Imam and thus were empowered to collect the zakat on the Imam's behalf and even to declare a jihad in defense of the faith. In the end, their ulama, particularly in Iran, had established a wide-ranging authority among the Shiites.

POLITICAL ISMAILISM: THE FATIMIDS

Sometimes called the "Seveners," the followers of Ismail, son of Jafar al-Sadiq, and of his descendants led an obscure existence in the Abode of Islam for most of the eighth and early ninth centuries. Then, in the second half of the ninth century, two diverse movements sprung from the same Shiite soil, the Qarmatians and the Ismailis properly so-called. Their "call" (*dawa*), as these early Ismailis referred to their movement, was heard in southern Iraq and Bahrain — this latter the proper locus of the Qarmatian "branch" of the larger movement — as well as in northwestern Iran and North Africa. The original substance of the call was the announcement of Ismail's son Muhammad's concealment and the promise of his eventual return as the Mahdi. It was precisely there, however, that the two groups parted company. Whereas the main body of the Ismailis believed that the return of the Imam had taken place in a person named Ubaydallah in Ifriqiyya (modern Tunisia), the Qarmatians continued to await the perhaps distant End Time return of their leader.

The Fatimids — as the dynasty was known, to stress its descent from both Ali and Fatima in contrast to the Abbasids, who claimed descent from Ali alone — soon vacated their eschatological claims. The End — the *qiyama*, or "resurrection," in Ismaili parlance — was not yet, and in the meantime there would be an indefinite line of caliph-Imams to rule the Abode of Islam. This meant that the traditional Islam of the "Pillars" and its traditional law (sharia) were still firmly in place. The Sunnis who were now under Ismaili political control were not constrained to embrace Shiism — such a course may have been far too dangerous, politically speaking — but the Fatimids did make strenuous efforts to convert them. Missionary dais were trained in the new dawa center in Cairo, al-Azhar, which eventually turned into Islam's largest, most prestigious, and influential (Sunni) school of religious studies and still dispatches Muslim missionaries all over the globe. From al-Azhar they were sent into the Fatimid provinces to instruct and persuade the Sunni majority and sent under cover into the caliph's domains to subvert the Sunni regime, which they attempted — unsuccessfully, as it turned out — with a combination of propaganda and terrorism.

The foundations of Ismaili Fatimid political power had originally been laid down among the perennially dissident Berber tribes, who had already bucked the tide in their adherence to Donatism in the fifth century and Kharijism in the seventh. The Ismaili call was not dissimilar to those earlier appeals and to the later ones that carried Berber fundamentalists into Muslim Spain: a heightened sense of community, a puritanical ethic, and a call to holy war against the "false" Muslims outside the movement. Within the new community of Ismailis a warrior class was recruited from among the Berber tribes, and the Berbers provided the bulk of the fighting force that carried the Fatimids across North Africa to conquer Egypt and nearly the caliphate itself.

The Fatimid claims to the Imamate varied over the period covered by the initiation of the call in Ifriqiyya, through the critical reign of the Imam Muizz (r. 953–975), down to the last fatal schism in the movement at the time of Imam Mustansir (r. 1036–1094), but varied, in any event, from the more straightforward call to apocalyptic revolution being broadcast by the Qarmatians. Muizz's reforms neither intended to nor succeeded in secularizing the office of the Fatimid Imam whose titles and ceremonial remained filled with echoes of Mahdism and quasi-divine powers. The "materialization" of these tendencies culminated in the divine claims of the Imam al-Hakim (d. 1021) and the creation of the Druze sect, named after one of its prominent missionaries, al-Darazi. Al-Hakim's view of himself as a divinized or divine Imam found little support among his subjects and his successors returned to a modest posture on the Imamate as simply a more authentic alternative for the Sunni caliphate. With the return to modesty came a turning as well to another Abbasid pattern, the delegation or loss of powers to more secular and military forces, the viziers and generals of the realm.

With the decline of the Fatimid power center in Egypt, the widely scattered Ismaili diaspora — the creation of those energetic dais — was increasingly left to its own resources. There was a considerable Ismaili apparatus in Iran, which, with schism and political impotence in Cairo, was taken over by the dai Hasan ibn al-Sabbah, who sometime before 1090 installed himself in the impregnable fortress of Alamut in Daylam, south of the Caspian Sea. Hasan never claimed the Imamate for himself; he was merely the *hujja* or Proof, here understood as the custodian of Ismaili doctrine until the return of the Imam-Mahdi. One of his more desperate, or optimistic, successors went considerably beyond that: the Mahdi had returned; the eschatological resurrection (*qiyama*) was at hand, and with it the abrogation of traditional Islam. It brought climax but no satisfaction. The entire movement went down under the deluge of the Mongol invasion.

THE SULTANATE

At the height of their power, the Ismaili Fatimids had extended their call from their base in Egypt westward across North Africa to Morocco—the Umayyad declaration in Spain that theirs was a genuine caliphate was a reaction to the approach of the Fatimids across the straits—and eastward through Palestine and parts of Syria that they held. Their agents were spreading the revolutionary message at the very heart of the caliphate in Iraq and Iran in the eleventh century. Sunni, caliphal Islam was under a grave threat and was likely saved by the arrival on the scene of intrepid warrior bands who were as loyal to Sunnism and the caliph as they were implacable soldiers. But they also brought a new element of power into the Abode of Islam: if the Turks saved the caliphate, the caliph had thenceforth to share his throne with the newcomers.

Sultan is a quranic term meaning simply power or authority, and early in Islam it came to be applied without a great deal of technical precision to sovereign political authority, frequently as a synonym of *mulk*, "possession," hence "kingship" or "sovereignty." The Abbasids used it that way, and it is noteworthy that they spoke of conferring *sultan* on the "amir of amirs." In the latter office, that of Grand Amir or commander-in-chief, lay the true origins of the sultanate as a distinct and autonomous power in Islam. In 936 the caliph al-Radi formally appointed as the first tenant of that office the Turkish general Ibn al-Raiq and so vested in him the highest civil and military functions of the state, functions that were formerly divided between a civilian vizier or prime minister and a military amir or commander. The grand amirate passed to successive military families who filled the post and exercised its functions until the arrival in Baghdad of the Saljuq Turks.

The coexisting caliphate and sultanate have been called "superimposed monarchies" in that both offices possessed a power that was at the same time personal and absolute. The sultan had to be invested by the caliph with his sovereignty—he was constitutionally the caliph's delegate—but once in possession of such sovereignty, the sultan's power was in fact unlimited. There was, of course, the Islamic law by which the sultan too was bound. But that point was largely moot since there was no instrument to guarantee its observance in the face of such sovereignty. What most severely limited the sultanate, however, was its failure to achieve the ecumenical status of the caliphate. While there was only one caliph, with the occasional anticaliph, there were in fact many sultans in the Abode of Islam, and within their domains their own amirs waxed powerful on the feudal system of land grants. But if the sultan could not speak for Islam, and if the caliph had long since ceased to do so, there were others who as a class were beginning to find their voice, the ulama, or scholars of the sharia.

THE OTTOMANS AND A UNIVERSAL CALIPHATE

The Abbasid caliph went down in the destruction of Baghdad by the Mongols in 1258. In Syria and Egypt, however, the Mamluk sultans—the Mamluks were military slaves who promoted themselves to sovereignty in Egypt in 1250 and held it until they were unseated by the Ottomans in 1517—turned back the Mongol advance. In the sequel, they provided themselves with an Abbasid "survivor" of the Mongol debacle in Baghdad and so could claim to possess, no matter what later historians might think, a legitimate caliph of their own in Cairo.

Note: There were other survivors of other debacles. The original Muslims invaders of Spain in the early seventh century were mixed Berber and Arab bands, and once they had stabilized Muslim control of at least central and southern Iberia, al-Andalus, as the Muslim territory was called, was ruled by a series of amirs, military men turned governors, and often rivals, who ruled in the name of the caliph in Damascus. In 750 the Umayyads of Damascus were overturned by a rival dynasty, the Abbasids, who engineered a wholesale massacre of the house of Umayya. There was a survivor, however, one Abd al-Rahman, who made his way, amidst almost legendary travail, to Spain in 756. He seized power there and gradually unified the Muslim domains into a single amirate based in Cordoba. It was a brilliant time, and the greatest of the Spanish Umayyad line was Abd al-Rahman III (912–961), who in 929 declared that henceforward he should be regarded not as amir but as caliph and Commander of the Faithful. There was a caliph in Baghdad, an Abbasid, but the gesture was not directed so much to Baghdad as to Abd al-Rahman's closer and far more dangerous enemies, the Fatimid Ismailis, whose caliph-Imam ruled all of North Africa from Qairwan and who were contesting control of the Mediterranean with the Umayyads of Spain. The Spanish caliphate finally expired, without much remark, in 1031.

The Ottoman Turks were not so nice in their pretensions, perhaps, and when in 1517 they absorbed the Mamluk sultanate into their own burgeoning domains — they already possessed Anatolia and a good part of the Balkans — they simply asserted that the caliphate had been bequeathed to them. Thus the reigning member of the house of Osman was both sultan and padishah, the political sovereign of the Ottoman Empire, but also caliph and Commander of the Faithful for the entire Muslim community, as they would claim to be for the next four hundred years.

Though the office continued and the caliph enjoyed a degree of spiritual *auctoritas*, already by the tenth century his actual political power was limited to what might be called the caliphal states in Iraq. By the next century even that had disappeared, and the only real power in the Abode of Islam rested in the hands of the various amirs who ruled, sometimes carefully in the caliph's name, at other times carelessly or defiantly not. Muslim theorists eventually made a place for this usurpation of power, as we have seen, under the rubric of the sultanate, but so strong was the notion of a single and universal umma that the traditionalists invariably spoke as if there were one sultan, the amir who executed the caliph's will, when actually there were many from Spain to India and beyond, and the will they executed was invariably their own.

Was the caliph a kind of Muslim pope? Even in his purely episcopal role, the bishop of Rome had, like the other bishops of Christendom, far more authority than his counterpart in Baghdad or Istanbul. Though a bishop's jurisdiction was limited to his see, he could speak out definitively on matters of faith and morals. But once the claim to primacy put forward by the bishop of Rome was accepted as such in the Western churches, the pope's jurisdiction became truly imperial, and from the eleventh century on, when the caliphs were yielding to their Turkish sultans, the popes were vindicating their claims to superiority over their own sultans, the emperors. The Eastern churches only fitfully, and usually under duress, accepted the papal claim to absolute primacy, but they recognized that the pope certainly spoke for Western Christendom.

Recognition of a universal caliphate was far more nominal. It was rejected in fact, at least in its embodiment in an Abbasid or Ottoman claimant, by the Umayyad caliphs in Cordoba, by the Ismailis in North Africa and Egypt, and by the Imami Safavids in Iran. Among the regimes that were Sunni, or even claimed direct linear descent from the Prophet — the so-called sharifs or sayyids — recognition of the caliph often included little more than the mention of his name in the Friday prayers. Foreign policy was not directed by, taxes were not sent to, or instruction requested or received from the vague eminence in Baghdad or Cairo or the caliph who lay all but concealed behind the sultan in Istanbul.

THE END OF THE CALIPHATE

By the early twentieth century Turkish rule was probably the most long-lived and vigorous of all the political realities of Islam, ancient and accustomed enough, at any rate, for some Sunni Muslim theoreticians to continue to maintain the notion of Islam as a universal and undivided theocratic community ruled by a succession of single and unique "deputies" (*khalifa*) of the Prophet descended from the noble clan of the Quraysh. The caliph, in the later, more pragmatic understanding — the one still current in the opening decades of the twentieth century — might, however, be any Muslim ruler who ensured that the principles and law of Islam were upheld. The Ottoman sultans certainly qualified under those conditions, and if they arrogated to themselves some of the titles, regalia, and perquisites of the earlier "universal" caliphate, there was no great harm in that: it strengthened the institution by affirming its', and Islam's, continuing connection with the glorious past. But the reality was understood by most Muslims, and the sovereign in Istanbul was invariably referred to not as "the caliph" but as "the sultan."

The name of caliph still had powerful associations, however — strong enough to tempt the Ottomans to invoke it on occasion, and in jurisdictions into which the theory did not quite stretch: to those Muslims, for example, who were once but no longer the political subjects of the Ottoman sultan, like the Muslims of North Africa or Egypt, or Muslims who had never been, like the millions of the Islamic confession on the Indian subcontinent and in East Asia. This was the aspect of the caliphate that was clearly being tested with the Ottoman call for a holy war in 1916. The lack of response to the caliph's summons illustrates the limits that most Muslims placed on their understanding of the Ottoman caliphate.

The Ottomans' call to holy war was never answered, and the Muslims of North Africa and India remained truer to their colonial masters than to their putative pope in Istanbul. In 1918 the Ottoman Empire went down in defeat along with its German and Austro-Hungarian allies, but out of the debacle arose the new state that called itself the Turkish Republic. On 28 January 1920 the deputies to the Ottoman National Assembly moved from Istanbul to Ankara. There they signed the Turkish National Pact declaring themselves in permanent session until the independence of the fatherland and the caliphate should be guaranteed. Two years later, however, the matter appeared somewhat differently. On 31 October 1922 the primary political institution of the Ottoman and Muslim past, the sultanate, was abolished, and though the office of the caliph was left untouched, its divorce from the sultanate effectively stripped it of whatever powers it may have possessed. On 17 November the last sultan, Muhammad Wahid al-Din, fled on a British ship to Malta, and two days later his cousin Abd al-Majid was elected to the vacant caliphate to preside, with severely limited powers, over a new, laicized Islam. On 29 October 1923 the revolution was accomplished: the Turkish Republic was proclaimed.

The laicization process went even further, as many of the traditionalists feared. On 3 March 1924 the Turkish National Assembly abolished the caliphate itself, an office the Ottomans had held for 407 years, and finally on 9 April 1928 that same body abrogated Article 2 of the Ottoman Constitution: Islam was no longer the religion of the state. Abd al-Majid was informed of the decision regarding the caliphate on the evening of the same day it was taken, and was told that he should prepare to leave the country forthwith. The family immediately began to pack its belongings, which were loaded onto trucks. At five the next morning all was ready. Abd al-Majid and his son occupied one car, the women and their attendants a second, and the cortege, escorted by the chief of police and patrolmen on motorcycles, left Istanbul and then, shortly afterward, the country itself.

Iran as a Shiite State

The destiny of Sunni Islam rested for centuries in the hands of the Ottoman Turks, who extended the borders of the Abode of Islam deep into the Christian Balkans and even to the gates of Vienna. Where they had less success was against their own Muslim rivals in Iran.

The community that later came to rule Iran as a dynasty, the Safavids began their career as a Sufi *tariqa*, or religious order, founded by one Safi al-Din (d. 1334) in northwestern Iran. His order, Sunni in its doctrine and sentiments, spread widely over southeastern Turkey and northern Iraq and Iran, and under its fourth sheikh managed to carve out for itself an autonomous political territory in northwestern Iran. Thus, by the mid–fifteenth century, the Safavid tariqa had become a political entity as well as a Sufi association. More, it veered sharply in the direction of a Shiism of the extremist variety — its sheikh was beginning to be regarded as himself a manifestation of God.

In 1494 a sheikh named Ismail (d. 1524) assumed the leadership of the order and of the still modest Safavid state in northern Iran. Iran at that time was still overwhelmingly Sunni in its allegiances and ideology, although there were already important Shiite influences at places like Qom and Neyshabur, and there were growing Shiite tendencies in some of the other Sufi orders, including the Safavid tariqa. By Ismail's time there was little doubt where Safavid thinking was. As the Fatimid Ismailis had claimed for their leaders in their day, in his followers' eyes Ismail was the Twelver Imam now returned from his concealment, and his troops reportedly cried out, on entering battle, "There is no god but The God and Ismail is the Friend of God." Battle they did, for ten years (1499–1509), until in the end Ismail and the Safavids ruled most of Iran. Already in 1501 Ismail had proclaimed Shiism the official version of Islam in his new kingdom.

The Safavids early possessed political sovereignty, bought at the end of a sword, but their claim to religious legitimacy was considerably less certain. The house, which was likely Turkmen or Kurdish in origin, claimed to have descended from Ali by way of the seventh Imam, Musa al-Kazim. This of itself gave Ismail prestige but no religious authority, and his claim that he was himself the Imam was entertained by none but his own most favored entourage of warriors. Most of his followers, and the population generally, appear to have known little about Twelver Shiism to begin with, and the more learned Shiite ulama whom Ismail and his successors invited to Iran seemed little inclined to unmask the pretensions of their benefactors. For most of the population, it was a relatively easy transition from Sunni to Shiite Islam, involving little more than heaping praise on Ali — never difficult among even the most devout Sunnis — and obloquy on his enemies, notably the Umayyads, and, where circumstances dictated, on the first three caliphs, who had usurped Ali's rightful position at the head of the umma. The only religious resistance that might in fact be expected would likely come from the Sunni tariqas. Ismail took no chances: the Sufi orders were disbanded.

The planting of deeper Shiite roots into Iranian soil was the work of Shah Abbas (1588–1629). His predecessors had already begun to disassociate the regime's ideology from its extremist origins, and Shah Abbas established more formal ties to normative Twelver Shiism by inviting Shiite ulama elsewhere to come to Iran and founding for the first time Shiite madrasas for the formal education of native ulama. Shah Abbas directed most of his attention to Isfahan, but under the next dynasty to rule Iran, the Qajars (1794–1925), similar colleges were opened, again with state support, in Najaf (now in Iraq), Qom, and Mashhad, which remain the chief centers of Shiite learning. The shahs' own connection with the Imams, meanwhile, fell increasingly into the background.

The Safavid regime managed to survive until 1722 when Afghans from the east penetrated the crumbling kingdom and took Isfahan. By their demise the Safavids had, however, established an apparently irreversible Shiite state, not the first in the Middle East but certainly the most powerful, and bound by strong ties to Iranian national sentiments, in an overwhelmingly Sunni world. Shiites have never constituted more than 10 to 15 percent of the Muslim population as a whole. They remain the overwhelming majority in Iran, but it is probable — it is to nobody's interest to count, or be counted, too accurately — that they also constitute more than half the Muslims in Iraq, Lebanon, and Bahrain and are a significant presence in Sunni Pakistan and multiconfessional India.

THE SHIITE ULAMA AND THE STATE

Shiites have always stood somewhat apart from the state. As a potentially revolutionary minority within an overarching system of Sunni sovereignty, Shiites have tended for most of their history, to regard "church" and "state," the Shiite community of "(true) believers" (*muminun*) and the Sunni caliphate of "submitters" (*muslimun*), as separate institutions. Tactically they might practice "dissembling" (*taqiyya*) toward the latter, but in what concerned their religious practices, their instructors were the ulama, Shiism's lawyers. The Shiite ulama were, however, neither as numerous nor as well trained as their Sunni counterparts until the sixteenth century. While the Sunni ulama were being formally trained in the expanding madrasa system — itself possibly a derivative of an earlier Ismaili Shiite experiment in Cairo — the Shiite lawyer-clergy received their instruction somewhat haphazardly in an apprentice arrangement, novice by master, with little certifiable competence on the part of either. Under Shah Abbas, however, the madrasa system was introduced into what was by then a Shiite Iran and thereafter the Shiite ulama, often known as mullahs, grew rapidly in skill, power, and prestige.

From about 1600, then, the Shiite ulama, who claimed for themselves the "general representation" of the Hidden Imam, had the option of cooperating with the government, resisting, or simply disregarding it. In most cases they have done the latter, which is obviously the most prudent course in Sunni-dominated lands and even when the regime is "secular," as in most of the modern states that constitute what was once the Abode of Islam. In Safavid Iran, in contrast, the newly invigorated ulama often dominated the government. Under their more secular successors, the Qajars and the Pahlavis (1925–1979), and particularly with the triumph of the "interpretationist" over the "transmissionist" wing among the ulama, Iranian mullahs forcefully intervened in politics, particularly from Iraq, where they were beyond government control, against the king and for constitutional reform in 1906, for example. The constitution that was finally adopted on that occasion recognized Twelver Shiism as the official religion of the Iranian state and appointed a board of five *mujtahid*s, or "interpreters," to screen all new legislation for its agreement with the sharia, an arrangement that was never put into effect. In more recent times, the Shiite mullahs were the single most potent force in unseating the shah of Iran in 1979 and establishing an Islamic republic.

THE ISLAMIC REPUBLIC OF IRAN

Ayatollah Khomeini, the prominent Shiite mullah instrumental in overthrowing the shah of Iran in January 1979, returned home in triumph from his Paris exile in February of that year to begin the momentous task not merely of putting in place a new government but of constructing a new state. What sort of state he preferred Khomeini had already made clear in his *Governance of the Cleric* (*Velayat-e Faqih*), which had appeared in 1970. In a referendum of 30–31 March 1979, the people were given the stark choice: an Islamic Republic, yes or no? The answer was an overwhelming "yes" and the Ayatollah proclaimed its establishment on 1 April of that year. At the end of the summer an Assembly of Experts, most of them from Khomeini's Islamic Republic Party, started work on a draft constitution, which was submitted to a popular referendum, again with a simple yes or no choice and again overwhelmingly approved by the electorate. The Islamic Republic was a reality.

Iran had had a constitution and some form of republican government since the Constitutional Revolution of 1906–1911, but this latest version, though it preserved some of the republican structure, was radically different. It was wrought to ensure that the rule of law would be the rule of the sharia (as understood by the Imami Shiites) and that governance would in fact be "governance of the cleric." The first principle is asserted in the preamble of the Constitution and often thereafter. "Legislation, which forms guidelines for the direction of society" must, the preamble dictates, "be based on the Quran and the sunna," and thus the Constitution is founded on "the fundaments of Islamic principles and guidelines." Article 2 ties state legislation to the sharia by describing legislation as a power reserved to God and acknowledging that revelation has a fundamental role in the promulgation of laws. Article 4 states that "all laws and regulations . . . must be based on Islamic principles." Article 72 forbids the parliament to pass laws that "contradict the principles and ordinances of the state religion and the land." The same restriction is imposed on local councils, whose resolutions must agree with "Islamic principles." Article 170 makes it incumbent on judges to refuse to implement government resolutions and decrees when these "contravene Islamic laws and regulations."

The clearest statement of principle is contained in Article 2 of the Constitution:

> 1. There is only one God . . . who by right is ruler and lawgiver, and man must submit to his command.
> 2. Divine revelation has a role to play in the promulgation of the laws.
> 3. The resurrection plays an essential role in the process of man's development vis-à-vis God.
> 4. God's justice is inherent in his creation and his law.
> 5. The Imamate will provide the leadership and will play a fundamental role in the progress of the Islamic revolution.
> 6. Man is endowed with nobility and elevated dignity; his freedom entails responsibility before God,

The governance of the Imami Shiite clerics is guaranteed by the most striking feature of the structure of the new Islamic Republic: side by side with the traditional republican institutions of elected executive, legislative, and judicial officials runs a parallel line of clerics, most of them appointed, who exercise a quite literal guardianship over the acts and enactments of their elected counterparts. Thus the president is "shadowed" by a religious leader, the parliament by a Council of Guardians, and the civil courts by religious ones. The purpose of this second, shadow government in the Islamic Republic of Iran is perfectly clear. As Article 2 of the Constitution expresses it, by means of "continual ijtihad ["interpretation"] exercised by qualified jurists on the basis of the Quran and the sunna of those who are infallible [that is, the Imams] (God's peace be upon them all), . . . justice as well as political, economic, social, and cultural independence and national solidarity will be achieved." That power is expressed chiefly in the appointed clerics' right to void any acts or legislation that are deemed contrary to the sharia.

7.

God's Way:

A Life and a Law for Muslims

WITH Muhammad's death, God's voice was stilled, and the community that "The Guidance" had brought into being had to turn to their recollection of what the Quran had pronounced were Muslim's responsibilities. But if the Quran declared the principles of a Muslim life, Muhammad exemplified these, and the community of Muslims has drawn on his example, as well as on his own personal teachings, from his own day to this.

MUHAMMAD AS MORAL EXEMPLAR

As the Christians looked to Jesus, who in his humanity was their peer, first in the flesh and then in the accounts of his life, the earliest Muslims had before them the example of Muhammad, in life to begin with, then in memory, and finally, and ever more dramatically, in legend. Muhammad lived in circumstances quite different from Jesus', of course. Mecca was a commercial center as well as a religious, albeit pagan, one. Given the importance of its shrine, religion was quite clearly the principal business, and as some modern interpreters would contend, business may have become the religion of Mecca as well. Muhammad had a modest but discernible role in at least the town's business: he married a local entrepreneur, Khadija, and tradition puts him in charge of her commercial caravan interests. The Quran, at any rate, is filled with commercial terms about humankind's accounts, God's reckonings, and painful audits at the End Time.

In the Gospels Jesus occasionally makes what seem to be disparaging remarks about wealth and the wealthy; the Quran is less interested in wealth as such than in the attitude it engenders. The Quran's earliest preaching to the Meccans was aimed directly at the arrogance and niggardliness of the wealthy who think that property is their due and who do not share their gains with the settlement's poor and needy. Circumstances were quite different at Medina, however. Muhammad and his community of believers came rather quickly to share the prosperity that was so dangerous to the Meccans, though it was now the Prophet's responsibility to say how it should be used (Quran 59:6–10). At Medina the Quran encourages the Muslim raiders with the promise of "rich spoils" (48:19), and tradition tells of the immense fortunes in loot acquired by some of the early Muslims. But those same raiders are warned not to be overly concerned with booty since God too has "spoils" in store for the faithful (4:94).

What of Muhammad himself? Muhammad was the exemplar of all human virtue for the Muslim, and though we are treated to a broad portrait of the man in the hadith that make up the "custom of the Prophet," we do not always know what to make of the details. Many of the Prophetic reports seem to be fighting a later war, some praising asceticism, others deploring it; some making the Prophet parsimonious, others lavish. The Quran granted the Prophet a large share of the spoils of his increasingly successful raids (59:6), and it permitted him as many wives as he chose to have, a "privilege granted to no other believer" (33:50–52). But for all that, Muhammad does not appear either self-aggrandizing or particularly concerned with personal wealth, either at Medina, when he possessed it, or at Mecca, when he did not. The Prophet's wives — and their exact number appears somewhat uncertain, perhaps as many as thirteen — represent a different issue, one dear to later Christian polemicists who found ample material in the hadith to paint the Prophet of Islam as a sensualist with an eye and a taste for women. As one famous hadith put it, "When it comes to this world (*al-dunya*), women and perfume have become dear to me," to which is quickly added, "but my heart's delight is in prayer."

Whatever the precise truth of all these reports, Muhammad was clearly no ascetic. He was neither excessive nor abstemious in his conduct, a rather remarkable trait in a man who knew both poverty in his early years and extraordinary worldly success in his middle life. "I am but a mortal like you," he is made to say in the Quran (18:110), and both the Quran and the sunna confirm that assertion. Nor did he preach to others any discernible degree of voluntary self-restraint or self-denial with respect to the legitimate pleasures of life.

THE GOODS OF THIS WORLD

If the Prophet of Islam was a "moderately sensual man" in person, his religious priorities were more radically defined, at least as they issue from the Quran. The Quran has a strong sense of the distinction between "this world" (*al-dunya*) and the "next world" (*al-akhira*). "Know," the Quran says (57:20), "that the life of this world is only a frolic and a mummery, an ornamentation, boasting and bragging among yourselves, and lust for multiplying wealth and children. It is like rain so pleasing to the cultivator for his vegetation which sprouts and swells, and then begins to wither, and you see it turn to yellow and reduced to chaff. There is severe punishment in the Hereafter, but also forgiveness from God and acceptance. As for the life of this world, it is no more than the merchandise of vanity." More, our desires are often displaced: "You want the frail goods of this world, but the will of God is for the other world" (8:67). There is no necessary contradiction between the realms; it is simply that the next world is where judgment will be passed on our use of the goods of this world — there that those who have used them well will find their place of reward, and those who have used them ill, their punishment.

The Quran's teachings differ little in this regard from the Gos-

pels', even though the exemplars in the two instances may be sending somewhat different messages by their personal conduct. And
though both men had the same concern for ritual purity — the Jew
Jesus arguably somewhat less than the more "Jewish" Muhammad — neither redrew the strict lines between the sacred and the
profane that are found in the Torah. If the Torah, looked on this
life as a dangerous place, it was not by reason of its attractions but
because its clustered yet clearly marked land mines of impurity
threatened (apparently) both God and humans. The Jew, properly
cautious of where the dangers lay, was free to enjoy the rest of the
terrestrial landscape. The Christian and the Muslim were under a
different kind of restraint, as we shall see.

Note: Though perhaps some small case might be made for an inclination toward the good things of the table (Luke 7:34), the Jesus of the
Gospels appears to be not so much denying himself as uninterested in
the pleasures and pursuits of the world. He was more focused on the
faith in God that made such a lack of interest and concern possible
than on the dangers of indulging in them. A craftsman in Nazareth,
Jesus gave up his profession to become an itinerant preacher, or perhaps even something of a scholar, in his native Galilee, supported, it
appears, by friends and followers, many of them women (Luke 8:3).
He was unmarried, we assume and the Christian tradition dogmat-
ically asserts, although at least one of his followers, Peter, is so casu-
ally revealed to have had a wife (Mark 1:30) that we must wonder
about all of them. Celibacy, at any rate, does not appear to have been
an issue with Jesus. He associated easily with women, some of whom
were devoted followers — Mary and Martha in Bethany (John 11:1–
2) and Mary of Magdala (Luke 8:2), for example — and it was women
who first bore witness to his resurrection, or at least to the empty
tomb (Mark 16:1; Matt. 28:9; John 20:11 ff.).

Although the distinction between this world and the next, each
with its own set of values, is clear, it is not fully fleshed out. The
sins of this world seem to be chiefly of the spirit: lack of trust in
God, lack of generosity toward the poor and needy. Intoxicating

wine is prohibited (Quran 2:219) — though it is served in Paradise (47:15) — and this is new; likewise forbidden are certain foods, most notably pork (5:3), and this is not. Judaism had gone there before, though the Muslim food menu is far less restrictive than the Jewish one. In addition, the Muslim had the example of the Prophet, which was, as already noted, not entirely unambiguous when it came to the licit things of the world.

THE TRADITION

Muhammad's example and, equally important, his instruction, was carried forward to succeeding generations of Muslims in a great body of anecdotes that professed to record his sayings and deeds. These Prophetic reports flowed steadily and powerfully into the still nascent Islamic tradition and, together with the Quran, gave it shape and definition. Out of this mix of Scripture and report, and the Muslims' interpretation of both, emerged the sharia, Islamic religious law.

There is more than one problematic element in the combination of Scripture, reports about the Prophet, and what the Muslims call ijtihad, or "personal effort." Something has already been said about the Muslims' probing the meaning of Scripture; here it is a matter of its complement, tradition. All three communities of Scripturalists recognize a continued or continuing form of revelation, whether in the form of texts or voices, to guide the community along the "right way " to its ordained goal. God's voice is not stilled, as it turns out, but merely turns into other channels. Generically, this other channel of divine guidance was understood as something handed down from an older and indubitable source, and so it is fair to describe it as "tradition." In English that word is used in the singular to describe a whole range of concepts, from a cast-in-stone practice, to authoritative counsels or exemplary guidelines, to mere customary action, with a semantic inclination toward the latter end of the scale. "Tradition" is being used here, however, in a rather precise, and perhaps unfamiliar, way. For all three Peoples of the Book, "tradition" is understood as a nonscriptural pronouncement, derived from an authoritative source, validated by trustworthy eye- or earwitnesses, transmitted by an authenticated chain of reporters, and so absolutely binding on believers as a standard of belief or conduct.

In Judaism, the tradition originated in the body of instruction or explanation given orally to Moses on Mount Sinai and then transmitted, again orally, through various groups in the community until it was finally committed to writing by Rabbi Judah circa 200 C.E. In that latter form it is called the Mishnah or, embedded in one of its two canonical sets of commentary, the Talmud. In Christianity, the tradition originated in the private teachings of Jesus to his immediate circle of followers (the Apostles), who then passed it on, in general fashion (what they passed on is called the *Apostolic Tradition*) to their immediate spiritual descendants (the linkage process is called the *Apostolic Succession*) who were then identified as the "overseers" (*episkopoi*, bishops) of the various Christian communities. This teaching (Lat. *doctrina*) becomes specific when it is defined, and it becomes dogma when it is prescribed, as is done most often in Christianity but only rarely in Judaism and Islam. In Islam, the tradition resides in the body of reports (*hadith*) that record, on the testimony of contemporary eyewitnesses (the Companions of the Prophet), the customary practice (*sunna*) of Muhammad and so serve as an authoritative guide to Muslim belief and practice.

This is what may be called the great tradition of the three monotheistic communities, a foundation stone in the construction of what we call Judaism, Christianity, and Islam. Adherence to the tradition as a standard of belief is part of what constitutes orthodoxy, and, as a standard of action, orthopraxy. Indeed, tradition in this sense — and it is used in this sense throughout — is so much a part of orthodoxy and orthopraxy that the great reform movements in Christianity and Judaism, which essentially attacked both the authority and authenticity of the great tradition, ended by recasting not only the content of prescribed belief and behavior but also the manner in which orthodoxy and orthopraxy were to be defined.

The authority of this elemental religious tradition derives in the first instance from its source. Scripture was primary in this matter: though there were traditions before Scripture, at least in Judaism and Christianity, once the Book was established as the revealed Word of God and its contents canonized, it enjoyed what appeared to be an absolute authority for believers. It was what the Quran calls "The Guidance." Tradition, which, as remarked, antedated Scripture and may in fact have eventually produced it, had in the end to carve out its own place in the face of this apparently unique claim of Scripture. In Judaism, and later in Islam as well, tradition is thought to have arisen at the side of Scripture and to have been transmitted through the same type of prophetic channel.

GOD'S WAY

Implicit in all that Muhammad did and preached was the notion that there is an Islamic "way" (*sharia*), which resembled the Jewish and the Christian way in that it came from God, and which stood in sharp opposition to both the religious paganism and degenerate tribal custom of the contemporary Arabs. But the Islamic way was no more explicit and formal than the random precepts of the Quran that defined it, and at Muhammad's death in 632, God's revelation was ended and the Quran had become forever a closed Book. At that very moment, however, the Muslim community, which was endowed with only the most rudimentary religious and secular institutions, was poised at the beginning of an immense military and political expansion that would carry it within a short space of time from Spain to the Indus.

The Islamic law or sharia is the prescribed pattern of Muslim behavior, and it originates in only one ground, God's will, which was made available to its intended beneficiaries either through his formal revelation in the Quran or, as it turned out, through the instruction or example of his chosen Prophet, Muhammad. But neither the Quran nor Muhammad's example are themselves sharia; the divine commands and prohibitions must be lifted or extracted from either or both. Law that is simply lifted from either of those two venues is constituted of the precepts lying, without ambiguity or contradiction, on the face of the text. All else must be extracted from beneath the received words.

Very little of the Quran was given over to what might be thought of as legal matters: by one count, only 350 verses, or somewhat less than 3 percent of the received quranic text, is legal in content. These verses have been further broken down, with some disagreement on details, into 140 on the regulation of prayer, fasting, pilgrimage, and the like, 70 on questions of personal status (marriage, divorce, inheritance, etc.), 70 more on commercial transactions (sales, loans, usury), 30 on crimes and punishments, another 30 on justice, and a final 10 on economic matters. This is merely a material description. Nor are all these verses in the form of explicit commands or prohibitions, and there are overlaps and even contradictions among them, the latter of which have to be resolved either by exegetical harmonizing, that is, by showing that the contradictions are only apparent, or else by invoking the principle of abrogation, whereby, as we have seen, a later command cancels an earlier (contradictory) one.

INSTRUCTION FROM ON HIGH: THE PROPHETIC REPORTS

There was more to Islam than the Quran, as it turned out. Muhammad, like Jesus, spoke with authority, not his own, to be sure, but God's and, at times, with God's very own words. The Quran was understood by Muhammad's followers as the *ipsissima verba Dei*, and we must assume that in this case too God's Prophet both volunteered and was requested to explain the sometimes opaque meaning of God's words and will, and even to give direction in other matters that were treated more generally, or perhaps not at all, in the Scripture. Muhammad, it is not difficult to believe, was Islam's first and most authoritative exegete and jurisprudent. Nor is it unreasonable to imagine that his respectful and perhaps awestruck contemporaries remembered his words of personal guidance and explanations with some of the same fervor and fidelity as they remembered his announcement of the words of God.

We can only guess how the Muslims conducted their legal affairs after the Prophet's death. The recognized head of the umma, the caliph, was also regarded as the chief judge (*qadi*) of the community, as Muhammad had been, and he delegated this judicial power to others in what were emerging as the provinces of the new Islamic empire. But how the *qadis* rendered their judgments to other Muslims — Muslim justice applied only to Muslims; Jews and Christians continued under their own juridical traditions, clerical and rabbinic — was likely on the basis of local custom, caliphal instruction, their own understanding of the Quran, and perhaps an embryonic sense of an Islamic way in what was recalled of the sayings and actions of the dead but still revered Muhammad. It was called the sunna of the Prophet.

Sunna, or "customary behavior," was a secular tribal notion of great power among the Arabs. Bedouin nomadism was a marginal existence at best, and the surest guide to survival in that hostile environment was adherence to time-tested procedures and practices summed up by the rubric "the ways of the elders." Sunna ritualized Bedouin life down to the finest details. It was both the moral and pragmatic template — at its high end, *bushido*, a code; at its low end, simply a recipe for staying alive — for tribal life on the pastoral steppe.

Sunna was perhaps less necessary or less desirable in the newly challenging environments like the meager urbanism of Mecca and the cramped and polymorphous oasis existence of Medina; indeed, the Quran may have been addressing itself to the troubling social and moral consequences of the crumbling tribal sunna in those two places. What the Quran proposed to substitute was God's own sunna. The principles proclaimed there were clear, and so too were some of its prescriptions, but the Quran hardly filled the social and moral void left by the expiring tribal sunna. To fill that, the early Muslims turned to something equally revolutionary, the sunna of a single charismatic individual. "This was our fathers' way" was replaced for Muslims by "This was the Prophet's way."

Exactly how the transition happened is not easy to discern. It is sensible to think that the first Muslims looked to Muhammad's words and example for guidance in the new life they had embraced. It is also plausible that memories of the Prophet circulated in some form, chiefly orally, as seems likely. That much is surmise. What we can say for certain is that there was in circulation, a century or so after Muhammad's death, a growing body of reports (*hadith* — in English the Arabic term is increasingly used as both a singular and a collective plural) that purported to record a saying or act of the Prophet. Though distinctive in form, they appear in very varied contexts, as the historical building blocks in what has become the biographical tradition concerning Muhammad, for example, as bits and pieces of the Muslims' earliest attempts at interpreting the Quran, and finally, and very consequentially, as a guide to Muslim behavior.

In the Muslim context, a hadith or (Prophetic) tradition may be defined technically as a report handed down, generally though not exclusively orally, by trustworthy witnesses concerning a saying or an action of the prophet Muhammad and so providing an authoritative guide to permitted and forbidden action or belief. Such a tradition is normally made up of a "chain" (*isnad*) of the names of those who transmitted the report and the text (*matn*) of the report itself. Taken together, these latter hadith were understood to constitute the custom or customary behavior of the Prophet in the same manner that individual tesserae are assembled to constitute a single mosaic. By the end of the eighth century the legal mosaic called the sunna of the Prophet was being put forward as nothing less than the archetype of Muslim behavior.

FROM PROPHETIC TRADITION TO LAW

The reports credited to Muhammad in the hadith would necessarily be explanatory or complementary to already revealed verses in the Quran, and hence it is this interpretation, the Prophet's own, and not some other imagined exegesis of the Book that should be followed. Shafii (d. 820), the most influential of the early Muslim jurists, tried to express this in legal terms. A Prophetic report may simply reaffirm or complement what is already in the Quran. Or it may render specific what is in the Quran only in general terms — the exact times of prayer, for example, or the precise terms of the alms-tithe. Finally, and this is where Quran and sunna are treated equally as revelation, there is the case "where the Prophet establishes a sunna (a custom) about which no part of the Quran has been revealed."

If the sunna of the Prophet, which had thus become normative in the matter of the law, unfolded in word and deed at Mecca and Medina under divine guidance, it follows that the hadith that severally express it must be regarded as a form of revelation. Generally, traditional Muslims have not shrunk from this identification, though some have attempted to distinguish between the Quran's direct and verbal "revelation" (*wahy*) and the more subtle and suggestive "inspiration" (*ilham*) given the Prophet in other circumstances. If nothing else, the stylistic and lexical difference between the Quran and the hadith is distinctive and unmistakable. Yet in legal terms, the sunna of the Prophet was a full partner with the Quran in prescribing Muslim behavior, perhaps even a senior partner since the hadith are far more detailed and prescriptive than the Quran on legal matters.

A GROWTH INDUSTRY

Once the hadith began to weigh more heavily in the lawyers' efforts at fashioning, if not a formal body of Islamic law, then at least a jurisprudence, such traditions not unnaturally began to multiply as supply went out to meet demand. Collectors fanned out across the entire Abode of Islam in search of these precious recollections and returned to the great legal centers in Iraq, Syria, and Arabia with their heads crammed with hadith. The enormous amount of material collected on these "hunting expeditions" was obviously quite inconsistent in quality. There were mutually contradictory traditions, those with incomplete chains of transmitters and others with multiple weaknesses. The reports themselves contained material that ranged on occasion from the trivial to the superstitious, or was transparently Jewish or Christian in origin. A great many were overtly and outrageously political in their inspiration, like the hadith that have Muhammad praising his uncle

Abbas, in fact a very late convert to Islam but, more important, the ancestor of the then reigning dynasty in Baghdad.

In their earliest form the hadith appear to have been offered with little more validation than "I heard it said that the Prophet, upon whom be peace . . ." Or "I heard from X, to whom it was reported that the Prophet . . ." With the multiplication of Prophetic reports, however, and the consequent jostling over their recognition as a basis of law, credentialing hadith became more explicit, and the Prophetic traditions were eventually cited with a fully articulated chain of transmitters (*isnad*) that extended from the most recent tradent, or transmitter, one who "hands down" (< Lat. *tradere*), backward to an eye- or ear witness among Muhammad's own contemporaries, the generation later canonized as the *sahaba*, or Companions of the Prophet.

Note: The Companions of the Prophet who stand at the eyewitness base of every hadith have been defined as any adult Muslim — though some wished to remove the qualification of adult — who had some sort of contact with Muhammad. The total number varies widely. One authority tallied them at 100,000, while Ibn Hajar (d. 1448), the Cairene scholar and judge who devoted himself to collecting every shred of evidence on the Companions, published critical lives of 12,267 individuals who qualified, 1,522 of them women. The number of Companions to whom authoritative Prophetic reports are actually attributed amounts to no more than 1,060, however. Even this figure is misleading. Five hundred related only one such report, and only 123 are credited with having witnessed twenty or more. At the very top of the list is a certain Abu Hurayra, whose chief claim to fame is that he transmitted 5,374 hadith. Close by is Muhammad's wife Aisha, who is credited with 2,210.

A SKEPTICAL REACTION

Many in the ninth century began to criticize the rising tide of hadith that was threatening to drown the still fresh enterprise of Muslim jurisprudence. Some resorted to mockery, while others, like the new rationalists in Islam who accepted the Quran as revelation but were averse to an authoritatively traditioned explanation to revelation, lodged even more trenchant criticisms against the hadith. To resolve the obvious difficulties of the tradition system, scholars devised a critical method for the study of hadith that would enable them to sort out the "sound" from the "weak" hadith. The work of criticism concentrated principally on the authenticity and reliability of the witnesses cited in the isnad of the report in question, and by the mid–ninth century the work had proceeded to the point where the newly authenticated hadith could be brought together for the lawyers' use. That they were in fact designed for lawyers is manifest in the earliest of the collections, that by al-Bukhari (d. 870), called *The Sound Collection*. All the reports in it — 2,762 of them, discounting repetitions, of an alleged 600,000 investigated — are certified as sound with respect to their tradents and so were usable in matters of law. To that end they are arranged according to their applicability to the categories of what was emerging as the science of Islamic jurisprudence, 97 divisions in all.

Note: Non-Muslim Western scholars first encountered the hadith in the nineteenth century when they took up the critical-historical investigation of Muhammad's life. The Muslim biographies of the Prophet are composed at base from hadith, though here they are historical rather than legal in content and are arranged chronologically rather than categorically. From the outset, there were doubts about their authenticity and soon Western scholarship turned its full critical attention to the question, particularly of the legal hadith, which had reportedly been sifted free of forgeries. The results were and remain overwhelmingly negative: according to Western critics, the great bulk of the hadith, sound or otherwise, appear to be forgeries and there is no reliable way of determining which, if any, might be authentic historical reports from or about Muhammad. This judgment may be the single most important bone of contention between modern Muslim and Western scholarship on the origins of Islam.

ISLAMIC JUSTICE: THE QADI

The Quran was sent down to restore justice to the world: to induce humans to recognize the "claims of God," as the jurists called them, as Creator and Lord, and, in consequence of that, to restore justice to human dealings with one another. The society to which this message was brought was not without its own version of justice. Mecca was in the process of urbanization, but, as already noted, the prevailing mode of justice there was still largely based on the Bedouin notion of a customary tribal law (*sunna*) administered, where necessary—the tribes frequently took justice into their own hands—by an arbitrator (*hakam*) chosen for his sagacity or, on occasion, his charismatic qualities.

The substitution of quranic norms of justice for Bedouin ones was neither a short nor an easy process. The tribal arbitrator, for example, continued to function side by side with fully developed Muslim institutions of justice for many centuries, though there were restrictions on the cases that could be submitted to such arbitration. The effort was made, somewhat haltingly at first, but eventually with great success, to convert Arab custom into Muslim law. The first sign of the intent to do so was perhaps a significant change in nomenclature. Judges appointed under Islamic authority were not called hakams or arbitrators, but qadis, decision-makers, a deliberate echo of *qada*, the verb used in the Quran to describe God's own divine power.

The Muslim tradition, which, like its monotheistic counterparts, attempts to legitimate its institutions by tracing them back to the origins of the community, credits the earliest caliphs—the Quran knows of no such official, or of any other, for that matter—with the appointment of the first qadis. Such may not be the case, but the practice of these early Islamic judges was of a very mixed quality: quranic injunction, local custom, their pre-Islamic predecessors' methods and norms, and their own discretionary powers all played a part in the judgments rendered by the Umayyad qadis. Though there was as yet no fully formed body of Islamic law at that point, the sharia was in the process of elaboration in various circles in late Umayyad times, not, however, in support of current local practices, but often in opposition to them.

In principle, the qadi's justice was the only justice for Muslims — and only for Muslims: the dhimmis, the Jews and Christians of the Abode of Islam, rendered justice in their own communities according to their own laws — and no person or class was exempt from it. No one is above the law in Islam. The qadi's judicial power was absolute within his own geographical jurisdiction, but as the rulers of the umma and its various successor states began to centralize the administration of justice, hierarchical arrangements eventually appeared, from local judges to the grand qadis of major jurisdictions.

The qadi's powers did not end with rendering judgment on cases brought before him. He possessed as well a kind of extraordinary jurisdiction that extended into such religious matters as superintending public prayer and mosques, the charge of orphans, widows, and the divorced, and even such secular matters as finances and administration. But the qadi's once broad jurisdiction has shrunk over the centuries. Even under nominally Islamic regimes there grew a body of secular or civil law, often disguised as one form or other of executive decree, that progressively narrowed the qadi's field to personal law, matters touching on divorce settlements and inheritances, for example. The process was hastened in the early twentieth century when many Middle Eastern regimes adopted a constitutional base with a full body of explicitly secular law and a secular judiciary, and it is in the newer, professedly Islamic states like the Kingdom of Saudi Arabia and the Islamic Republic of Iran that the sharia has been restored to some semblance of the law of the land and the qadi reestablished as a primary judicial authority.

ISLAMIC MORALITY AND ISLAMIC JURISPRUDENCE

As a manual of behavior the Quran is obviously incomplete, at least in the sense that its general principles of morality have not been drawn out into every one, or indeed many, of the forms that human behavior might take. A great deal more detailed instruction was provided by the body of traditions handed down about the Prophet's own behavior, but there remained the considerable task of explaining, ordering, and adducing into their particulars the general moral principles provided by revelation. This fell to the science of jurisprudence (*fiqh*), which Ghazali (d. 1111) defined as "the science of scriptural rules established for the regulation of the acts of those who are obliged," that is, the Muslims. Muslim dialectical theology (*kalam*), in contrast, took up the investigation, explanation, and defense of the principles themselves, among them the not inconsiderable task of reconciling God's all-determining Will and humans' responsibility for their own acts.

Note: The behavioral codes of the three monotheistic communities are thought to rest on God's will, as expressed in the commandments and teachings he had laid down in Scripture. The matter, as it turned out, was far more complex. There was, to begin with, a powerful competing vision of what constituted the good for humankind. What the Greco-Roman ethical tradition principally contributed to the moral systems of the monotheists was the fruit of a long, richly detailed, and highly intuitive scrutiny of human character. Plato, Aristotle, and the Stoics lay bare the wellsprings of human action and devised a typology of human personality. Sin, the concrete reprehensible act — *hamartia*, "missing the mark," the Greeks called it — interested them far less than vice, the habituated and habitual character trait that produced such an act. The formation and content of monotheistic morality had a strongly personal cast: sin is an offense against God or, more specifically, against something God had willed. The motivation for such acts was somewhat problematic. An "evil impulse" or Satan was sometimes fingered as the immediate culprit by the rabbis, whereas for the Christians, Original Sin provided a more general explanation.

Once the Jews and Christians, and latterly the Muslims, came in contact with Greek ethical theory, these explanations of why humans acted in despite of God's express will became somewhat less than satisfactory. The monotheists did not need the Greeks and Romans to tell them that "the good that I would do, I do not" (Rom. 7:19), that

> your head (or Scripture) tells you one thing and your heart (or some-
> other part of your anatomy) tells you quite another. What the Helle-
> nic ethical tradition did do was explain to the Scripturalists, who
> were very good at keeping score, the rules of the game. But first the
> monotheists had to explain to themselves why there was a game to
> begin with.

General Muslim fiqh had as its subject the "roots of the law,"
whereas particular jurisprudence, the "science of the branches,"
was devoted to placing a moral template atop the range of conscious human activity to provide guidance for the Muslim. Accordingly, at one end of the spectrum of human acts are those, like
prayer, that are judged "mandatory" or "obliged" (*fard*) and so
are morally incumbent on the believer. At the other end are practices that simply forbidden, like usury (Quran 3:130). Between the
absolutely required and the absolutely forbidden stand three inter-
mediary moral categories. In the middle is the morally neutral
(*mubah*) act, which lies entirely in the discretion of the agent. Toward the side of virtue lies a field of acts that are "recommended"
(*mandub*) and, verging toward vice, the "cautioned" or "discouraged" (*makruh*) acts. In all cases, however, it is the internal state,
the agent's intention (*niyya*), that is crucial in determining the morality of a given action.

The lawyers divided prescribed actions into those directed toward God as his due, the "worshipful acts" (*ibadat*) that constituted Islam's ritual code, and the "deeds" (*muamalat*) that described
and evaluated transactions between individual Muslims, where the
notion of consensus played a powerful role. The ritual acts that
constitute one category of the Muslim's obligations are based on
God's rights and humans' consequent obligations. The deeds,
however, are acquired obligations. They had their pre-Islamic origins in transactions, chiefly having to do with land use, and they
never quite lost that original sense even as they broadened into a
moral category. For Ghazali, for example, the muamalat, which
form the heart of Muslim ethics, are constituted either of ex-
changes like trading, selling, lending, debt, and the like, or of con-

Note: The categorization of foods stands somewhat obliquely on that of human acts. Some foods are indeed forbidden (*haram*) to Muslims by reason of their substance, like pork (Quran 2:167) or wine (5:92), or, in the case of meats, by the manner of their preparation, if they are scavenged, for example, or not properly slaughtered. Foods that meet these latter criteria are termed *halal*, "kosher," and so permitted. Here, as elsewhere in Islamic law, circumstances condition the obligation: where ritual slaughter is impossible, Muslims may use Jewish butchers, and where no other nourishment of any type is available, they may eat nonhalal foods.

tracts and their dissolution, hence matters of marriage and divorce, slavery and emancipation, and so on.

The categories envisioned by Ghazali as the matter of Islamic ethics is a rather notable narrowing of the field of moral activity — the matter submitted to the muftis for their opinion was, of course much broader — and what widened Muslim moral sensibility was its inclusion of the very typical Arab notion of *adab*, a kind of social etiquette that included both a style and a body of information. Adab was what was expected in a polite society; what actually occurred was *adat*, the community's customs or manners. Thus, throughout Islamic history, consideration of the morality of the muamalat has had a powerful sociological constituent, one that took account of both adab and adat in determining how a Muslim should act in given circumstances.

A Society of Law — and Lawyers

The qadi was a functionary, a government functionary to be sure, appointed to resolve issues between individual Muslims, to settle, either by the consent of the parties or the power of the state, civil and criminal disputes between plaintiffs and defendants. Cases were adjudicated on the basis of equity or according to what were understood as the principles of Islamic law. That latter was somewhat problematic, however. There was no Codex Juris Civilis as there was in the Roman Empire and no Codex Juris Canonici as there was in the Christian Church. There was only a (barely) emerging consensus of an ill-defined body of individuals who interested themselves in legal questions and who could be found in informal circles in the major Muslim centers. They were not judges in that they did not adjudicate, nor lawyers in that they did not plead, but what we might call law school professors, had there been at that point any law schools or anything resembling professors. They were simply Muslims whose avocation was sharia — Islam's rabbis, though without either the judicial or the liturgical functions of the latter.

Traditional Muslim societies have been as dominated by lawyers as the parallel Jewish ones, and it may be useful at the outset to lay out some of the modulations in which Muslim jurisprudence appears. The common Arabic term for one learned in the law is *alim*, plural, *ulama*, quite simply, "the learned" or "the experts." But their learning is formal: they have been trained — at first they seem to have trained themselves — in the science of jurisprudence (*fiqh*), hence the ulama are also more functionally known as *fuqaha* (sing. *faqih*), "jurisprudents." Islamic jurisprudence is a scholarly and academic subject, eventually pursued in the madrasa, an institution formalized in the eleventh century and designed, like the Jewish yeshiva, to provide such scholastic training. But the faqih might don two other caps; though not simultaneously. He could be recruited by the political authorities to render justice and so assume the state-sponsored and salaried position of judge (qadi); or he might, if requested, consent to render an opinion on a practical matter of the law, a *fatwa*, as it was called, or indeed many such, and so serve in the generally unofficial, though widely recognized, position of mufti.

JUDGMENTS AND OPINIONS

Sharia emerges into our line of vision early in the ninth century, and with it, the profile of those experts, the ulama, who produced and glossed it. Their glosses were, in the main, scholastic and theoretical, new building blocks in the edifice of the sharia, but ordinary Muslims had other, more concrete concerns. In matters of contest, they had perforce to go to the qadi for a binding judgment, but in matters of conscience, on whether this or that act was licit or not, they turned, as we might expect, to one of the ulama for guidance. The response given by a qualified alim constitutes a fatwa. It is the application of the sharia, as understood by the jurisprudent in question, to a practical matter of conduct, and those who render them have been called, with justice, "the creative mediators of the ideal and the real of the sharia."

There was one class of Muslim jurisprudents who, by their position in the great madrasas, or simply by community assent, were looked on as capable of rendering a fatwa or an informed opinion on a matter of that law. Like rabbinic *responsa*, the Muslim fatwa is generally nonbinding and enjoyed only as much authority as the person issuing it. Since there is no case law in Islam, the judgments of qadis in no way constituted a precedent for future decisions nor did they extend the purview of the sharia. A fatwa, in contrast, though nonbinding and unenforceable in the context in which it was originally delivered, had a more profound effect on the sharia. Fatwas were recorded and collected, and some — those that expressed a new interpretation of a point of law rather than a mere recitation of the appropriate scriptural and hadith texts — have constituted, no less than the conclusions reached by the academic ulama, an extension of the sharia. Indeed, the mufti has been described as holding a position on the Islamic legal spectrum somewhere between the practice-normative qadi and the faqih or academic jurisprudent exercising his personal initiative or interpretation (*ijtihad*) within the walls of the madrasa.

PRIESTS AND RABBIS

Between Constantine and the beginning of the Reformation, Christianity, like temple Judaism, operated within a system of dual authority symbolized by the Gospel image of the "two swords"

(Luke 22:38). Those two swords represented the temporal power of the emperor, (which was neither entirely secular, since from Constantine's day he was understood to rule over some sort of idealized Christian commonwealth, nor entirely spiritual, since both the emperor's feet were firmly planted in the Roman imperial tradition) and that of the head(s) of the Church, in the East the patriarch of Constantinople and in West the pope in Rome. At its highest level that duality often appears like hand-to-hand combat between powerful individuals, but in the ranks below, the elite of prestige and power in Christendom was unmistakably its clerics, who controlled its sacramental system and, through their possession of the magisterium or teaching authority, shaped the behavior and beliefs of all Christians.

The ministry of the principal sacraments and the magisterium were both spiritual powers possessed by the Christian clergy not by training, habit, or experience but through the conferred gift of the Holy Spirit. Neither Judaism nor Sunni Islam had a clergy in anything like the same sense, and in both those cultures lawyers were and remain the leaders of the religious community. Rabbis were the uncontested elite of Jews living in both Christian and Muslim societies, where they had no genuine secular competition and very few religious rivals — the holy man (*tzaddik*) was one, and the later "pietist" movements (Hasidism) also challenged mere legal learning. The rabbi's prestige arose from his mastery of the law, which could be certified by the masters or school (yeshiva) he had attended or simply by the community's recognition.

JEWISH RABBIS AND ISLAMIC ULAMA: A COMPARISON WITH A DIFFERENCE

It is tempting, then, to see in the Muslim ulama the rabbis of Islam. In a sense the comparison is just. Both groups constituted a relatively well defined class that enjoyed the power and prestige of a religious elite by reason of their mastery of religious law, and both received a standardized education in jurisprudence in an institutionalized setting. Neither were legislators in the strict sense, but both rabbis and ulama were at the same time the conservative guardians and the cautiously innovative exegetes of a long and complex legal tradition.

But there were important differences. Jews were granted a degree of community autonomy, first in the Roman and Sasanian Empires and then in the dhimmi and later the millet systems under which they lived for long centuries in the Abode of Islam (see chapter 8). That freedom was a concession dictated from above, and within it the rabbis served, by delegation and with the acceptance of their coreligionists, as the administrators of that restricted autonomy. They not only maintained a legal tradition; they also administered it, as judges and surrogates of a higher judicial authority, that of the patriarchs who ruled the Jews of the Roman Empire, the exilarchs who governed the Babylonian communities, and the *geonim*, or heads of the great yeshivas.

The Muslim ulama, in contrast, at least the Sunni variety, were only one element among the classes and elites contesting for power in the Abode of Islam. Before Ottoman times they neither possessed nor delegated any political authority, and they eschewed the administration of the sharia, a task that fell to the government-appointed and supported qadi. Their power lay elsewhere, in the prestige they enjoyed as the custodians of the obviously Islamic component in what was professedly an Islamic society; in their independence of the state, which they could castigate or applaud as circumstances dictated; and in the network of marriages by which they could forge ties with other powerful classes like the large landowners and the wholesale merchants. Unlike their episcopal counterparts, the ulama did not hold the keys of the kingdom in their hands; they could neither bind nor loose nor force a caliph to his knees or out of the Church. But power they possessed, a genuine political power. Like their Jesuit contemporaries in Europe, they educated an Islamic intelligentsia in their school system. After the eleventh century higher education across the face of Islam was uniquely ulama-inspired and directed in madrasas, where Islamic consciences and indeed Islam itself were shaped through the instrument of the sharia.

Until relatively recent times, the law school or yeshiva was the exclusive form of Jewish higher education, and the same is almost as true of Islam. But whereas the yeshiva was a financially marginal institution in Christian and Muslim societies where Jews themselves were politically marginalized, in Islam, where religion and empire were two sides of the same community, the madrasa, its faculty, and students generally enjoyed adequate to lavish financial support. This came, however, not from the state but from private individuals through the institution of *waqf* (endowment). Almost every Muslim intellectual from the eleventh to the nineteenth century received his higher (and increasingly standardized) education in the Quran, hadith, and jurisprudence in the all-male classrooms and courtyards of the madrasa.

Note: As an institution waqf falls under the general heading of charity (*sadaqa*), in this instance a voluntary one, in contrast to the alms-tithe (*zakat*) obligation of all Muslims. The Muslim jurist al-Kasani (d. 1189) defined it as "a continuous or closed charity for the sake of God and his religion." From the legal point of view, waqf was a complex contractual institution. By his public and witnessed declaration the owner of a property or of an object with value surrendered his right to proprietorship of that same property or object: he deeded its ownership and, more important, its income, to God, inalienably and forever. But before the transaction was completed, the donor exercised his right to specify the disposition of its continued income, after expenses, which included the upkeep or continued operation of the property and the fees of the waqf executors.

The difference between the rabbis and the Sunni ulama rests finally in the latters' conviction that they are the interpreters of the sharia, whereas the rabbis regard themselves as the custodians of a Torah that is "no longer in heaven" but rests instead in the hands of the rabbinate. As a result the rabbis have through the centuries practiced ijtihad with far less hesitation and far fewer qualms than their Muslim counterparts. Although both groups think of themselves as competent to render responsa on specific questions of law, the rabbis' ready issuance of both *gezerot*, or decrees, to protect the law and *taqqanot*, or rulings, to advance the common good has no parallel among the Sunni ulama.

THE SCHOOLS

The early evolution of Islamic law took place in widely scattered centers across the Abode of Islam, and not even Shafii's attempts at imposing a kind of order on its development eradicated or even inhibited the continued growth of different schools of legal interpretation, each of them recognized as orthodox and legitimate by the others. Thus the Shafiite, Malikite, Hanafite, and Hanbalite "schools," which were founded by and named after early masters of Islamic jurisprudence, flourished, and continued to flourish, among Muslims. They differ on specific points of theory and practice, but their differences are not very substantial, nor do their practices much differ from the positive precepts of Shiite law, although this latter has a considerably divergent view of what lawyers call the roots of jurisprudence. The four major Sunni schools recognized, with varying degrees of enthusiasm, the Quran, the sunna of the Prophet (as expressed in the hadith), the consensus of the community, and a measure of personal interpretation (ijtihad) as the basis of Islamic law; whereas the Shiites relied heavily on the infallible teachings of the Imams and rejected out of hand community consensus which had in fact betrayed them and, in their view, ignored both God's will and Muhammad's explicit intentions.

Shiite law is based on a foundation quite different from that of the Sunnis. Shiites too extended the law beyond the givens of the Quran—not on the authority of the traditions reported from Muhammad's Companions, who had deprived Ali of his lawful claim to leadership of the umma, but on those from the divinely appointed and infallibly guided Imams. The latter passed down traditions regarding the Prophet, it is true, but they could also pronounce on their own authority, something denied to later generations in Sunni Islam. Thus the Imams, down to their Great Concealment among the Twelver Shia in 941, represented the same kind of ongoing revelation on matters of faith and morals as claimed by Christian bishops and in particular, after the erosion of their powers and the growth of his, by the pope, the bishop of Rome.

There are no great divergencies between Sunni and Shiite law in practice, but two examples deserve notice. Unlike, the Sunnis, the Shiites permit the practice of temporary marriage (*muta*), a sexual union for a limited period of time, even hours, in exchange for a fixed sum of money. The Sunnis regard this as mere prostitution; the Shi'ites claim, perhaps correctly, that the Prophet himself allowed it and that it was only outlawed by the caliph Umar. Since the Shiites do not accept the authority, political or legal, of any of the first three caliphs, muta stands. Taqiyya, or dissembling, is a characteristic Shiite teaching born as a reaction to living as an often persecuted minority under Sunni sovereignty. Indeed, Muhammad himself had lived under such circumstances, and according to the Shiite understanding of Quran 16:106, which promises the wrath of God will descend on those who disbelieve "except for those who are compelled but whose hearts are firm in faith," it is permissible to dissemble one's beliefs, specifically one's Shiite beliefs, when there is danger of losing life or property. Though generally associated with Shiites, taqiyya was also permitted to the Sunni Muslims of Spain, for example, when they were threatened with death if they did not convert to Christianity.

IJTIHAD

Since the lawyers of Islam were essentially rabbis and not bishops speaking comfortably *ex cathedra*, they had early begun to employ various forms of legal reasoning that have been the staples of lawyers always and everywhere. The earliest generations of Muslim jurisprudents had often simply rendered an "opinion" (*ray*) on a matter of practice in the still ill defined field of Islamic law, and more often than not this was sufficient to settle the matter. By the generation of Shafii, however, things had become considerably more complex, and the Egyptian lawyer was clearly attempting to rationalize legal thinking when he insisted that "opinion," which was nothing more or less than the lawyer's using his own interpretative powers (*ijtihad*, or "personal initiative," from the same polymorphous root as *jihad*) on a disputed or uncertain point of law, should become more rigorous by being based solely on a text of the Quran or a hadith—as opposed, say, to some local custom—and that it follow a recognized procedure. That procedure was generally some form of analogy: the present case resembles or is identical to an explicit commandment or prohibition in the Quran or the hadith and so may properly be judged as commanded or prohibited.

Analogy was acceptable procedure to Shafii, as it was to most subsequent jurists, but only if it was used to erect "hedges for the Law," to use the talmudic phrase, and not to extend exceptions into general rules; that it start from the literal and not the allegorical understanding of the text; and that, finally, it be regarded as the fourth and weakest of the "roots of the Law" after the Quran, the custom of the Prophet, and the consensus of the umma. Where personal initiative became considerably more problematic—one lawyer ungraciously described it as "carrion, to be eaten only when no other food was available" —was when it was extended to pronounce something licit or forbidden in the name of equity (*istihsan*) or public interest (*istislah*) of the umma, whereby the letter of the law was relaxed in the name of the common (i.e., community) good.

THE CLOSING OF THE GATE

After Shafii, and as a result of the debate over the validity of independent reasoning, the freedom granted to earlier jurists to elicit legal conclusions from even the most traditional material was severely circumscribed, and by about 900 c.e. a new consensus was developing that the "gate of ijtihad" had closed. Lawyers might dispute matters common to the schools, but the Quran and the hadith were henceforward off the table. Interpretative ijtihad was replaced by *taqlid*, "imitation" or "adherence," whereby the jurist was now bound to follow the teachings of the jurists of the classical schools of the classical era.

The "closure of the gate of ijtihad" has an ominous ring to it, but should be understood in a sense not very different from the closure of the Talmud. As a herald for the advent of scholasticism, scholars had to couch their legal speculations in the form of commentary and explication on an established body of masters, in this case the developed doctrine of the canonical schools. The analogy with the Talmud should not be pressed too closely, however. In a sense Islamic law was fundamentally in place by the beginning of the tenth century, just as the Mishnah was complete in the third, and the two Talmuds in the sixth. But all these latter were formal texts, whereas the sharia continued to exist, even after the tenth century, in the form of a somewhat inchoate, if consensually agreed on, mass of propositions whose exact formulation had only as much authority as the jurisprudent from whose pen it came.

One lawyer who attempted to pry open the gate of ijtihad—and successfully in the eyes of some increasingly influential modern Muslims—was Ibn Taymiyya (d. 1328). This Syrian jurist belonged to the Hanbali school, the most conservative of the Islamic legal traditions. The Hanbalis resisted "innovation" on all fronts, and yet they were uneasy with the notion of the closure of the gate of ijtihad. It was not so much because they favored the sometimes dangerous personal effort but rather because they doubted the possibility of any real consensus of scholars. Consensus was, as we have seen, the validating principle of ijtihad but many Hanbalis thought of consensus as a literal majority of all of the ulama, which was unlikely in the best of circumstances. Thus, the door of ijtihad still remained theoretically ajar for Ibn Taymiyya, the most prestigious of the Hanbali jurists.

Note: Today the gate of ijtihad seems agape rather than merely ajar. Early in the nineteenth century, some of Islam's progressive intellectuals used the Hanbali arguments about the impossibility of a consensus to assert their own right to practice ijtihad to modernize Islamic practice. The argument and its conclusion also proved useful to modern Muslim states that required, or at least desired, some Islamic underpinning for their reforming legislation. Thus, in 1957 Tunisia passed a Law of Personal Status that argued that the Quran permitted polygamy only if all the wives could be treated with absolute impartiality and that this should be regarded as a precondition of a polygamous union — a position never previously held by the ulama. Since that was practically impossible, polygamy was declared illegal.

More recently, fundamentalist Muslims have likewise asserted the right to ijtihad, though for very different ends from those envisioned by the modernists.

Consensus on Moral Matters

Absent an authoritative defining authority on religious matters, Muslims have often been troubled by the differing opinions offered by the experts on moral questions. Just as often, the problem has been resolved, eventually if not immediately, by consensus (*ijma*), which is the often unacknowledged key to the sharia. It arose of necessity from a system based on a revelation that was closed by a single definitive event — the Prophet's death — rather than by community agreement, as happened in the case of the Jews and Christians, who themselves signaled the end of the incremental growth of their Scriptures by gradual but nonetheless effective community consensus. The sudden closure of the Quran occurred as the umma was beginning its astonishing growth into a community linked by little else than monotheistic faith, possession of the Arabic document that had proclaimed it, and certain ethnocultural ties. The absence of detailed behavioral and institutional norms was in part met by the equally astonishing growth of Prophetic reports purporting to supply moral guidance from the Prophet's own example. As a legal instrument, the hadith soon collapsed under their own weight. For ninth-century Muslims there were too many to be convincing, just as for the modern non-Muslim they are too good to be true. The attempt to reground the certitude of the proliferation of Prophetic reports led to the canonical collections of sound or healthy hadith. Muslim scholars then had in hand a "closed" body of and authoritative data from which to fashion a workable code of Muslim behavior.

Quran-based reasoning on moral matters has always been selective in the sense that all the verses of the Revelation, like its counterpart in Judaism and Christianity, are of equal truth, and so citation of any one of them is in theory definitive. The fastidiously trained jurist might recognize the contradictions between one quranic verse and another and seek to justify them by applying the principle of abrogation (see chapter 5), but for most the quranic *Ipse dixit* was enough, and the same attitude seems to have prevailed in the matter of the hadith. Such an attitude, that "all's fair in Quran and hadith," leads to moral probabilism — namely, that a defensible position is a permissible one, and however attractive a notion that might be to radical or amateur moralists, it never was such to Muslim jurists. How, then, in the absence of a determining moral authority, was the Muslim to decide among the varying probable positions founded on Quran or hadith or, more disconcertingly, on the opinions of jurists who attempted to work out solutions to moral questions on the basis of their own personal effort? The answer turned out to lie in consensus, the agreement of the community of Muslims.

The agreement of the community of Muslims had its own seeds of anxiety, in the suggestion, for example, that moral truth was what most Muslims thought it was rather than what God said it was. A solution was quickly forthcoming. The authority of consensus rested with God, as explained in the Prophetic saying that inevitably appeared in all discussions of the subject: "My community will never agree in error." Another aspect of the problem was addressed in a second hadith: "You are better judges than I in temporal matters," the Prophet is reported to have said of himself, in addressing future generations, "and I am a better judge than you in what concerns your religion." In matters of faith, then, the Quran and the *hadith* rule alone; in matters of morality, community consensus may also provide a reliable guide.

The operation of consensus is apparent in the matter of circumcision. The pre-Islamic Arab practice of circumcision had no warrant in the Quran itself, and yet there are sound hadith that seem to prescribe it for both men and women. The Muslim consensus decided early on that male circumcision was indeed an obligation, whereas there was no general agreement on the matter of female circumcision, which is, consequently, practiced by some Muslims, ignored by others, and decried by still others.

Consensus is clearly mutable, though such changes occur slowly and only with difficulty. The arguments for change take the traditional form of a debate over the "true" and hence "only" interpretation of quranic passages that are often opaque and occasionally contradicted (or "canceled") by others, or of summoning up hadith that appear to resist the current consensus. What has changed is not the evidence but moral sensibilities: they drive the attempt to change the consensus, just as another set of moral sensibilities shaped it in the first place. Where an earlier generation of Muslims preferred to veil its women and make divorce solely a male prerogative, some more recent Muslims prefer women to be unveiled and to make the initiation of divorce a right of both members to the marriage contract. Both groups resort to quranic exegesis and hadith citation to support their preferences; what distinguishes the more modern arguments is the often unacknowledged presumption of historical conditioning.

8.

Defining and Defending

the Community of Believers

IT IS sometimes pointed out that there is no such thing as "Judaism," or "Christianity," or "Islam" save what we construct as such in our own minds: there are, in truth, only Jews, Christians, and Muslims. To put it somewhat more accurately, however, those names are what the believers constructed in their own minds. The three group designators were devised not by modern social scientists but by members of the groups themselves, early on. The conceptualized "Judaism" first appears, in Greek, in 2 Maccabees 2:21; in 14: 38 the phrase "practicing Judaism" is used. It is echoed by Paul (Gal. 1:13–14). "Christian" is used quite self-consciously as a very new membership marker in Acts 11:26, and "Christianity" (Gk. *Christianismos*; Lat. *Christianitas*) appears, now as a fully domesticated term, in Ignatius and Polycarp at the end of the first and beginning of the second Christian century. "Islam" has the most exalted pedigree of all. It was God's own designation of the "religion" to which he had summoned the believers. Here, as often in the Quran, God himself is speaking: "If anyone desires a religion (*din*) other than Islam (*al-islam*), never will it be accepted of him, and in the Hereafter he will be in the ranks of the losers" (Quran 3:85). Muhammad is made to say to the pagans of Mecca, "You have your religion (*din*) and I have mine" (109:6).

The believers thus saw themselves as members of an identifiable group, and they organized themselves as such, even at times in a form close to something we might call a state. The three faith communities are in fact metasocieties whose special quality derives from their being founded by divine decree and as part of a divine plan. The famous covenant concluded by God with Abraham is the founding charter of that sense of community, and all subsequent claims of monotheist affiliation go back to it. Although this covenant was initiated and in a sense dictated by God, its adherents must, like Abraham himself, assent to it.

IDENTITY MARKERS

We have just seen the overarching religious context of the monotheist communities' identification. But from the beginning, each had also to define itself against its immediate neighbors and rivals. Muhammad's first concern was, like that of the early Israelites, to mark his community by its monotheism, in contrast to the prevalent idolatry and polytheism of Mecca and Arabia generally: we are "believers" (*muminun*) and "submitters" (*muslimun*); you are "unbelievers" (*kafirun*) and "associators" (*mushrikun*), the Quran asserts at every turn. As the Muslim community took shape around that basic marker, other identity issues arose, in the first instance by the presence in Medina of a Jewish community that could, and apparently did, deny Muhammad's implicit inclusion of his submitters in some supposed community of monotheists — what later came to be called, with a somewhat different marker, the Peoples of the Book. In its Medina suras the Quran thus takes up the task of distinguishing the Muslims from both the Jews and the Christians by recourse to the notion of a "religion of Abraham," a faith community that antedated both Judaism and Christianity and of which the Muslims were the most authentic representatives.

BUILDING THE UMMA: CONVERSION

Even during Muhammad's lifetime, the armies of the community of believers had passed north, west, and east out of Arabia into the heartlands of the empire of Byzantium and Sassanian Islam. Their successes were astonishingly rapid and, as it turned out, irreversible. Most of the conquests of the first century of Islam are still Muslim in their loyalties and Arab in their culture. The armies of conquest were small; cadres of Arab camel troopers peeled off occupation garrisons as they passed through their conquests, and then replenished their ranks with new converts and old opportunists as they pushed ever farther afield. Some of the garrisons of occupation attempted to keep themselves apart from the local population in Near Eastern camp towns, but eventually they moved into the older and prosperous cities of Syria, Egypt, North Africa, Iraq, and Iran with their overwhelmingly non-Muslim populations of People of the Book. Those same Jews, Christians, and Zoroastrians converted in growing numbers to both the faith and culture of their rulers in the ninth and tenth centuries and thus made the conquered territories Muslim in faith and Arab in culture.

Conversion to Islam was readily done but difficult to realize. The standard *Life* of Muhammad is filled with accounts of the Prophet's instructing delegates of this or that tribe on the new beliefs and practices to be followed, but the process of substituting the practice of the Prophet for the venerated "sunna of the ancestors" was not accomplished quickly or easily. Surely the best that could be hoped for in those early days was that the tribesmen should stop sacrificing to and otherwise venerating their idols and learn some verses of the Quran, which they could then use as prayers. But the spread of Islam quickly passed beyond the Bedouin into the sown lands of Syria, Egypt, and Iraq where their faith did not sit so lightly on Jews and Christians who had been attacking each others'—and variant versions of their own—faith for centuries. We have little clue as to how the Muslim conversion process proceeded here. It must have been slow, but some of its results can be observed fairly soon in the career of Islam. The accounts of early Muslim writers, chiefly historians and quranic commentators, are filled with biblical and postbiblical tales filling out the Quran's sketches; they most often seem to come from very early Christian, and particularly Jewish, converts to Islam. These were later lumped together as Israelite tales with the attached label "Do Not Use." The warning came too late in most cases. The "Israelite tales" from the People of the Book were an influential contribution to the formulation of Islam in the first obscure century of its existence.

The Making of a Muslim

Many if not most pre-Islamic Arabs practiced circumcision, and though the Quran is silent on the subject, Muslims soon began to understand it as a religious mandate, probably in imitation of the Jews, just as Christians, with a little help from John the Baptist, took over baptism from a Jewish conversion ritual. But despite the Islamic (or Arab) affinity to Judaism, which some even saw as tribal—their identification with "Ishmaelites" has already been noted—Islam is more like Christianity in that it is not a kinship society but a community of believers. Muslims too are made, not born. The Quran could easily echo Paul's sentiments that "there was neither Greek nor Jew, slave or free, man or woman" among the Muslims, but the social realities of seventh-century Mecca differed from those of first-century Jewish Palestine. Muhammad lived, whether in Mecca or Medina, in a combatively tribal society, and in the Prophet's preaching there is a good deal of space and energy devoted to taking down that mind-set. The Muslim umma was intentionally designed to replace a kinship society with a faith-based one. The program was successful, at least during Muhammad's lifetime. The umma of the Muslims was in fact an egalitarian society open to all believers, but only as long as the overwhelming number of believers were Arabs, it soon appeared.

At God's command, then, Muhammad founded a community that took as its identity marker a submission (*islam*) to total monotheism, an acceptance of Muhammad as the envoy of God and, in consequence, of the Quran as God's words. Though the Quran frequently referred to the members of that community as submitters (*muslimun*), an even more frequent designation for them was "those who have faith (*iman*)," thus, the "faithful," or *muminun*. Later some who drew on this distinction between *islam* and *iman*, "submission" and "faith," to further distinguish the community's true and marginal members, but, as a matter of actual fact, becoming a Muslim depended directly and exclusively on making the profession of faith (*shahada*) — "There is no god but The God and Muhammad is his envoy" — and a consequent sharing in the Friday community prayer and annual contribution of the alms-tithe, though in the beginning failure to pay the zakat seems to have had more serious consequences than the neglect of prayer, presumably because it was more willful.

Those adults who renounced paganism at Mecca and Medina had presumably to do nothing more than pronounce the shahada as an affirmation of monotheism and an acceptance of the divine mission of Muhammad and, by implication, of the divine origin of the Quran. There were baleful social consequences of such a profession in hostile Mecca — the Quran clearly reflects them — but notably less so in Medina, where the community moved inexorably to a Muslim majority. Where we begin to understand the long-term problem in conversion, however, is in the instance of a Medinese Jew choosing, as some did, to become a Muslim and leaving his highly marked Jewish community for the equally distinct society of Muslims. Until Muslims became the majority over the entire Abode of Islam, leaving one's original community and joining the umma carried with it a profound social dislocation and often painful consequences.

Though we can broadly calculate and weigh some of the social and economic incentives to conversion, it is impossible to measure the spiritual ones, except in the rare individual cases where someone undertakes to explain. We do know that Muslims were at first a very small minority in the lands they so rapidly conquered but that eventually, after two or three centuries perhaps, they became the majority. We know too that the people who became Muslims from Spain to Iraq were originally Christians and some Jews, and farther east, Zoroastrians. Muslims were the rulers of those people, their superiors in power and wealth, if not in sophistication and learning. Surely the first two qualities and not the latter — the possibility, that is, of sharing in the Muslims' power or wealth (or at least in not suffering the liability of being excluded from the perquisites of the new order) — prompted at least some of those other Peoples of the Book to leave their home communities and join the triumphalist Muslim umma, even given the disabilities and derogation that being a non-Arab began to carry with it early on.

AN ARAB, AND ARABIC, ISLAM

In its earliest manifestation, Islam was the faith of Arabs revealed by an Arab prophet whose message was, it boasted, "in a clear Arabic." In the earliest conversions, it was a matter of Arabs passing from tribe to umma, of losing their tribal identity (though only briefly), but not, as it turned out, any of the cultural markers of language, dress, food, and so on. Islam was at first measured by prayer, which could not be monitored always and everywhere, and by payment of the alms-tithe, which could. When the call to Islam passed among other peoples — the Greek- and Aramaic-speaking people of Syria-Palestine, the Greek- and Coptic-speaking peoples of Egypt, the Greek-, Aramaic-, and Pahlavi-speaking peoples of Iraq and Iran — it may have seemed theologically familiar to the monotheists, but culturally it was unmistakably Arab. And it continued to be such for a very long time — the anchor of the Arabic Quran secured it — so that Muslim converts had to assimilate to a new culture as well as assert a new faith.

The converts' cultural assimilation to Arabism was astonishingly rapid; within thirty or forty years the language of the Bedouin was being used as the language of state. Assimilation also occurred so thoroughly that it transferred the entire North African–Near Eastern land mass into an Arab cultural *oikoumene*. There were a few survivors — Persian culture, for example, held its breath long enough under the Arab flood that it could revive after a century or so, though with strong Arab overtones — but the transformation was sufficiently complete that those Christians,

Jews, and others who declined to embrace Islam were in the end content to speak its language.

The new converts' assimilation to Arab tribal society was considerably more difficult. Differences between peoples had always existed, of course, save in that pre-Babel world when all humankind was one (Quran 2:213; 10:19), but conversion had a particular significance in an essentially tribal society where identity and its consequent social and political protections were claimed on the basis of birth. There are ways of associating with tribal societies even if one is not born into them, but one of the most common, fictive adoption and its resultant patron-client relationship, provides the *cliens* with status of a decidedly inferior quality. What the cliens was to vestigial Roman tribalism, the *mawla* was to pre-Islamic Arab tribal societies: a freed slave, protected but dependent. It was a kind of juridical adoption whereby the newcomer became a client of the tribe, with limited membership privileges and a considerable menu of obligations.

The Arabs too were organized tribally before the coming of Islam, and though the Quran attempted to create a new type umma where spiritual merit replaced the old blood ties — "the noblest among you in God's sight is he who is most righteous," Quran 49:13 announces in a bold reversal of tribal values — the Muslim society that emerged after the Prophet's death continued to display much of the same tribal organization and many of the status markers that had prevailed in pre-Islamic days. Thus new Arab converts could be assimilated into the rapidly expanding umma without difficulty, but non-Arabs who submitted were accessioned only through the pre-Islamic institution of clientage known as *wala*. Thus the new Persian Muslim, for example, was attached to some Arab tribal lineage as a mawla, or client, who depended on his patron (*wali*) for protection and, in some larger sense, from whom he took his identification as a Muslim. This condition of clientage, a tribal hangover in a religious society that in theory recognized no tribal distinctions, though it created serious social problems in the eighth and ninth centuries, and even later in Spain, eventually passed out of Islam.

"There Is No Coercion in Religion"

This celebrated phrase is the Quran's own (2:256), and as an apparent charter of religious tolerance, it is often cited in modern discourse on that subject. But as occasionally occurs in the Quran, other statements on the subject suggest a different view, most famously perhaps the command to "Fight against those who do not believe in God or in the Last Day, who do not forbid what God and His Prophet have forbidden or practice the true religion, among those who have been given the Book, until they pay the poll-tax from their hand and are humiliated." The last phrase is open to some interpretative doubt, but the general thrust of the verse is clear: the People of the Book must be fought until they capitulate and pay the tribute required of the conquered. The verse does not say what is to occur if they do not capitulate, but that is equally clear from the parallel case of the pagans. The Quran gives no instruction on this subject, but there was a well-known Prophetic report that addressed it rather precisely. It was passed down on the authority of Ibn Abbas, a very much younger cousin of the Prophet.

> I asked [the Prophet]: "If the Arab polytheists refused to adopt Islam, do you think they would be allowed to make peace with the Muslims and become dhimmis?" He replied: "They would never be allowed to do so. They would be invited to accept Islam. If they became Muslims, that would be acceptable on their part; otherwise they would be forced to surrender because it has been related to us that such was the ruling and they should not be treated like other unbelievers." [I then asked:] "If [they refused to capitulate and] the Muslims attacked them and took their women and children as captives and their men as prisoners of war, what would be the ruling concerning them?" He replied: "The women and children would become booty and be divided up as spoil, out of which a one-fifth share would be taken; but of the men, those who adopt Islam would be free, but those who refuse to adopt Islam would have to be executed."

How are these clear statements in theQuran and hadith to be reconciled with "There is no coercion in religion" or even the Prophet's apparent resigned tolerance early in his Meccan days? "You have your religion," he was instructed to say to the pagans, "and I have mine" (109:6). Muslim exegetes and lawyers were quite as capable as their Jewish and Christian counterparts at harmonizing the apparent contradictions of Scripture, but in this instance they felt there was little need. The consensus opinion was that the later verse, "Fight against those who do not believe in God," abrogated or canceled the earlier, "There is no compulsion in religion." Officially, then, there was no religious tolerance in Islam save for Jews and Christians and then only under the negotiated capitulation contract called the dhimma.

DHIMMA AND DHIMMIS

Muhammad's attitude toward the People of the Book, as he called those who shared the same scriptural tradition with Islam, was generally favorable. Early on, in fact, he had called on them to verify his message. But as time passed, the Quran came to look on Jews and Christians as adherents of rival rather than collegial faiths. Some of this change in attitude was dictated by events at Medina itself, where Jewish tribes made up part of the population. Not only did the Jews of Medina reject Muhammad's prophetic claims; they began secretly to connive with his enemies in Mecca to overthrow him. Muhammad's own reaction was determined and progressively more violent. As the Prophet's political strength in the oasis grew, the Jewish tribes of Medina were first banished, then taken and enslaved, and finally executed on the spot. This quite extraordinary behavior is matched by nothing in the Quran, and is quite at odds with Muhammad's treatment of the Jews he encountered outside Medina. We must think then that his action was essentially political, that it was prompted by behavior that he read as treasonous and not some transgression of the law of God.

That later encounter with Jews took place in 627 in the course of a raid on Khaibar and Faydak, two oases north of Medina whose population was mostly or wholly Jewish, including some that Muhammad himself had exiled from Medina. He settled terms on them, and this and other similar arrangements rather than his own conduct at Medina provided the model for the Muslim community's disposition of the non-Muslim peoples who were, in the late 620s and early 630s, being rapidly swept under Muslim political sovereignty. Beginning with the capitulation of Khaibar to Muhammad himself, settlements in the path of the Muslim raiders were offered quite specific terms: either submit peacefully or be conquered by force. Those who resisted could expect little mercy for themselves or little respect for their possessions. Most, however, appear to have submitted on the Muslims' terms. The newly conquered had to pay to their new political masters (as they had to their old) a tribute in the form of an annual head tax (*jizya*; Quran 9:29), in addition to the traditional land tax. If they were pagans, they had perforce to become Muslims. Jews and Christians, however, — and later the Zoroastrians — though they too had to pay the jizya, were under no compulsion to convert. As People of the Book, Jews and Christians were offered a kind of concordat or pact (*dhimma*). According to the Prophet's own terms, the vanquished recognized Islam's political sovereignty and in turn were permitted the free practice of their religion, subject to certain limitations.

The limitations waxed and waned in number and specificity in the early decades — many of the Christian versions claimed their parentage in the spurious Covenant of Umar, the terms reputedly granted to the Christians by the second caliph, Umar ibn al-Khattab, when he accepted the surrender of Jerusalem in 635 — but most of them are rather self-evident. The dhimmis, as they were called, were forbidden to attempt to convert the Muslims, to build new places of worship, or to make public display of their rituals. But in other instances, depending on the circumstances of time, place, and ruler, the social and financial disabilities imposed by dhimmi status were more severe and more humiliating. Jews and Christians were not persecuted within the Abode of Islam, but neither did they enjoy the full rights and privileges of the Muslims.

People of the Book is a theological category and describes peoples who have received a genuine revelation; dhimmi is a peculiarly Muslim politico-theological category and refers to those People of the Book who have been offered and accepted the dhimma and live with its protection under Muslim sovereignty in Muslim-ruled territory, the so-called Abode of Islam (*Dar al-Islam*). People of the Book may be found inside and outside the Abode of Islam dhimmis only within it.

> *Note*: The Christians recognized no such affinity with Islam. They permitted the Muslims to live at peace among them (however briefly) for social and economic, not theological reasons, and one group of them, the Muslims living under Christian sovereignty in Spain, underlines the religious and theological significance of the dhimma. The dhimma concluded by the Muslims with their Christian and Jewish subjects was a religious pact, guaranteed by God and sanctioned by the practice of the Prophet himself; as such it formed part of the body of the sharia, the canon law of Islam. The Christians' arrangement with their Muslim subjects in Spain, in contrast, was a political agreement concluded by secular authorities as an affair of state. It could be abrogated by the dictating party, as it shortly was in fact by Ferdinand and Isabella in 1502 with respect to the Muslims living in Castile, who were then, absent any statute, given the inevitable choice between exile, death, or conversion. The same choice was extended in 1526 to cover the far more assimilated Muslim dhimmis living in the Christian Crown of Aragon. We do not know how many Muslims chose death in the aftermath of the abolition of their tolerated (Sp. *mudéjar*) status, but many did in fact leave for Muslim-ruled North Africa and others converted to Christianity.

THE MILLET SYSTEM

The dhimma defines and regulates the status of the People of the Book living under Muslim sovereignty. It makes no distinctions, however, among them: Jews, Christians, and later, Zoroastrians, were all equal before the Islamic law, granted the same privileges and subject to the same restrictions. In 1453, the same year that he took Constantinople from its last Eastern Christian defenders, the Ottoman sultan Mehmed II organized his "flock" (reaya), that is, the 90 percent of his subjects who were not part of the Ottoman ruling institution. The flock was divided horizontally according to profession and occupation, but Mehmed introduced a new vertical distinction by *millet*, or religious community. In theory, the Muslims of the flock constituted a millet along with the others, but in reality the millet organization applied only to the Jews, the Armenians, and Orthodox Christians.

Or so they were called. The Orthodox millet was headed by the newly appointed Greek Orthodox patriarch of Constantinople, George Scholarios, known as Gennadius II, a monk strongly opposed to all plans for reunion with the Roman Church. His millet jurisdiction included not only the Greek Christians but the Churches of Bulgaria, Serbia, and Bosnia, whose liturgical language was not Greek but Slavonic. The members of these latter Churches all spoke Serbo-Croatian as their vernacular, and all of them were at the time of the Ottoman conquest well on their way to becoming jurisdictionally independent (autocephalous) Christian Churches. Likewise, the Armenian patriarch in Constantinople presided over the fortunes not only of his own Church but of the bundled Monophysite Churches in the Ottoman lands, notably the Copts of Egypt and the Jacobites of Syria and Iraq. The Jewish millet was presided over by the chief rabbi of Istanbul and included both Sephardic and the less numerous and influential Ashkenazi Jews of the empire.

The sultan dealt with his non-Muslim subjects through the heads of the millets, who naturally favored their own proper constituents. In the Balkans this led to increased estrangement between the Slavic Churches and the Greek Orthodox Church under whose jurisdiction they were now placed. For their part, the three millets became in effect Ottoman institutions, organs of administration in the sprawling bureaucracy of the empire.

Note: The dhimmi issue is generally moot in modernizing Middle Eastern states with Western-style constitutions, which guarantee freedom of religion and equal political rights for all citizens. Yet the dhimma remains an active — and provocative — component in many Muslims' vision of the Islamic state, whether in being, as in Iran or Saudi Arabia, or as a prospect, as in the program of the Muslims called fundamentalists or Islamists.

DEFINING THE TRUTH

Unlike the Jews, who regarded themselves as an ethnic as well as a religious community united by ritual and behavior, Christians and Muslims were both solely religious communities who ended up defining themselves as much by their beliefs (orthodoxy) as by their behavior (orthopraxy). The normative teaching or doctrine of the faith community can take several forms. First, it is the body of teaching explicitly set forth in Scripture and upon which there is an agreed interpretation. But this handing down of doctrine occurs in other less formal terms, as we have seen, whether through the Jews' Sinai-based oral tradition, the Christians' conviction that their bishops were enunciating a true Apostolic Tradition, or the Muslims' acceptance of the Prophetic traditions as a veritable second revelation. Finally, doctrine may rest on a consensus, when the community was unanimously agreed, or so it seems, on some point without scriptural warrant, for example, the canon of Hebrew Scripture, the divinity of Jesus, or that there should be a leader (caliph, Imam) after Muhammad.

Christianity defined and redefined itself in a series of credal statements, and in the positive dogma and negative anathemas issued by the councils of the Church. Among the Jews and Muslims were officials who might respond to queries, particularly on matters of correct behavior, but none could pronounce with the same authority as the Christian bishop, singly or in council, and none ever enjoyed the authority of the bishop of Rome. Yet both communities were concerned with matters of belief, what a Jew or Muslim must believe or may not believe. Islam had neither bishops and councils, and its closest approximation to a creed in the sense of a baptismal formula is the simple shahada: "There is no god but The God and Muhammad is his envoy." By the mid–eighth century, however, longer statements in the form of a creed (*aqida*) began to appear anonymously in legal circles. Contrary to what one might expect, they have nothing to do with the two basic elements of the shahada, which are the affirmations required of the individual Muslim, but rather addressed themselves to the issues in current religio-political disputes. All these so-called creeds were manifestly not documents to live by but somewhat sectarian statements on problems troubling the early lawyers and theologians. Many of the points were still in contention at the time of composition, but if one moves forward to the period of Ghazali (d. 1111) and beyond, when a consensus of sorts had developed in Sunni Islam, the Muslim creeds have much the same appearance as a Christian catechism, that is, of highly stylized, albeit abbreviated and simplified treatises of scholastic theology, like the catechism inserted by Ghazali himself in his *Revivification of the Sciences of Religion*.

The creeds are the closest the community of Muslims ever came to defining orthodoxy. Like their Christian counterparts, they arose in the context of dispute, as a response to other views about God, humans, and the universe that the community, or at least its religious leaders, judged at variance with the Quran, the sunna, or, simply, Muslim sensibilities. In place of these deviant beliefs, the creeds express propositionally and affirmatively what it seems fair to call a Sunni Muslim consensus. It may be summed up as follows.

Regarding God, His Nature, and Attributes:

> God is one, unique, without associates or offspring; He is eternal and unchanging; His existence can be proven from the contingency of the world; God is other than humankind; incorporeal, hence the quranic descriptions of Him should be accepted "without asking how" (*bila kayf*). And yet God will be "seen," *bila kayf*, by the

faithful in the world to come. God enjoys preeminently the qur-
anically attested attributes of omnipotence, omniscience, life, will,
hearing, seeing and speaking, as well as all those others that constitute His "most beautiful names." The Quran is the uncreated
speech of God.

Then, God's Will:

God's will is sovereign in the world and is always and everywhere
effective; indeed, as many hold, God predestines events beforehand.
All human acts, like all events, are created by God but they are
attributed to humans, or as some say "acquired" by them, since
they proceed from an internal power created in humans at the moment they act.

The Last Things:

The signs of the End Time are all genuine and real, including the
questioning by Munkar and Nakir and the torments of the tomb,
and when the End does arrive, God will judge all humankind. Some
few people, Muhammad chief among them, will be permitted to
intercede for sinners among the Muslims at the Judgment; prayers
and alms offered by the living will also avail the dead; Paradise and
Gehenna exist now and will forever.

Revelation:

God has sent both apostles and prophets to humankind. Muhammad is the "seal" or last of them, and he and the other prophets
have been preserved from sin (though perhaps only grave ones).
Against the Shiites, it must be held that after Muhammad the first
four caliphs were the best of men; only good must be spoken on the
Companions of the Prophet.

Belief:

Faith is knowing in the heart, confessing by the tongue, and, according to most, performing good works. Faith is due solely to
God's guidance and unbelief to abandonment by Him.

THE UMMA DIVIDED: EARLY MUSLIM SECTS AND SECTARIANISM

The issue of the "genuine Muslim" and so of membership in the community arose as early in Islam as it did in Christianity, where it already concerned Paul no more than twenty-five years after Jesus' death. The Medina suras of the Quran speak often of "hypocrites" (*munafiqun*), and though the allusion, like much else in the Quran, is not entirely clear, it seems reasonably certain that the reference was to Medinese Arabs who had at least nominally professed Islam but were not Muslims in their heart. Some hearts were easier to read. At the death of the Prophet in 632, many of the opportunistic Bedouin tribes of Arabia bethought themselves of leaving Islam, at least to the extent of not paying into the Muslim treasury the alms-tithe that was a sign of their submission. Muhammad's successor as head of the umma had to make an immediate decision: was it possible to secede from the Islamic community? The answer was a decisive "no." The "secession" (*ridda*) was put down when armies were sent against the tribes to coerce their once declared and now irrevocable adherence to Islam.

It was clear, then, that entry into the community of Muslims was regarded, as it was among Christians, as an only partially reversible act: a Muslim may be banished from the community, that is, denied the means of salvation, but may not willfully withdraw from it. That latter act is called apostasy and is viewed exceedingly gravely in all three faiths. In most cases apostasy requires a formal act of disavowal on the part of the believer, but the question was raised in Islam, as it was among radical Reform Christians we lump together as Anabaptists, as to whether nonobservance was, in fact, a kind of apostasy. The early Muslim sect called the Kharijites certainly thought so, and were willing to visit the fatal consequences of apostasy on those who did not pray daily or fast during Ramadan.

In the classic form cited above, the shahada is purely a verbal formulation and leaves open the questions of interior intention and of the relative importance to be placed on interior faith and external good works. The Kharijites, a group that was part of Ali's support up until shortly before his death and then broke with him, had greatly emphasized the latter: whoever did not act like a Muslim was in fact not a Muslim, and should be treated accordingly. "Accordingly" in this context meant as an apostate, the penalty for which was "termination with extreme prejudice." In the few places where Kharijites actually gained political control of the community, they were, as one might suspect, exceedingly circumspect about killing off all the other Muslims who did not share their view of Islam.

INNOVATION AND HERESY

In a society that possessed no institution or office capable of defining "orthodoxy" in the familiar Christian sense, one norm against which a Muslim's actions or, somewhat less certainly, his opinions could be judged as to rectitude was the custom of the Prophet. The notion that the sunna might serve as an Islamic yardstick gained widespread currency in legal circles only in the early ninth century, but neither it, nor deviations from it — bida, "innovation" — serve as a very useful guide for understanding what was actually happening within the Islamic community in the first century and a half of its existence, nor even, perhaps, thereafter.

On a closer inspection of the notion of bida, with its attractive heuristic possibilities as an Islamic equivalent of "heresy," it soon emerges that the term covers both more and less than is historically useful. The Quran presents itself as both a permanent and a closed revelation, and the Muslim believer, no less than his Jewish and Christian counterpart, is invited to accept the notion that God had here laid out, definitively, immutably, and exhaustively, his will for humankind. To add, subtract, or otherwise change God's Word was, therefore, an "innovation," whose Arabic expression stands suggestively close to the etymon for "creation," a power reserved exclusively to God.

God, as it turned out, had not said his Last Word, even in the believers' eyes, and what followed in Islam was an attempt to interpret, to flesh out, and, somewhat less ingenuously, to modify the divine message. That is clearly the function of the hadith, to gloss and explain the revelation, and there is innovation enough vis-à-vis the Quran's pronouncements within the extraordinarily flexible limits of the "custom of the Prophet." Some of this had in the end to be accepted as permissible innovation in grudging acknowledgment of at least some evolutionary energy at work within the community. At the other end of the belief spectrum, however, stood *ghuluw*, "extremism," a type of innovative practice or belief that violated even the elastic limits of the lawyers' patience. And beyond that lay only total and irreconcilable unbelief, the damnable *kufr*.

The question remained what to do about such aberrations. Excommunication or banishment from the company of one of its members is a corollary of the very notion of community. Members may depart of their own volition, either by drifting off and away by the kind of silent attrition that affects all communities or through a formal renunciation, the act that is, in this religious context, called apostasy and that often carried with it the most severe penalties. Neither is the issue here, however; the present concern is with those members of the faith community whom the rest judge unfit or unworthy for continued association and so ban or excommunicate, cutting them off from community membership and from sharing in whatever considerable benefits may flow from that affiliation. Though it was put into these precise words only by the medieval Latin Church, the belief that "Outside the community there is no salvation" was a long and profoundly held conviction among Jews, Christians, and Muslims alike. To thrust someone outside the Church of the Saints, to declare that this believer or this class of believers "has no share in the Afterlife" was to pronounce a grim sentence indeed.

SUNNIS AND SHIITES

Before adherence to the custom of the Prophet became a criterion for orthodoxy, there was another, older idea to which many Muslims could rally and which, by its choice of issue, effectively set political limits against "sectaries." This was the principle of a united community, *jamaa*, and it survived in the common centrist conjunction of "people of custom and the united community" (*ahl al-sunna wa al-jamaa*), briefly characterized as "Sunni." The connection between the two notions of custom and community may go back to the days of Ali (r. 656–661), when that caliph refused to accept the extension of the sunna concept, the notion of normative behavior, beyond the Prophet to his immediate successors. The partisans of *jamaa*, in contrast, regarded the community and its sunna as a continuous process and so were willing to accept the sunna of the first three caliphs as authoritative and normative as that of the Prophet himself.

What was important in the Sunni view was, then, staying close to "catholic" Islam as defined by consensus, first in a political sense by following the Commander of the Faithful or leader of the community: praying with him, paying the alms-tithe into his hands, following him into holy war if he so decrees, abiding by his application of the punishments prescribed by the Quran. "Whoever secedes from the Imam of the Muslims," said Ahmad ibn Hanbal (d. 855) in his *Creed*, "when the people have agreed upon him and acknowledged his caliphate . . . , that rebel has broken the unity of the Muslims and opposed the tradition coming from God's Messenger." But there is an even more profound sense in which consensus defines the community. The Prophet is reported to have blessed Muslims who "kept close to the community," a phrase that for Shafii, Islam's most influential jurist, meant deviation "from what the community of Muslims maintains. . . . Error arises in separation. In the community there can be no total error concerning the meaning of the Book, of the Prophetic tradition," and, taking a large step outside the cover of revelation, he adds, "or of analogical reasoning, please God."

If the Kharijites were thereby willing to exclude the grave sinner as well as the unbeliever (*kafir*) from their midst, there were others such as the early jurist Abu Hanifa (d. 767) who regarded faith (*iman*) as something separate from the moral activity of the individual Muslim. Neither view entirely prevailed in the end. The definition of faith as "confessing with the tongue, believing with the mind, and knowing with the heart" was generally accepted by Sunnis as applicable to membership in the community of believers whose profession rendered them subject to the Islamic law. All agreed, moreover, that the one unforgivable sin of polytheism (*shirk*; "association," that is, of other gods with *the* God) excluded one from that community. As regards other grave sins such as murder and fornication, eternal punishment in the Afterlife was probable but not inevitable. The sinner could only put his hope in God's goodness and the Prophet's intercession; for their part, the other Muslims here below must suspend judgment.

The Shiites would not have it entirely so. In Shiite eyes, the Sunnis are assuredly Muslims (*muslimun*) in that they have professed the essential monotheism of the shahada; but it only the Shiat Ali were muminun, or true believers. Shiites have not hesitated to enforce this conviction on Sunnis when they have had the power to do so — in Safavid Iran, for example — but more often the power shoe was on the Sunni foot. To avoid having Sunni practices forced on them under threat, Shiites, despite their deep veneration for the martyr, have resorted to the practice of dissembling (*taqiyya*) their true beliefs. Neither Sunnis nor Shiites, however, despite their often antagonistic feelings toward one another — often most openly and violently manifested on the hajj or annual pilgrimage, when they are in close quarters and religious emotions run high — have read the other out of the umma.

Obvious deviance apart, the Sunnis' tolerant attitude of suspending judgment on the moral conduct of one's neighbor had some extremely disagreeable political implications that were, in fact, the chief point in the discussion. Postponement of judgment effectively removed the religious and moral issue from the political life of the Islamic empire, and the acceptance of this principle marked another stage in the secularization of the caliphate, whose tenants could no longer be challenged on the grounds of their personal morality. The predestination argument led in the same direction — *de facto* was in fact *de Deo*. The predestination versus free will argument drifted off into quite another direction, into the metaphysical thicket of atoms, accidents, and "acquisition," but the postponement thesis held because it represented some kind of ill-shaped Muslim consensus that custom and the community were more important than tossing dead sinners into hell and live ones out of office or out of the community.

THE ENEMY WITHOUT: JIHAD

The complex of concerns and conditions that have collected around the Muslim notion of holy war (*jihad*) reduces itself to a discussion of the circumstances under which an individual Muslim or, more commonly, the community of Muslims, is faced with the obligation to use force against an enemy. Although some considerations are directed to the extent or degree of that force, the main thrust of the discussion in Muslim circles from the Prophet down to the present has been about the enemy and the hostile act that triggers the use of force.

In the quranic passages on jihad, there is certainly a wider dimension to the term than the use of force. The believer must energetically strive "in the path of God" to overcome the temptations of the world and his own inclinations to sin; that ethic of striving, the jihad of the heart that is not terribly far from the Christians' *miles Christi* or Moral Rearmament, is built into the Muslims' moral code. The question at hand, however, deals with the other component of jihad, the jihad of the sword, the use of force, or "killing" (*qital*), as the Quran calls it in what appears to be the earliest revelation (22:39) to address the issue: "Leave is given to those who fight because they are wronged . . . who were expelled from their dwellings without right." The date must have been soon after the Hegira, and the verse obviously looks to the cause of the Migrants who had recently had to take refuge in Medina. Permission was granted to take up arms against their Meccan oppressors.

If the Meccan suras of the Quran are circumspect on the subject of violence — the few and defenseless Muslims there would almost certainly have suffered in its use — and generally appear to counsel its avoidance (Quran 15:94–95; 16:125), the mandate for force granted at Medina was eventually broadened (2:191, 217), until, it seemed, war could be waged against non-Muslims at almost any time or any place. Quran 9:5 — "Slay the idolaters wherever you find them" — is as broad a permission for war against the infidels as can be imagined. In the traditional Muslim understanding of the passage, it was thought to have abrogated all earlier limitations on the use of violence against nonbelievers.

It was the thrust of these texts, and of the body of hadith that grew up around them that led Muslim jurists to divide the world into the Abode of Islam (*Dar al-Islam*), where Islamic law and sovereignty prevailed, and the Abode of War (*Dar al-Harb*), lands that were not yet subjected to the moral and political authority of Islam, as inevitably they must in this triumphalist theology. In theory, the Abode of Islam is in a permanent state of warfare with the Abode of War, as the very name suggests, at least until the latter submits, and jihad is the instrument by which that subjection will be accomplished. Hostilities between the two spheres may be suspended by armistice or truce, but they can never be concluded by peace, only by submission.

A systematically framed doctrine of jihad emerges in the work of the Muslim jurist al-Shaybani (d. 804). His *Law of Nations* became one of the foundation texts of Muslim thinking on the subject, and it was often glossed and expanded by later lawyers. It is worth noting that this formulation of a doctrine of jihad occurred during the full tide of Muslim expansion, when the Abode of Islam was growing ever larger by conquest. But it was also a period when the unity of the original umma was being replaced by local Muslim polities whose rulers found the conduct of a jihad a convenient and persuasive way of establishing their Islamic legitimacy.

Al-Shaybani and other early jurists appear, however, to have exercised a certain caution on the matter of hostilities with the unbelievers, which is the essence of holy war, and required that some degree of provocation be present. This was not so with his somewhat younger contemporary Shafii (d. 820). In his view, war with the Dar al-Harb was not an occasional circumstance but a permanent and continuous state since the cause was precisely the others' unbelief (*kufr*). Jihad was, in the words of a later commentator, "a duty enjoined (on Muslims) permanently till the end of time." It was in fact this notion of obligation that much exercised the jurists. The obligation to wage jihad was, Shafii explained, a collective one (*fard kifaya*) since all that was required was that *some* Muslims — the obligation bound "adult, free men who had the means and the health" — take up arms against the infidel. If no one does, the punishment will fall on all, however.

The discussion of warfare is prolonged and detailed among the jurists, who tried to make sense of what the Quran said about such matters and what the hadith revealed about Muhammad's own counsel and practice, though obviously in quite different circumstances. The degree of harm that might be inflicted on the enemy, to his person, his property, or his liberty, was a major concern. The caliph had large discretion in such matters, whether to pardon, ransom, enslave, or kill prisoners of war. All agreed that adult males might be slain during hostilities but not women and children, provided they were not involved in the actual fighting. There was, however, a sharp division of opinion — the Quran and Prophetic example were unclear here — on whether or not it was legitimate to execute prisoners of war. At issue was the reason there was warfare in the first place: if it was, as many alleged, because of unbelief, then there should be no exceptions to the death sentence. If, however, it was all about war, then the capacity to fight was the determinant, and so the elderly, infirm, monks, and perhaps many others might be spared.

Finally, there is a nice discussion that finds a later juridical echo in the Christians' *Requerimiento* with regard to the infidels of the New World who had to be "invited" to become Christians before they could be attacked. According to some Muslim jurists, the infidels of the Abode of War had also to be read a version of their Miranda Rights before they were assailed. The Quran has God say, "We never chastise them until We send forth a Messenger" (17:15), a statement that, when taken with the pertinent hadith, was understood to mean that hostilities with the unbelievers could not begin until they had been formally summoned to Islam and had refused. This was not a majority opinion, however. There were enough reports of Muhammad's own unannounced attacks to make most jurists conclude that in this instance, "the practice of the Prophet had abrogated his words."

In the centuries after Muhammad, the combination of juridically imposed conditions and political realities has diminished the
effectiveness of jihad as a practical instrument of policy, though it
remains a potent propaganda weapon both for Muslim fundamentalists to brandish and for their Western opponents to decry. Muslim jurists have rarely agreed on the exact fulfillment of the conditions they have laid down for a genuine jihad (and Muslim public
opinion even less often), while the umma on whose behalf it is to
be waged has now been divided, perhaps irretrievably, into nation-
states that generally subscribe to a quite different (and decidedly
non-Islamic) version of international law.

Just Wars and Crusades

While the classical Islamic legal tradition prohibits all war (e.g.,
tribal warfare, raids, blood feuds) except on religious grounds,
Western ethical theories, on the contrary, have sanctioned "just
wars" on certain natural law grounds but never on the basis of
religious ones. This latter attitude is altogether quite modern and
altogether secular since most religious communities have permitted and even encouraged war in the name of God. Yahweh was a
warrior God (Exod. 5:3; Isa. 42:13), and the Bible is not unnaturally filled with conflicts that are palpably holy wars. The Israelites, quite like the pre-Islamic Arabs, even carried their God with
them into conflict on occasion (Num. 10:35–36). Deuteronomy
20–21 provides rules for war, with God as the leader, and its terms
are not very dissimilar from those dictated by Muhammad, except
there is no agreeable dhimma status granted to the Israelites' enemies. With the progressive loss of Jewish sovereignty (and so the
capacity to employ force against its enemies), war eventually became an anticipated eschatological event among the Jews, and
then, with the diminution of messianic enthusiasm, a school exercise for the rabbis.

With the 1948 foundation in Palestine of a "Jewish state" — the
ambiguity of the expression is as profound as it is in "Islamic
state" — the question has been reopened for Jews. Israel's battles

have been parsed by some as national wars but by other Jewish mujahideen as genuine crusades fought to realize the divine pledge of "next year in Jerusalem" or, even more grandly, to take and hold Eretz Israel, the "Land of (or for) Israel" that was promised in the Bible and never foresworn.

The Christian Church is not a state as such and so cannot formally declare or conduct a war. It has, however, on occasion permitted and even encouraged both warlike acts and formal wars in the name of religion. An example is the Crusades, the first of which was called for by Pope Urban II at Clermont in 1095. The Crusade—its formal title was *peregrinatio in armis*, "armed pilgrimage"—had as its stated objective freeing the Christian holy places in Jerusalem from the Muslims (Jerusalem fell to the crusaders in 1099, was retaken by the Muslims in 1187), and it was garlanded with the Church's spiritual rewards and indulgences for those who voluntarily participated in this and later attacks against Muslim lands.

Originally the Crusades had nothing to do with attempts to persuade or force the Muslims to convert—European Christian missionary activity among the Muslims was rarely attempted and notoriously unsuccessful—but the later Crusades began to adopt it as an objective, particularly as attempts at taking and holding Jerusalem and Palestine began to seem increasingly illusionary. Coerced baptism never found much favor among the Church's canon lawyers. It was just such a canon lawyer, however—Innocent IV, as he was known when he was elevated to the papacy in 1243—who defined the Church's position: though nonbelievers might not be coerced into conversion, the pope, as vicar of Christ on earth, had the authority to order even non-Christian powers to admit preachers of the Gospels into their lands, and, if they refused, to authorize Christian states to use force to effect their entry. Thomas Aquinas, in his *Summa Theologica* (1265–1271), echoes Innocent's reason and adds three other grounds that justify a state's use of force against the infidel: the latter's hindering the Christian faith by "blasphemies, evil suasions, or open persecutions."

The Enemy Within: Ibn Taymiyya

Holy war is, then, a religious obligation for Muslims, a duty whether for the community or the individual, forcefully to resist the enemies of Islam. The division of the world into the Abode of Islam — the territories under Muslim political sovereignty — and the Abode of War — the lands beyond that pale — draws a rather precise line between the community and its enemies. But the early Muslim jurists who laid down those boundaries were aware that the political and religious reality they sought to define was far more complex. The very first problem faced by Abu Bakr (r. 632– 634), Muhammad's immediate successor as the head of the umma, was whether to use force, in effect, whether to invoke jihad against those Arabian tribes who, at Muhammad's death, refused to pay the alms-tithe required of all Muslims. This was judged apostasy (*irtidad*), and so the use of force to coerce the defiant tribes was legitimate. The decision to do so redrew the boundaries of jihad: holy war, the only war permissible to Muslims, might also be waged against God's enemies within the umma.

The attack on the faith to which jihad is a legitimate and necessary response most often came from external enemies, from that area designated by classical jurisprudence as the Abode of War, whether because its inhabitants were in fact hostile to Islam or were constantly in a state of war among themselves. But as soon became apparent, Islam had its enemies within, those who likewise threatened the faith, either as apostates, like those who had refused the pay the zakat, or dissenters like the Kharijites. Jihad was waged against both groups.

By the thirteenth century the problem of internal enemies had changed not so much in kind as in scale. Central Asian newcomers called Mongols had entered the Abode of Islam and threatened to destroy the very fabric of the umma. In 1258 Baghdad, the heart and seat of the caliphate, was taken, sacked, and so thoroughly destroyed that the city never quite recovered. But the Mongols, who were inexorably pushing westward toward the Syrian and Egyptian heartlands, were by then themselves Muslims and so not enemies but members of the umma; indeed, its de facto rulers. Might they be fought?

The question was posed to the most eminent, and notorious, jurist of the day, the Syrian Ibn Taymiyya (d. 1328). In his tension-filled lifetime, he had fought against both state and church and paid for it with spells in prison; he died a prisoner in the Damascus citadel. The issue now was the Mongols, whether a jihad might be fought against these new, powerful, and destructive Muslim warlords. In two fatwas, or judicial responses, and then more systematically in his treatise *Public Policy in Islamic Jurisprudence*, Ibn Taymiyya rendered a judgment that still resonates today among fundamentalist Muslims. Profession of Islam was not enough. Though by the criterion of the shahada they were Muslims, the Mongols violated the broader requirements of Islam. They still lived according to their own pagan law, which rendered them, in effect, unbelievers. Jihad against them was not only licit but required. The duties of Islam are both explicit, like those detailed in the Pillars of Islam, and implicit, Ibn Taymiyya argued in his *Public Policy*. The true Muslim must not marry his sister, eat impure foods, or, significantly, "attack the lives and wealth of the Muslims." "Any such trespasser of the Law should be fought," he concludes, "provided he had a knowledge of the mission of the Prophet. It is this knowledge that makes him responsible for obeying the orders, the prohibitions, and the permits (of the sharia). If he disobeys these, he should be fought."

Despite his own problems with some of the rulers in Islam, Ibn Taymiyya was a firm believer in the two swords of temporal and spiritual power and responsibility, distinct but firmly linked in Islam. The Islamic state, whose function is described in the popular phrase "to command the good and prohibit evil," possessed, and was obliged to use, its coercive might to protect the integrity of the faith and the observance of the law, while it was the function of sharia and its guardians to maintain justice in the community.

Note: In the case of Islam, a distinction must be drawn between a Muslim state, one in which the majority of the population is professedly Muslim, and an Islamic state or society, whose laws are based to a greater or lesser extent on the sharia. Syria, Egypt, Iraq, and Turkey would be examples of the first, whereas Iran, Saudi Arabia, Taliban Afghanistan, perhaps, from a certain perspective, the Sudan and Pakistan, and fitfully Libya might all be argued — and disputed, chiefly by each other — as Islamic states. "Jewish" and "Christian" do not allow the same distinction. It is of no matter in the first case since there is only one state or society that qualifies in either sense of the word as "Jewish," the State of Israel, even though it has no constitution and many Jews cannot or prefer not to imagine it as Jewish in the religious sense. There are, however, still many states where the majority of the population professes Christianity, but only one surviving state, the Holy See or State of the Vatican City, population 870, is governed by a version of Church law.

Fundamentalists As the Faithful Remnant

Ibn Taymiyya has been a powerful ideological model for the theoreticians of the modern movement called Islamic Fundamentalism, or, as some prefer, Revivalism. Whatever the appropriate name, this is the Muslim version of what is in fact a much broader phenomenon called fundamentalism, a term that was originally applied to Evangelical Christian sects in the 1920s. Fundamentalism, whether Muslim or any other variety, is generally (though not invariably) characterized by a series of positions that are at the same time theological (Scripture is infallible); philosophical (Scripture is not subject to so-called critical analysis); historical (it envisions a return to origins); political (it advocates revolution in the name of religion); and, of chief interest in the present context, sociological (the movement is a "Church" within the "Church").

Muslim political power, or better, the political power of Muslim states has been on the wane for many centuries. One reading of the descent from world empire to "developing states" sees it as the result of an ideological attack from secularism, which is represented in modern times by Western nation-states. The effects of the onslaught are everywhere apparent: the era of colonialism, the West-abetted foundation of the State of Israel and continued Western dominance of the political economy, the erosion of Islamic political, judicial, and educational institutions. Two basic and contrasting solutions have been offered (with many compromises in between). One is to adopt Western ways, in short, to modernize Islam—the position is called Modernism—and bring it into conformity to the needs and demands of the modern era. The other is to return to Islam, either to struggle for the preservation of the best of the past, what is called Traditionalism, or to seek, as the Fundamentalists, or Islamists, as they are now often called, do, a renewal or revival (*tajdid*) of the past.

It is from this latter perspective that Fundamentalism has arisen in the Islamic world. It has issued its "call" for a moral and social movement to establish the Islamic order, realized in the Jamaat-i Islami in Pakistan and the Muslim Brotherhood in Egypt. It is firm in its denial of nationalism and its repudiation of the nation-state in the name of a single umma. Islamic Fundamentalism struggles — not always successfully; consider Saudi Arabia and the Islamic Republic of Iran—to be nonsectarian. It seeks the reconciliation of Shiite and Sunni differences. And if it is willing and eager to embrace the technology of modernity, it is resolute in its denial of the ideology of secular and pluralistic modernism. It points, with great effect, to the failure of two modern Muslim experiments in modernism and Westernization, republican Turkey and pre-revolutionary Iran.

What distinguishes Fundamentalism from Traditionalism is the flexibility of the former, its willingness to practice ijtihad (as Ibn Taymiyya did) and to adapt sharia to the modern world. It is a critique not only of the West but of the Muslim status quo. Islamic Fundamentalism understands Islam as a totalizing experience and so rejects the separation of Islam from politics or any other aspect of modern life. The Islamists, like all other such groups, see themselves as a faithful remnant, the true Muslims, who stand in sharp contrast to others who profess Islam but who follow the values of the derogatory *jahiliyya*, the "era of barbarism" used to characterized pre-Islamic days. Hence they are also willing to follow Ibn Taymiyya's lead with respect to the Mongols and to condemn other Muslims as unbelievers, most notably the rulers of other "Muslim" countries, a conviction that led directly to the assassination of Anwar Sadat, president of Egypt, in 1981.

9. *The Worshipful Acts*

THE QURAN is part preaching directed toward conversion and part instruction, where the Book lays out, sometimes generally, sometimes specifically, what it is to be a muslim, one who has submitted to God. The quranic picture of what makes up a Muslim life grew far more detailed at Medina, where Muhammad was the head and authoritative guide of a Muslim community (umma), a community now free to practice its beliefs in public. Part of that instruction is liturgical, that is, it describes the rituals—in Arabic *al-ibadat*, "the worshipful acts" — by which God wishes to be formally and publicly acknowledged.

To Be a Muslim

The Torah is as highly detailed in its prescriptions on how, when, and where God wishes to be worshiped as the Gospels are spare in their instruction: the Lord's Prayer and the Eucharist stand out as almost unique exceptions. Otherwise, we are left to suppose, Jesus' followers were simply to carry on their Jewish liturgical practices. The Quran stands somewhere between the two. It provides some new specifics regarding prayer, almsgiving, and fasting for the believers and, in the case of the pilgrimage, a liturgical practice already in use among the pagan Meccans and their neighbors, it modifies and corrects this ritual that, the Quran instructed the new converts, went back to Abraham's day and was not only permitted in the new Islamic dispensation but required. Finally, those newly submitted had the practical example of the Prophet himself to guide them.

Later generations filled out the picture, based on the preserved recollections of the Prophet's sunna, and from these efforts emerged the Pillars of Islam, a summary statement of what constituted, in very broad terms, the Muslim's obligations. Interestingly, of the five only the first is about what a Christian might call orthodoxy. It is the profession of faith (shahada) or "bearing witness" and it is brief indeed: "There is no god but The God, and Muhammad is his envoy" (la ilaha ill'allah wa muhammad rasul allah). The first part is a straightforward affirmation of monotheism; the second, of the validity of Muhammad's mission and message. The other four Pillars have to do with acts incumbent on the Muslim: prayer (salat) five times daily; payment of an annual alms-tithe (zakat) calculated on income; fasting, that is, complete abstention from any form of food or drink (or sexual activity) from dawn to dusk during the twenty-eight days of the lunar month of Ramadan; and realization at least once in a lifetime of the hajj. Only two of these are properly liturgical, prayer and pilgrimage, and will be examined further.

WOMEN IN THE RITUAL LIFE OF ISLAM

If all Muslims are bound to perform these so-called Pillars, the obligation is limited by considerations normal to most moral systems: generally speaking, the subject has to be competent to discharge the obligation. Defects of age or condition exempt from the duty; various forms of "commutation" — the performance of another virtuous act, like alms to the poor, in place of the prescribed one — are recognized; and finally, a greater good may override a religious obligation, even including the profession of faith. Religious dissemblance was permitted, for example, to Muslims living under Christian sovereignty in Spain when the shahada might mean their death, and Shiites exercised the same privilege vis-à-vis their Sunni persecutors.

Women represent a special case. In some respects they are "defective" individuals in the face of the sharia. Their testimony in court does not carry the same weight, for example, as that of a man, despite the notorious fact that a great deal of the testimony regarding the custom of the Prophet on which the sharia is built was transmitted by a woman, Aisha, Muhammad's wife. Lawyers also invoked the notion of the higher good to excuse women from performing of many of these ritual duties. The bearing and rearing of children, which in Muslim society was a woman's responsibility until the child was about seven, when, at least in the case of male children, the father took over, was thought sufficient cause to keep a woman at home, and occupied.

What actually barred a woman from full participation in the liturgical life of Islam was rather, it appears, her occasional but not always predictable states of ritual impurity: questions of (enabling or disabling) ritual purity (*tahara*) always precede discussion of the obligations in Muslim legal handbooks. Like her Jewish counterpart, the Muslim woman was rendered ritually impure by childbirth and by menstruation and so unfit to perform the ibadat or even to touch a Quran. In Judaism — and among the Christians who emerged from it — such impurity prohibited a woman from becoming a priest or even approaching the sanctuary. Islam had no priesthood, but the prospect of ritual impurity was enough to bar a woman from participation in ritual acts, from prayer to fasting during Ramadan.

But if women are seen only rarely in mosques — there are many Prophetic reports advising them to absent themselves — and then only in the same kind of sheltered enclaves as appear in traditional synagogues, the reason is not merely a male — or divine — fear of ritual contamination. It was also a matter of gender segregation. Women were not notably empowered in pre-Islamic Mecca — the Quran dictated improvements in their standing in society — but there is no indication that they were segregated. A degree of female segregation was, however, practiced among the urbanized classes of both Byzantine and Sassanian society, where women lived in separate quarters in the great houses and were often veiled in public, which Bedouin women never were. As Muslims moved out of their original Arabian environment into the great cities of the Fertile Crescent, they adopted, and adapted, the social mores they found there, including the segregation of women. But what was a social custom rapidly became religious as well in the totalizing environment of Islam. Quranic texts were uncovered and unpacked—most notoriously the famous "veiling" (*hijab*) verse, 33: 53, where the context seems to refer to the privacy of the Prophet's wives, who may have been bothered by unwanted visitors to this famous Medina household. Far more pointed Prophetic reports were eventually adduced in great numbers to support the contention that the Muslim woman was a taboo object excluded not merely from participation in the *sacra* but from any share in the public life of Muslim society.

The public social segregation of women was not simply borrowed custom, to be sure. The Quran, not less than the Bible and the New Testament, urges modesty on women. Quran 24:30–31, which begins, "And say to the believing women that they cast down their looks and guard their private parts and do not display their ornaments except what appears thereof, and let them wear their head-coverings over their bosoms, and do not display their ornaments except to their husbands and fathers," is a famous example. Women's being rendered "unavailable" in various ways also has its obvious parallels in the two other monotheist communities. But though Islam and Judaism have valued as highly as Christianity women's chastity, they have never celebrated the virginity of either men or women as an ideal. Where Christians adopted the Virgin Mary as the feminine ideal, Muslims (who revere "Maryam," though not for her virginity) look rather toward Fatima, the Prophet's daughter and the mother of his two favorite grandchildren, as the embodiment of Muslim womanhood.

Muslim Prayer

The Quran shows no interest in the earlier Jewish temple cult, though there is good evidence that Muhammad himself originally prayed facing Jerusalem. The Quran's one possible reference to the

Eucharist (5:117–118) suggests that it was thought of as some kind of meal sent down from heaven to sustain the believers. Islamic liturgy lay not in those directions, however; it was more akin to that of rabbinic Judaism in that it was grounded in prayers. The pagans at Mecca had prayed, after a fashion, a practice the Quran characterizes as "whistling and clapping of hands" (8:35). Muhammad substituted, on God's command, formal liturgical prayers (*salat*). These daily prayers are largely unspecified as to their content, frequency, and times in the Quran, but the details were quickly supplied from the Prophet's sunna. Muslim prayers are made up principally from God's own words in the Quran. They are preceded by a ritual ablution and accompanied by appropriate gestures and prostrations. Though private prayers (*duat*; "callings" on God) are approved and encouraged, the formal salat are the heart of the Islamic liturgy and the chief form of divine worship that lies on the Muslim.

Muslim liturgical prayer is composed of units called "bowings" (*rakas*). The first in any series always begins with the phrase "God is great" (*Allahu akbar*), recited with the hands placed, palms outward, at each side of the face. This is followed by the recitation of "The Opening" (*al-Fatiha*), the initial *sura* of the Quran, and one or more other passages from that Book. Next is a bowing from the hips, after which the worshiper returns to an erect position. The worshiper then kneels and touches forehead to the ground, then sits back on the haunches. This is followed by a second bowing like the first. Though the practice is still somewhat fluid in the Quran, prayer soon became standardized at five times a day—Jews are required to pray three times a day—when the faithful are summoned by a "caller" (*muadhdhin*; English, "muezzin") at the appropriate times. These were at daybreak (*subh* or *fajr*), noon (*zuhr*), midafternoon (*asr*), after sunset (*maghrib*), and finally, the early part of the night (*isha*). At first, the prayers were said facing Jerusalem, as the Jews did—Christians faced toward the east—but later the direction of prayer, the qibla, was changed toward the Kaaba at Mecca.

FRIDAY PRAYER AND THE MOSQUE

The Muslim's daily prayers might be said in private in any decent and dignified setting, but the noon prayer on Friday had a special liturgical significance in that it was a prescribed congregational prayer. Friday came to be called the "day of assembly" (*yawm al-juma*), and the place of that congregation was known as the "assembly" (*jami*). This latter is what we call a mosque, though the English word goes back to another Arabic word describing another function of the same place: *masjid*, a place of prostration or worship.

The Muslim Friday began its career as a reaction, Muhammad's own reaction, it appears, to the Jewish Sabbath, once again in the sense of deliberately choosing a day for common prayer that would distinguish the Muslims of Medina from the Jews there. On that day the community prayer is celebrated, and though it is not formally a day of rest, in the sense that normal activities, usually commercial, had to be suspended, it is becoming assimilated by Muslims worldwide into an expanding notion of the "weekend" as nonworking days.

The first mosque in Islam was the courtyard of Muhammad's own house in Medina. Its successors in the Islamic diaspora served much the same purpose as the original building, a simple structure used indifferently for political assembly and liturgy. There were few architectural requirements: flowing water for ablution before prayer in an open court and a tower or minaret from which the muezzin might summon the faithful to prayer; within, a niche (*mihrab*) to note the qibla, or prayer direction (toward Mecca), and a raised throne (*minbar*) — as opposed to the Christian pulpit, which is a kind of raised podium — which originally served as a sort of political rostrum but which developed, with the progressive restriction of the mosque to liturgical functions, into a pulpit for the Friday sermon.

The mosque is the single most distinctive sign of a Muslim community. In the Islamic lands the cities are filled with them, generally built by private rather than public funds from the already noted waqf, and sited wherever the will and the wealth of the builder chooses. Technically, there is only one "Friday mosque" — the assembly mosque for the Friday community prayer; all others are merely oratories — in each community, just as there is one cathedral in each major Christian community, but the size of the Muslim population soon outstripped that notion. Now the common custom is simply that there must be at least one Friday mosque in each community.

The conceptual centrality of the Muslims' Friday mosque is its only connection with the Christian cathedral. The latter is the seat of a bishop in a juridically constructed diocese. Islam possesses no bishops (or priests, for that matter) and has neither dioceses nor even parishes. More basically, the Muslim mosque is the functional equivalent of the Jewish synagogue, an assembly place for prayer; the analogue of the Christian church is the now defunct Jerusalem temple, the site of sacrifice. The most distinctive furniture of a church is an altar of sacrifice, absent in both mosque and synagogue, and its most distinctive official is the sacrificing priest, who is nowhere to be found in Islam. Although the ongoing line of Jewish *kohenim* or priests may be identified by their kinship caste markings, they can no longer, absent the temple, perform their primary function of sacrifice on the altar of the Lord.

THE HAJJ

Daily prayer is one of the liturgical Pillars of Islam; the other is the hajj, the pilgrimage to the holy places of Mecca and its environs, which every Muslim must make at least once during his or her lifetime, if circumstances permit. This complex ritual, much of which is both time- and place-tied, unfolds between the eighth and thirteenth days of the lunar pilgrimage month (Dhu al-Hijja).

The hajj was a long-standing pre-Islamic ritual in the environs of Mecca; how long we cannot say, although its rites seem redolent of primitive Semitic practices. They antedated Muhammad's lifetime, at any rate, as did the umra, a more local Meccan festival celebrated by the townspeople in and around the Kaaba. Though Muslims are loathe to imagine the Prophet in any connection with paganism, we have no real reason to think that Muhammad did not participate in the hajj before his call to prophecy in 610, nor indeed even after that date, at least until his departure for Medina. He made the umra at Mecca in 629 and 630, and there were Muslims on the hajj of 631, though not Muhammad himself. His first and last Muslim hajj occurred in 632, the so-called Farewell Pilgrimage. It was on that occasion that by word and example — his sunna — he made whatever modifications were deemed necessary to purify this ritual that in Muslim eyes had originally been instituted by Abraham himself (Quran 22:27).

The hajj was not, at any time we can observe it, a single, unified ritual act in the manner of a drama but a concatenation of barely connected activities spread over a number of days. Or so it appears to us since whatever etiological myths the Arabs once possessed to explain these now baffling rituals are entirely lost. Perhaps they had already disappeared by Muhammad's own day. The Quran provided the believers with their own properly Muslim explanations. The hajj rituals were now understood in reference to Abraham and his sojourn in Mecca. Here at Arafat Abraham stood and prayed before God. Here at Mina he was bidden to sacrifice his son and then given an animal in substitution. Here too Abraham was tempted by Satan, and so the three "Satans" in the form of pillars are stoned. And so on.

Besides the Haram or sanctuary area in the middle of town, Mecca is surrounded by a larger taboo area that is marked by points or "stations" along the main roads leading into the Holy City. At or before he or she reaches one of those points, the pilgrim must enter a taboo state, *ihram* or "haramization," by undergoing a complete ablution, donning a special garment made of two simple white sheets, one tied around the waist and reaching the knees and the other draped over the left shoulder and tied somewhere beneath the right arm. Head and insteps must remain uncovered. This is for the men; no particular dress is prescribed for the women, though most are fully covered, head to toe, in white. This garment and this alone is worn throughout the pilgrimage, and no further washing or grooming is permitted. Nor are sexual relations: any indulgence in the latter renders the hajj void.

224 ◈ CHAPTER NINE

To Mount Arafat and Back

On entering Mecca, the pilgrim should proceed as soon as possible to the performance of the *tawaf*, the sevenfold, counterclockwise circumambulation of the Kaaba, the first three at a somewhat quickened pace. Pilgrims attempt to kiss or touch the Black Stone embedded in the eastern corner of the Kaaba as they pass it, though the pilgrimage throng often makes this impossible. The tawaf completed, the pilgrim goes to the place called Safa, beyond the southeast side of the Haram, and completes seven "runnings" between that and another place, called Marwa, a distance altogether of somewhat less than two miles. Today both places, and the way between, are enclosed in an air-conditioned colonnade. The tawaf originally formed part of the umra or Meccan spring festival, but the running between Safa and Marwa was connected to it by Muhammad himself, as we can still read in Quran 2:153.

There is a certain flexibility in the performance of those Meccan rituals—some prefer to do them very late at night when the weather is cooler and the crowds thinner—but precisely on the eighth of Dhu al-Hijja the hajj proper begins. The pilgrims proceed to Mina, a village five miles east of Mecca, where some pass the night, while the rest proceed directly to the hill called Arafat in the midst of an open plain eleven miles from the Haram, where they spend the night in what becomes, for that solitary evening, one of the largest cities in the Middle East. The next day, the ninth, is the heart of the hajj. The pilgrims, now many hundreds of thousands, assemble and stand around the rocky hill of Arafat. At times sermons have been delivered during this interval, but they have nothing to do with the ritual, the point of which is precisely the standing before God, as Abraham did, from noon to sunset. Just before sunset occurs the "dispersal," a sometimes pell-mell rush to Muzdalifa, a village halfway back toward Mina. The night is spent here; then, the next morning, the tenth, there is another dispersal as the pilgrims hasten to Mina, where the ritual Stoning of Satan, the casting of seven pebbles at a stone pillar, occurs.

With the Stoning of Satan, the hajj has reached its official term, but there remain a number of rites that are part of the pilgrims'

desacralization. As already noted, the pilgrim must sacrifice an animal — this is the *id al-adha* celebrated by the entire Muslim
world — though some Muslim legal experts permit, on the basis of
Quran 2:196, ten days of fasting (three on the hajj, seven later) as
an acceptable substitute for this blood sacrifice.

Note: Sacrifice, precisely animal sacrifice, which was the primary
form of worship in temple Judaism and, in its eucharistic transformation, is still at the liturgical heart of Christianity, was a feature of pre-
Islamic ritual at Mecca. Although it was given to humankind by God
through Abraham, and the ritual is even described in its pages, the
Quran expresses certain reservations regarding animal sacrifice (22:
32–36; cf. 5:106). The practice was nonetheless imposed on Muslims
(sura 108), principally in the performance of the now prescribed pilgrimage. At the "festival of the sacrifice" (*id al-adha* or *id al-qurban*)
that occurs at Mina on the tenth day of the hajj month, the offering
must be a herd animal — it is possible to share the expenses of offering
a large animal — whose head is turned toward the Kaaba and whose
throat is slit, much in the manner and intent of Jewish temple sacrifice, so that the blood drains out on the ground. Though it is permissible to eat its flesh afterward (Quran 22:33), it is regarded as mer-
itorious to give it as food for the poor. At the same time this is being
done at Mina, other Muslims around the world join in the celebration
of the id al-adha by making, if they wish, their own animal sacrifice,
sharing the food with neighbors and the needy.

After the sacrifice the men's heads are shaved, the women's locks
lightly clipped, to signal the end of the ihram state — the sexual
prohibitions remain a short while longer. The pilgrims return to
Mecca, perform another tawaf, are sprinkled with water from the
well of Zamzam, and then bathe. The next three days, the eleventh, twelfth, and thirteenth of the month, complete the desacralization. The pilgrims return to Mina, now entirely freed of all ta-
boos. On each of the three days the pilgrims again stone the great
pillar there, as well as two smaller ones. The hajj is then complete,
and though it is in no sense part of the ritual, many pilgrims pro-

ceed to Medina to pay their respects at the Prophet's tomb before returning home.

INTERCALATION PROHIBITED

The hajj of 632 completed, Muhammad turned to other connected matters. It was probably soon after the Farewell Pilgrimage that Muhammad announced the revelation banning the practice of intercalation (Quran 9:36–37). In modern societies the establishment of an accurate and useful calendar seems like a purely civil act controlled by scientists at best and politicians at worst. This is not so in religious societies where the calendar controls most of the community's ritual activities.

The Christians, under Roman influence, adopted a solar calendar to mark the cycle of their liturgical year, a choice that further distanced them from Jewish roots, though Easter continued to have a lingering connection with the lunar Passover. For their part, the Jews continued to use, at least for religious purposes, their traditional lunar calendar, which the Bible itself had enshrined by making the appearance of the new moon a festival celebration. The pre-Islamic Arabs too followed a lunar calendar and, like the Jews, practiced intercalation. For the Jews the agricultural festivals of Sukkoth and Passover continued to mark the fall harvest and the spring sowing respectively, whereas for the Arabs the umra remained a spring feast like Passover and the hajj was, like Sukkoth, always observed in the fall.

But no longer, the Quran ruled. God had abolished intercalation, and so what were originally seasonal festivals and holy days, the hajj, umra and the month of Ramadan, now moved freely across the solar year, each cycle falling ten days earlier in the solar year than in the preceding one. Indeed, the umra grew so detached from its original seasonal celebration that Muslims often simply attached it to the beginning of the hajj and celebrated both together. We can only speculate what was behind this ban. Most likely it was intended to disconnect Muslim religious practices from all their pre-Islamic associations, pagan or Jewish, since those earlier holy days were seasonal. The Christians broke their religious ties to the past, and redefined themselves, by going solar; the Muslims, by dropping intercalation.

THE ENSHRINEMENT OF JERUSALEM

Holy cities like Mecca have always invited the politically minded to gain some political advantage by making public and visible investment in the place, particularly its holy locales. David, Solomon, and Herod all engaged in such enterprises in Jerusalem, with varying results, as did various Muslim rulers in Mecca and Medina as well as Jerusalem. But the two who achieved the most lasting effects in Jerusalem, if not to their reputation, then to the city, were David and Constantine. Each took a settlement that was not particularly regarded by their subjects and converted it into something very different. David's achievement is quite complex in that it had both political and religious results that last to this day. By moving himself and his court there and by bringing the Ark of the Covenant into the town and making arrangements for its permanent housing there — though his son Solomon actually built the dazzlingly sumptuous House of the Lord — the king of Israel made the Jebusite settlement of Jerusalem into the political and religious capital of the Israelites. It has always remained such for the Jews, even absent both sovereignty and shrine from that place.

David was only the second king of Israel, but Constantine rested on even less certain terrain: he was the first Christian emperor of a political enterprise, the Imperium Romanum, that stretched, in one form or another, a millennium into the past, a thousand pagan years by Christian reckoning. In the 330s, at Constantine's express command, the site of Jesus' execution and burial, which had been outside Herod's wall on that side of the city but now lay well within the Roman city, was excavated and cleared. Not only was the site found, but in the excavation were discovered three crosses, one of which was miraculously demonstrated to be Jesus' own.

Both the rock-hewn tomb and Golgotha, the mound upon which Jesus was crucified, were laid bare. Over the tomb was built a circular domed edifice, which opened on its eastern side to an uncovered courtyard where Golgotha stood, now surmounted by Jesus' cross. On the eastern side of this porticoed court lay Constantine's enormous basilica, with its monumental entry opening onto the *cardo*, the main colonnaded street that ran north-south through Jerusalem. A similar building was constructed over the grotto identified as Jesus' birth site in Bethlehem, another at the place where Jesus stood on the Mount of Olives, and finally a shrine was built around Abraham's oak near Hebron. Where Constantine led, the nobility followed: the Christian holy places of Jerusalem and Palestine were richly endowed and enshrined over the next three centuries.

In 735 or 738 the Muslims took Jerusalem, together with much else around the Mediterranean, almost effortlessly and without bloodshed. They left the Christians pretty much as they were, but the new Muslim masters of the city seem to have struck up what appears to us an odd symbiotic relationship with the Jews. The Jewish community was permitted to return to Jerusalem, which it did, soon moving the rabbinic circles that directed Jewish legal and religious affairs from Tiberias, where they had been for more than five centuries, back to Jerusalem. Moreover, the Muslims built their first place of prayer in the city not in or by one of the Christian churches or shrines but atop the temple mount, a place ignored and neglected by the Christians but obviously still important to the Jews. Indeed, the Jews may have been permitted to pray once again on the mount. Within a generation the Muslims had greatly enhanced their first crude mosque there and constructed atop the same Herodian platform a magnificent domed shrine over the rock that was said to have been the temple's foundation stone. This Noble Sanctuary, or Haram al-Sharif as the Muslims call it, the Herodian platform with the Dome of the Rock and the Aqsa mosque placed atop, not only dominates the cityscape of Jerusalem to this day; it may be the single most impressive architectural expression of Islamic sanctity in the entire Abode of Islam.

The Distant Shrine

Why did the Muslims choose that place? If we are willing to jump
forward from the seventh to perhaps the eighth or ninth century,
there are answers in abundance, since by then the traditions on the
subject were well established. The Haram, it was said, was holy for
two reasons. There were its biblical associations, which, by reason
of the Quran's certifying them as God's true revelation, became
Muslim sacred associations as well. The Quran never mentions
Jerusalem by name, neither as such nor by any of the titles by
which it was later referred, The Holy House (*al-Bayt al-Maqdis*) or
simply The Holy (*al-Quds*), though it almost certainly is referring
to the city and its temple when it speaks of the two destructions
that God visited on it (17:4–8). The Muslim tradition found more
than that, however. It rather quickly understood the Quran's reference to "the distant shrine" (*al-masjid al-aqsa*)to which Muhammad was miraculously carried by night (17:1) as a allusion to Jerusalem, and the subsequent mention of "the prayer direction you
once had" (2:142, 143) as a reference to Muhammad's originally
praying toward Jerusalem.

Once Jews began to convert to Islam and open to the Arabs the
riches of Jewish midrashim on the Holy City, Muslims had good
reason to glorify Jerusalem. There stood the temple of Solomon,
one of the Quran's most tantalizingly interesting and mysterious
figures. Before him David had prayed there in his oratory on the
western side of the city, Jacob had had his vision of God there, and
Abraham was bade to sacrifice Isaac there. But if the Jerusalem
Haram is biblical and therefore Muslim, it is also Muhammadan,
as we have just seen, by reason of its connection with the life of the
Prophet. "By night," sura 17 of the Quran begins, "God carried
His servant from the holy sanctuary [of Mecca] to the distant
shrine." The Quran says no more about this "Night Journey" or
the location of the shrine, but the Muslim tradition soon enough
identified it with Jerusalem and, more precisely, with the platform
atop the temple mount. It was from this same spot, the tradition
continues, that the Prophet was straightway taken up to the highest heaven and granted a supernal vision.

THE CHRISTIAN ASSAULT ON JERUSALEM

Thus Jerusalem became a Muslim holy city by reason of the biblical and Muhammadan associations of its Noble Sanctuary, though for the next four centuries it remained overwhelmingly Christian in its population. Around the Haram was a Muslim population whose interest in living there was in part administrative and in part simple piety. A modest Jewish community lived somewhere in the southeast corner, rabbis many of them, who enjoyed the prestige of constituting the principal yeshiva of the Jewish world but who otherwise shared little of the prosperity of their coreligionists in Islamic urban centers like Fustat/Cairo or Baghdad. The reason was not oppression; it was simply that Jerusalem was not a very prosperous place. It was of secondary political and administrative importance; it had little share in the burgeoning trade and commerce that was beginning to enrich other cities in the Abode of Islam. Jerusalem remained what it had been since the second century, a provincial backwater that now possessed major Christian and Muslim shrines and a Zionist recollection of a Jewish one. Pilgrims still came and went, more and more of them Western Christians.

The eleventh-century Palestinian city called al-Quds, "The Holy," was, then, neither a very prosperous nor indeed a very safe place to live. It was in the center of a three-cornered Muslim war zone amid Egypt, Syria, and Iraq, and like some ancient Belgium or Armenia, Palestine was often overrun by armies heading elsewhere, with the additional hazard that when the dust cleared, the predatory Bedouin who infested the area often moved in to pick over the bones. The Muslims did not often visit Jerusalem in those days; indeed, they could scarcely defend the place. When tyranny descended on the land, it was usually all three communities that shared the oppression. For the Muslims that oppression was largely economic; for the Jews, and particularly the far more visible Christians, it frequently cast itself in religious raiment. Thus al-Hakim, the eleventh-century ruler of Egypt whose memory is fragrant in no one's annals, Muslim, Jewish or Christian, and who was disturbed, if not entirely deranged, had destroyed the Church of the Holy Sepulcher in 1009 in an act of senseless malice, unwittingly setting in train events that are still unfolding to this day.

There is no need to rehearse the First or Jerusalem Crusade, or better, the Pilgrimage, as its participants called it. The Western knights, most of them French, took Jerusalem in 1099, slew the Muslim defenders down to the women and children — the fate of the Jewish community is less clear; some were doubtless killed but many others were ransomed by their coreligionists in Egypt — and so found themselves in possession of a city that was filled with holy places but had no inhabitants other than themselves. The Dome of the Rock was converted into a church, the Templum Domini, and the Aqsa mosque, renamed the Templum Solomonis, after a brief career as the palace of the Latin king, was handed over to the new Order of the Knights Templars who began to subdivide, enlarge, and adapt the building to their own uses. Some Eastern Christians were lured back into the city, and eventually too a few Jews and Muslims must have made their tentative and modest reappearance in Jerusalem.

This extraordinary interlude in Jerusalem's history lasted less than a century, from 1099 to 1187, when the crusaders were driven out by Saladin's armies. The fighting was savage once again, but this time there was no massacre in its wake. The Haram buildings were of course reconverted to the Islamic cultus, but the Church of the Holy Sepulcher, which the crusaders had extensively rebuilt, was left untouched, as were most of the city's other major Christian shrines. Saladin did, however, convert the convent attached to the Church of St. Anne into a madrasa, or law school, and part of the palace of the now departed Latin patriarch into a Sufi convent and hospice.

MUSLIM JERUSALEM IN THE MIDDLE AGES

The Old City of Jerusalem as it appears to the visitor today is Ottoman on the outside — the walls were built by Ottoman Sulayman in the early sixteenth century — and largely Mamluk within. The careful eye can catch a considerable number of crusader traces in the city, and the design of the Haram complex dates back of

course to the earliest days of Islam. But the Muslim public buildings were mostly built between about 1250 and 1450 by the successor dynasty to Saladin's own, the Mamluks. These structures
are, overwhelmingly, madrasas, Sufi convents, and related institutions, most of them with boarding facilities, for the teaching of
Islamic law and the cultivation of Islamic piety. They cluster like a
frame around the Haram and on the streets leading north and west
from it, since in Jerusalem, as in all other holy places, nearer is
better. These institutions were founded chiefly by sultans in Cairo,
their governors in Damascus — during most of the Middle Ages
Jerusalem was an appanage of Damascus, which was in turn a
provincial center for the capital in Cairo — or Mamluks banished
for reasons to what was judged to be the healthy but politically
impotent climate of Jerusalem.

There was considerable Mamluk investment in Jerusalem in the
fourteenth and fifteenth centuries, as there was in Mecca and Medina in the same era. One reason was that the Mamluks had problems with their Islamic legitimacy — they were former military
slaves — and as the Jewish Herod, the Christian Justinian, and many
other rulers had observed, there is no better guerdon of legitimacy
than the generous endowment of a holy place or a holy city. And
Jerusalem was now in fact a genuine Islamic holy city. If after that
first extraordinary gesture of the Dome of the Rock, succeeding generations of Muslims had grown careless of the Haram and even
somewhat indifferent to Jerusalem, the Frankish Crusades and the
sentiments they eventually provoked had refocused Muslim attention on the city. The Merits of Jerusalem tracts had leavened Islamic
thinking about Jerusalem. One ruler after another left his architectural signature on the increasingly crowded Haram, and around it
monumental gates, arcades, and stairways were set up to frame and
enshrine the Dome of the Rock and the Aqsa mosque.

THE PIOUS VISIT al-QUDS

Two general types of activities are called "pilgrimage." The first
refers to the performance of certain acts of worship that can be

done only at certain times or places. These time- and place-tied rituals are exemplified in the Jews' obligation to celebrate the three great annual festivals of Pesach, Shabuoth, and Sukkoth in Jerusalem at the appropriate seasons and the Muslims' once-in-a-lifetime obligation to perform the hajj on the appointed days in and around Mecca. Properly speaking, these may be better thought of as liturgies. Pilgrimage is also used of voluntary journeys in the three religious communities and is in effect a pious visit — what the Muslims call a *ziyara*, in opposition to the liturgical hajj — a voyage from here to somewhere else, as the Latin name *peregrinatio* signals. That "somewhere else" is a holy place of a number of different types. It might be a locale where salvation history has unfolded, Sinai, for example, or the site of the crucifixion in Jerusalem, where the pilgrim might relive and, indeed, liturgically reenact that event. It might be the dwelling of a holy man or woman, where one might attend and gaze on one of those friends of God thought to embody perfect virtue. And finally, and most generally, it might be one of the sites sanctified first by the earthly presence and now by the sacred remains of the martyrs and other heroic witnesses to the faith.

The line between the hajj, the obligatory and highly ritualized annual liturgy at Mecca, and a ziyara, an informal and quite voluntary visit to Jerusalem or the Prophet's tomb at Medina or even to Mecca, might be perfectly clear to the Islamic lawyer, but it was surely not so in popular devotion, and so at least some Muslim voices were raised protesting the somewhat novel exaltation of Jerusalem to the status of a Muslim holy city. In the period immediately preceding the Frankish Crusade against Jerusalem, and particularly after it, a kind of pious competition developed among Mecca, Medina, and Jerusalem for the palm of Islamic sanctity. Or so it seemed. Actually afoot was a deliberate campaign to raise Muslim consciousness toward this neglected holy city. In Judaism, Jerusalem and the temple had no real competitors, and Christians take their holy places where they find them. But against Muslim Jerusalem there was always Mecca and Medina, which had long enjoyed the privilege of being al-Haramayn, "The Twin Sanctuaries," the blessed sites of Islam's very origins. The campaign to raise Jerusalem's Muslim profile — which was reinvigorated after 1967 — must be judged successful. After Saladin's restoration of Muslim sovereignty in the city in 1187, both Muslim investment in and Muslim pious visits to Jerusalem dramatically increased.

By far the most common practice of a Jerusalem ziyara was a visit to the city en route to Mecca. The hajj caravan that marshaled in Damascus peeled off an excursion to Jerusalem on its way southward, and many other pilgrims made the relatively easy detour to Jerusalem on their own since a visit to al-Quds was thought to enhance the sanctification of the subsequent hajj. None of this is unexpected, given Jerusalem's deliberately enhanced reputation as a holy city, nor is it surprising that, with the increased investment in madrasas and Sufi convents in the city, many of Islam's "friends of God" should choose to settle there and that many more of the pious should come to Jerusalem to sit at their feet and gain their blessing (*baraka*).

More surprising — perhaps even startling — is the growth of a kind of pilgrimage ritual in the Noble Sanctuary. What is merely surprising is that there should begin to develop a kind of stational liturgy in and around the Haram al-Sharif. Some of this was obviously generated by stories of where and how the Prophet prayed during his celebrated but brief Night Journey to the Noble Sanctuary, and some of those places were soon enshrined with small domed oratories clustered around the Dome of the Rock. What is startling, however, and somewhat perplexing, is the persistent tradition that in late-seventh-century Jerusalem was intended to replace Mecca as the site of the Muslims' mandatory hajj and the unmistakable evidence that throughout the Middle Ages a number of Muslims did just that. The early tradition is connected to the caliph Abd al-Malik (r. 685–705), who was confronted by a stubborn rebel who had taken possession of Mecca. The caliph, it was said, built the Dome of the Rock, which he assuredly did, to divert the hajj from rebel-held Mecca to *his* holy city of Jerusalem. Modern scholarship has discounted the story, but it persisted in Islam, and we do know that in subsequent centuries at least some Muslims — 20,000 were reported on one occasion — performed their obligatory "standing" atop the Jerusalem Haram while their fellow Muslims were doing the same at Arafat outside Mecca, and that they and others performed the ritual hajj sacrifice in the Noble Sanctuary in Jerusalem.

MUSLIM DEVOTIONS

Christianity early institutionalized the veneration of its holy men and women. The martyrs were the first to be so honored, but with the end of the persecutions and the execution of Christians, the same veneration was soon extended to the "confessors," those holy men and women whose lifelong pursuit of virtue proclaimed their sanctity as eloquently as the blood of the martyrs did theirs. They too might be venerated, though never adored, and it was permissible to request their intercession with God—Islam is particularly firm in its denial of intercessory powers to any human, excluding Muhammad—but the line between veneration and adoration is thin indeed. Augustine had warned about crossing that line, and the Church Council held in Nicaea in 787 made a careful distinction between the worship (*latreia*) and adoration owed to God alone and the respect and veneration (*douleia*) that might be paid to the saints. However complex the matter might be, there was a small attached rider: Mary, the Mother of Jesus, might be paid a kind of superveneration (*hyperdouleia*).

There is nothing remotely like these Christian devotions in Sunni Islam. Its liturgy, principally the five-times-daily salat, is as fixed in performance as its Christian counterpart, the Eucharist, but is far less dramatic since the Eucharist is essentially a reenactment, and Muslim prayer a recitation. Islam has neither stational liturgies like the Christians' annual ritual celebration of the events of Jesus' last days in Jerusalem, nor commemorative liturgies like the daily celebration of the basic eucharistic liturgy in honor of some saint, the mass for the dead, and the marriage mass. Sunni Islam's only "seasonal" liturgy—as already noted, Muhammad's ban on intercalation rendered true seasonal celebrations impossible—is the time- and place-tied hajj. Despite occasional attempts, however, the ritual has not as a whole been successfully "translated" to other places save the sacrifice made at Mina on the tenth day of the hajj month, which, as we have seen, is replicated elsewhere in the Muslim world, though more as a custom hardened into precept than as a commandment.

Not only does the Muslim salat suffer no liturgical expansion; the avenues for the spread of local piety are missing in Muslim religious culture. There are blessings (*barakat*) in abundance in Islam, but they are diffused over a wide variety of persons and objects. There is no sacramental system to channel and regulate their dispensation, no clergy to propagate them, no Church to institutionalize them, no authority or faculty to validate their orthodoxy. Sunni Islam's sole commemorative holy day is Mawlid al-Nabi, the Prophet's birthday, the twelfth day of the lunar month called First Rabi. The first mention of its formal celebration among Sunnis is not until the beginning of the thirteenth century, as a court celebration, but soon the common people and most notably the Sufis had taken up the celebration. The liturgical heart of the feast day is the recitation of a lengthy poetical panegyric, likewise called a mawlid, recounting the creation of the preexistent Muhammad, the "Muhammad Light" (*nur muhammadi*), the genealogy of the Prophet, the "annunciation" to his mother, Amina, that she will bear the Prophet, and a description of his actual birth. The day and its celebration are, however, still regarded in some circles as something of an "innovation" (*bida*), a somewhat more opprobrious term in Arabic than in English. The underlying cause may be its widespread adoption in Sufi circles, a move that rarely enhanced the orthodoxy of anything in Islam.

THE FRIENDS OF GOD

The cult of saints, living or dead, was not an entirely natural development in Islam, which placed an almost infinite gulf between a transcendent God and his creation here below. It occurred nonetheless, and with some speed. Note has already been taken of the opposition to the Mawlid al-Nabi in honor of the Prophet's birthday. Muhammad, who never claimed to be anything other than mortal (Quran 18:110), and stoutly refused to produce supernatural signs to verify his claims as a prophet, was soon after his death credited with marvelous powers, and those gifts and graces (*karamat*) bestowed by God on his Prophet were quickly extended to God's "friends" (*wali*; pl. *awliya*), male and female. The cults of these friends of God, whether the founder of a Sufi order, a local holy man, or the Prophet himself, were popularly patronized, and the devout were richly rewarded with generous "blessings" ranging from medical cures or fertility to luck in marriage — which were attached to visitations to the tomb shrines of saints, generally called *qubba*s by reason of the distinctive small domed building over the site. Women in particular, who, as we have seen, were not encouraged to participate in public prayer, and generally did not find the mosque to be a welcoming place, often made pilgrimages to local tomb shrines or cemeteries with petitions for favors or intercession. All of this combined to make such places and their rituals a center and focus of Muslim spiritual life, particularly in the countryside.

These cults did not pass unremarked. The school of jurisprudence founded by Ahmad ibn Hanbal (d. 855) was particularly outspoken in its criticism of the cult of saints, particularly at their tombs. The greatest Hanbalite eminence of the Middle Ages, Ibn Taymiyya (d. 1328), issued fatwas and wrote broadsides against them. Though he was not in a position to do much about this extremely common practice, many of his opinions found an echo in the preaching of Muhammad ibn Abd al-Wahhab (d. 1791), the conservative ideologue behind the rise of the House of Saud in Arabia. In 1813 the Wahhabis emerged from central Arabia to destroy the tomb shrine of Husayn ibn Ali at Karbala, in Iraq, and when they took Mecca and Medina early in the nineteenth century and again, more permanently, in 1926, the zealous Wahhabi "brethren" destroyed the tombs of many of Islam's earliest and most venerated heroes. They did not, however, touch the largest tomb shrine of them all, that of the Prophet Muhammad at Medina. Indeed, the Saudis have enlarged and elaborated it.

THE PASSION AND THE DEATH OF HUSAYN

Pious devotions in Sunni Islam were nourished by neither popular literature nor popular art. Drama was not among the arts that found a distinct place in traditional Islamic culture, though in more recent times all the popular forms of drama, from grand opera to soap opera, are performed in Muslim societies. Traditional Islam had its dramatic narratives, to be sure, the encomia of the Prophet on his birthday, for example, and the laments recited or chanted on the tenth of Muharram in memory of the martyrdom of Husayn at Karbala in 680. These latter "garden recitals" — they derived mainly from a Shiite work titled "The Garden of the Martyrs" — were stationary and delivered by a professional reciter, but they were processional liturgies as well. There is evidence for public processionals in honor of Husayn in Baghdad from as far back as the tenth century, when mourners with tattered clothes, streaming hair, and blackened faces circled the city walls on the tenth of Muharram, beating their breasts and chanting their dirges. This took place when there was an Alid-leaning dynasty ruling in the capital, but when an out-and-out Shiite regime was established in Iran in the sixteenth century, the processions became full-scale pageants — with many of the participants dressed as characters in the Husayn-related events being portrayed.

In the mid–eighteenth century the Husayn pageants and the garden recitals fused and produced in Iran, and in Persian, a genuinely dramatic performance in a fixed place before a stationary audience, the *taziyeh*, or "consolation." At first these dramas were performed at street intersections or open areas in the town, but eventually, in the nineteenth century, special arenas were constructed, either permanently or temporarily, for their performance.

Though the liturgical event may have begun merely to commemorate Husayn's slaughter, soon other themes and other figures from Shiite history were introduced. In the end, the taziyeh proved to be a more open-ended performance than its Christian passion play counterpart. The latter remained closely tied to the Gospel texts and to faithful presentation of events that were not only historical but sacramental. Taziyeh, in contrast, knew no such textual or theological restraints. Like the Passover haggadas, which are readily altered by Reform Jews to reflect changing perceptions, conditions, and needs—the Orthodox hew faithfully to a text whose central core goes back to the ninth century—the taziyehs vary greatly in their textual and dramatic presentation.

ISLAM AND THE GRAVEN IMAGE

Among the laws given to Moses on Sinai, one expresses a concern about the Israelites' use of "images." "You shall not make for yourself a sculpted image, or any likeness of what is in the heavens above, or on the earth below, or in the waters under the earth," God says (Exod. 20:4–5), in what has come to be known as the Second Commandment. The defiantly aniconic God of the Israelites had good reason for his concern, as it turned out. Throughout most of their history down to the Exile, the Israelites were plagued with their penchant for idols and idol worship. The Bible makes no effort to dissemble their attraction, from the golden bull set up during Moses' absence with the Lord on Sinai (Exod. 32:1–10) to Jeroboam (1 Kings 12:28–31) and his successors as kings of Israel making a similar cult the official policy of the state. How seriously the problem was taken by some of God's spokesmen emerges clearly from this witheringly sarcastic attack on idols that occurs in the forty-fourth chapter of Isaiah: "The makers of idols all work to no purpose; and the things they treasure can do no good, as they themselves can testify. They neither look nor think, and so shall they be shamed" (9–10). Indeed, the Quran attributes many of the same sentiments to Abraham (Quran 21:51–67), the first to turn away from idols to the One True God. He upbraids his idol-worshiping father and the rest of his family with the taunt "Do you worship, besides God, these things that can do you neither good nor harm?" (21:66; 26:73).

If the Israelites had an inclination toward idolatry, the Meccans seemed to run and embrace it. The first generation of Muslims had to explain how the Mecca that Abraham left in the hands of Ishmael and his monotheistic progeny had become a pagan center of idol worship by the Prophet's day. Each of those early inhabitants, whenever they left town, we are told, took a stone from God's house in Mecca and venerated it wherever they happened to be. Eventually, however they no longer remembered the point of the practice and ended up worshiping the stones for their own sake. So perverse they became, Muhammad's biographer disdainfully continues, that the ordinary Arab would pick four attractive-looking stones, use three of them to support his cooking pot, and worship the fourth as a god.

From the outset, the Prophet made no secret of his intentions regarding the omnipresent idols of the Arabs. Tribes that embraced Islam during his lifetime were required to destroy their idols or, if they were incapable of bringing themselves to perform such an act, the Prophet dispatched some more convinced Muslims to do the demolition work for them. When Muhammad finally entered Mecca in triumph in 630, he put his intentions into action in his native town. The scene is described in the traditional biography:

> The Messenger entered Mecca on the day of the conquest and it contained 360 idols which Iblis (or Satan) had strengthened with lead. The Messenger was standing by them with a stick in his hand saying, "The truth has come and falsehood has passed away" (Quran 17:81). Then he pointed at them with his stick and they collapsed on their backs one after another. . . . When the Messenger had prayed the noon prayer on the day of the conquest (of Mecca) he ordered that all the idols which were around the Kaaba should be collected and burned with fire and broken up. . . . The Quraysh had put pictures in the Kaaba including two of Jesus son of Mary and Mary herself, on both of whom be peace. . . . The Messenger ordered that the pictures be erased, except those of Jesus and Mary.

We know little of what to make of that last curious event; the Kaaba was later rebuilt and there is no further trace of the pictures (icons?). What we can say, on the basis of the Quran, at any rate, is that, for all Muhammad's opposition to idolatry, there is no sign in the Book of any preoccupation, no open approval or disapproval even, of pictures or images. But conditions must soon have changed, since by the time we come to read the collections of Prophetic traditions, they are filled with condemnations of images and image-making: "Abu Talha reported the Prophet as saying, 'The angels do not enter a house which contains dogs or pictures.'" Or again, "Aisha told that she had screened a store room of hers with a curtain on which there were figures and the Prophet tore it down. So she made two cushions out of it and had them in the house for sitting on." And, much more circumstantially,

> Said ibn Abi Hasan said: "When I was with Ibn Abbas a man came to him and said, 'Ibn Abbas, I am a man whose livelihood comes only from the work of my hands, and I make these representations of things.' Ibn Abbas replied that he would tell him only what he had heard from God's Messenger. He had heard him say, 'If anyone makes a representation of anything, God will punish him until he blows a spirit into it, and he will never be able to do that.' Then when the man gasped and became pale, he said to him, 'Out upon you! If you must do so, make representations of these trees or of anything which does not possess a soul.'"

We do not know when those traditions were put into circulation. If they are authentic, we are faced with the same kind of dilemma that the figuratively decorated synagogues of Palestine posed to a supposedly aniconic Jewish tradition. Muslim coinage as a matter of fact bore representations of the caliph down to the reign of Abd al-Malik, and even after that date Muslim sovereigns continued to build Syrian steppe palaces decorated in a style that was not merely figurative but even aggressively and suggestively secular. It is perhaps safer to conclude that Islam came to its iconophobia gradually, and that the Prophetic traditions reflect a later and not a primary stage in that evolution.

The later official Islamic sentiment on images is clear enough, however. This is how it is expressed in one of the standard Islamic law books, that written by the Syrian jurist al-Nawawi (d. 1377). Now all fear of idolatry is gone, and the reasons for the prohibition are overtly theological:

> The learned authorities of our (Shafiite) school and others hold that painting a picture of any living thing is strictly forbidden, because it is threatened with grievous punishment as mentioned in the Prophetic traditions, whether it is intended for common domestic use or not. So the making of it is forbidden under every circumstance, because it implies a likeness to the creative activity of God. . . . On the other hand, the painting of a tree or of camel saddles and other things that have no life is not forbidden. Such is the decision on the actual making of a picture. . . . In all this there is no difference between what casts a shadow and what does not cast a shadow. This is the decision of our school on the question, and the majority of the Companions of the Prophet and their immediate followers and the learned of succeeding generations accepted it.

The practice of Islam forbade, then, figurative art as surely as it did the imbibing of wine and indulgence in homosexual love. "Islamic" poetry is awash nevertheless with both wine and beloved boys, and not occasionally or slyly or embarrassedly, just as "Islamic" art is filled, from its exquisite Persian miniatures to the "holy cards" of popular Shiite piety, with the likenesses of humans, mythic, historical, or the Muslim next door. The appearance of such themes in a religious culture that quite explicitly banned them seems not so much a willful flaunting of God's law as the rising to consciousness of another, quite different sensibility that found accommodation in certain places and certain circles in Islam.

THE WORD AS DECORATION

Jews and Muslims have a particular attachment to the Word as expressed in terms of language. Hebrew and Arabic are both sacred languages, and both are in a sense the language of God himself. But there is an important difference. The Jews lost their Hebrew as a living language while the Bible was still in the process of formation with the result that some of the last sections of the Book of Daniel are not in Hebrew but in Aramaic, the related

Semitic language that had become by post-Exilic times the lingua franca of the Jews and many others in the Middle East. Ezra had the Scriptures translated, presumably into Aramaic, at the ceremony renewing the Covenant at the return from Exile (Neh. 8:7–8), and by the second century B.C.E. its seems that many Jews, like the Greek-speaking Philo and Paul as well as the authors of the Gospels, were getting their Scripture from either the Greek Septuagint or else, like the Aramaic-speaker Jesus, the Aramaic Targums, and without a great deal of comment. There were some complaints, of course, but not about the fact of translation; merely, in the case of the Septuagint, of its lack of accuracy.

If the Jews turned to the vernacular, the Muslims did not. Their Scripture frequently boasted that it was "an Arabic Quran," and while Muslim piety might regard the Book's style, diction, and syntax as paradigms of perfection, Muslim theologians soon converted them into miracles. Muhammad had been instructed to respond to his critics by challenging them to "bring a sura like it" (Quran 1:13; 10:38; 28:49). They could not, of course, and thus was born the notion of the Quran's inimitability, and, more specifically, of its language and style, which was, at base, the validating miracle of Islam, the theological counterpart of Jesus' resurrection from the dead.

Veneration of text and language thus went hand in hand in Islam, and the emphasis on both was strengthened by their already noted aversion to figurative arts. As we have just seen, Muslims took God's prohibition against idols as seriously as the Jews, and, like the Jews, they extended it, though certainly not at all times or in all places, to figurative and pictorial art generally. Muslim decoration frequently took the form of repetitive geometric or vegetal patterns, the so-called arabesque. This type of decoration was not original with Islam; it can be observed on many of the Roman monuments of the Middle East, in Syria, for example, which antedate Islam by many centuries.

The other Muslim alternative to figurative art seems to have been Islam's own special creation, or at least emphasis. Large, elegantly inscribed writing appears unmistakably as decoration, and not merely to provide information as it did on Greek and Roman buildings and in more miniature form on coins. Muslims too put inscriptions on their coins — from which figures were eventually removed — and early on in their buildings, like the Dome of the Rock (692), which has mosaic inscriptions in the interior. But as time passed, the writing on buildings in particular, though it still conveyed information, had taken on a life of its own as it was transformed from writing to calligraphy. Extraordinarily ornate writing runs around the portals, across the facades, or up and down panels on the walls of most of the great Islamic monuments of the Middle Ages. Its design is often stunningly intricate and complex, almost unreadable in fact, in the manner of modern graffiti. In most cases the literate viewer probably needed little help in understanding the content since the texts were usually familiar quranic ones. It was purely and simply the Word that was being magnified by artistic enhancement.

There is little parallel among the equally aniconic Jews. From the tenth century onward Jews produced artistically illuminated manuscripts in Muslim Egypt, though without figurative representations. But two centuries later, when Jewish manuscript illumination began in Christian Europe, representations of sacred or ceremonial objects were portrayed, and later, in the seventeenth and eighteenth centuries, figures of rabbis and others began to appear. But there is no exaltation of Hebrew into the monumental public calligraphy of Arabic. It is not difficult to understand why. Islam was official: it controlled the public life of the Middle East and what was permissible in it; Jews lived under the dhimma, which would have made the public display of Hebrew not only unlikely but dangerous.

10. *This World and the Next*

ALL THREE monotheistic movements grew out of a perceived distinction between God, "who alone is holy," and the present circumstances in which humankind finds itself. These circumstances are often referred to as "the world" or "this world." Though God had looked on this world, which was, after all, his creation, and pronounced it "good" (Gen. 1:4, etc.), his devotees sometimes took a somewhat more pessimistic view of their circumstances, as did God himself on occasion, since there were elements in that creation, some manmade but others quite natural, that he wished to keep distant from his presence.

The Pillars of Islam (see chapter 9) are bare bones, a catechetical summary of the Muslim's ritual obligations, and though they became the point of departure of a vast body of prescription regulating Islamic behavior, they reflect neither the tone nor the urgency of Muhammad's message, particularly of the earliest revelations. The Meccan suras of the Quran have a dramatic eschatological emphasis, expressed now in commercial terms and now in the vivid images of Jewish and Christian apocalyptic. The God who created the world will also be its judge. When the Day of Judgment comes, accompanied by chaos and confusion, the Lord of the World will open the accounts of all humankind and reckon each at his or her worth. For those who have gravely sinned or hoarded their goods out of meanness of spirit, there awaits a fiery Gehenna of ex-

treme suffering. But the magnanimous person who has submitted
his will to God and committed her goods to the needy and the
downtrodden will be rewarded in a garden Paradise of luxurious
ease and splendor. Indeed, this is why the Prophet was sent, to be a
"warner" to humankind that the reckoning was close at hand.

THE BEGINNINGS OF MUSLIM ASCETICISM

How and why the world that seemed so pristinely good in Genesis
became so dangerous and even so evil a place was variously explained.
Genesis offered its own reasons, humankind's moral delinquency chief
among them, a theme elaborately glossed by the Christians into the
doctrine of Original Sin. However it was parsed, the view that this
world was morally dangerous settled deep into the religious sensibilities of Christians, Muslims, and, to a somewhat lesser extent, Jews.
Christians and Muslims could contrast the toils and dangers of this
world with both the rewards and punishments of the next world,
whereas for the Israelites generally, and for many Jews thereafter, the
perfect justice of the Afterlife was simply not available.

What prompted the first Muslims to separate themselves from the
world and their fellow Muslims by practicing asceticism (*zuhd*), that
is, a lifestyle with a notable degree of self-denial, appears to have
been a sense of contradiction between the increasingly successful
and extravagant ways of many Muslims and the general simplicity
and otherworldliness of the quranic message. That disparity did not
appear to bother Muhammad himself, who suffered neither pangs
nor nostalgia over his Meccan poverty, though the prosperity enjoyed by him and his companions at Medina was merely a thin
shadow of what followed in the first century of Islam. There appear,
in any event, here and there among the persons known to us in that
first century, some few individuals who "withdrew" from contemporary society, not in the manner of the Christians' headlong flight
into the wastes of Egypt, but more cautiously and circumstantially.
A number of them bore the title of Sufi.

Certain devotional practices characterized those early Muslim
pietists, but the virtue that was their principal goal is best resumed

in the Arabic word *tawakkul,* or "trust in God." It meant placing oneself completely in the hands of God, "like a corpse in the hands of its washer," a phrase and a notion not very different from Ignatius of Loyola's advice to his Jesuit companions to be "much like a corpse" when it came to the will of God, that is, to have no desires of one's own. A Sufi who had achieved this was in fact a "mendicant" (*faqir*), literally "a poor man," or a "child of the moment" (*ibn al-waqt*), according to another dramatic phrase. The early Sufis strove to be indifferent not in the manner of Stoic *apatheia,* a state of being immune to affect and that required an active regimen; rather, they were careless of them, as careless as "the birds of the air" or the "lilies of the field," Jesus' own exemplars of God's providing the wherewithal for his creation.

We know little besides some biographical details about the earliest Muslim Sufis, but we can observe almost immediately the differences and similarities between them and their Christian monastic contemporaries, of whom they must generally have been well aware. There was no Muslim flight to the wilderness; their ancestors had just recently come in from the wildernesses of Arabia. The cities of the new Islamic empire were filled not with pagans and paganism, as the Roman Empire was in early Christian times, but with Jews, Christians, and Muslims of their own faith. Sufis by and large remained in the cities: their "flight" was personal and interior. Nor did their practices of self-denial have the fiery ascetic edge so notable in the Christian holy men and women of the Middle East. Muslim Sufis practiced asceticism, to be sure, occasionally of a severe type, but it was always more occasional, more temporary, and more self-forgiving than its Christian counterpart. One reason may be that it passed far more quickly from an end to a means. Sufi asceticism found its mystic vocation far more quickly than did the Christian version of self-denial.

THE SUFI WAY

There are numerous scholastic tracts in Arabic on the theory and practice of Sufism (*tasawwuf*), on Muslim ascetical and mystical theology, as they might be called in Christianity, but for most Muslims the reality of Islamic spirituality was the tariqa, or brotherhood, into which Sufis began to assemble themselves. As in Christianity, the earlier eccentric "hermit" saints of Islam came to Sufism as a social enterprise, which took shape within the various community houses that were the counterparts of the Christian monastery. In Christianity, the cenobitic life may have been more sustainable in the depths of the wastelands than the eremitic, but the *koinobion*, or convent, soon developed its own moral character with obedience to a superior, and later to a rule, as its most highly prized virtue. In Islam, Sufis seem originally to have come together under one roof by reason of the attraction of a single master, with the master and his circle often moving from place to place. In the end, these circles became more stationary, with a fixed abode variously called a *khanqah*, *ribat*, or *zawiya*, a *tekke* among the Turks, and a *dargah* in the Persianized Sufi circles of India.

There is ample evidence that there were Sufi convents for both men and women in medieval times. The females may have been older women, many of them widows and poorer than their male counterparts. Though socially somewhat different, the women practiced the same *dhikr* exercises as the men, had a religious guide of their own, a shaykha, and even had their own prayer leaders and preachers. But there were inevitably differences. Circles of female Sufis tended to be local in nature, centered around the tomb of a local (male) saint, whereas the men belonged to associated circles that spread, many of them, across the entire Abode of Islam. When the men adjoined to the Friday mosque to join the entire body of Muslims in the weekly communal prayer service, women were unlikely to join them there; rather, they returned once again to the local tomb shrine.

The point of Sufi associations, like their counterparts in Christianity and Judaism, was essentially the imitation of and instruction by a recognized holy man. In the tenth century communal Sufism was a vocation for the few and the elite. There was no question at first of rules or a formal way of life. Tasawwuf was everywhere different, everywhere centered on a recognized master whose task was to show forth the Sufi's intimate union with God rather than to explain or define it. As Ghazali was later to remark, the Sufi life "cannot be learned but only achieved by direct experience, ecstasy, and inward transformation."

In Christianity, the rule governing the community of ascetics can be either "constructed," as it was in the case of a Basil, a Benedict, or an Ignatius of Loyola, or else, as in the case of the Franciscans, inspired directly by the living example of the founder. Sufi orders almost universally followed the second paradigm. The sainted man who stood at the head of the file of Sufis was not so much a founder as a paragon or paradigm around whom followers collected in the original khanqahs in the hope of sharing, by association and imitation, his baraka, the blessing or grace he possessed. The rule evolved from an attempt to recollect and emulate at least his behavior. But two things must be noted. The rule did not come from the saint, as it did in Christianity, and it required no one's formal approval or approbation. In Christianity, there was no "order" until it was approved, and, in the West, approved by the highest authority, the bishop of Rome.

The Sufi initiate took an oath of allegiance (*baya*, the same word used for the pre-Islamic oath of fealty to the tribal sheikh and then to the earliest caliphs) to the founder of the order and to his present-day earthly successor and deputy, the current link in the same spiritual chain (*silsila*) that led uninterruptedly back to the saintly founder. The initiate in a Christian religious order made three permanently binding vows to God: one of personal poverty, one of celibacy, and one of obedience to the rule, as expressed in the will of the superior. It is precisely in this matter of the oath/vow that the difference between the Christian monk and the Sufi becomes clearest. The latter swears allegiance to an individual, the former to a rule, or an ideal. Even more telling, perhaps, is the fact that the Sufi initiate receives, again at the baya, the *wird*, or prayer formulary proper to his order. Part of the wird is like the monks' "office" and will be recited in common and in public at the dhikr of the tariqa. But part too is personal and secret. The secret formulary is imparted to the Sufi initiate, is expanded by degrees, and will become complete on the occasion of his final oath of allegiance. Members of a zawiya met regularly for a "session" (*majlis*) where,

besides the prescribed liturgical prayers (*salat*), the dhikr and the
wird were performed, the latter often with the help of a Muslim
"rosary," a beaded cord called a *subha*. Sometimes there was a
common meal eaten either in silence or while listening to spiritual
reading.

Sufi tariqas had immense popular appeal in Islam, not least because they were a social and spiritual reaction to the increasingly
clerical and legal character of what had come to be official Islam,
which was dominated by a rabbinate with powerful economic, social, and political connections. Functionally, the Sufi orders filled
many of the same roles as the Christian clergy generally in the
medieval West. Like the diocesan or local clergy of the Western
Church, the Sufi "brethren" (*ikhwan*) were drawn from and remained close to the local community and its people, and they offered, like their Western clerical counterparts, a variety of spiritual
and corporeal services to their fellow Muslims. Their dhikrs in
town and countryside provided an ongoing liturgy with an emotive, dramatic, and mystical content not present in the daily salat,
which was, in essence, a private devotion. Finally, the tombs of
holy Sufis became, as we have already seen, a rich source of blessings (*barakat*) and graces (*karamat*). What the dead saint delivered
from beyond the tomb, so too could the living sheikh of the tariqa
as the recipient of the founder's own charismatic karamat. Both
were channels through which blessings, favors, and protections
against ills and tragedy might flood to the ordinary Muslim. The
Christian Church directed those blessings through the highly institutionalized and depersonalized sacramental system; Sufism accomplished the same end through its personalized and decentral-
ized rituals celebrating the friends of God, both living and dead.

The Path to God

In the tenth century Sufism found its literary voice, in both hagiography and theory. The masterpieces of Sufi literature, however
much they differ among themselves in scope and emphasis, share a
common understanding of the purpose and methods of Sufism: to

experience the "unity of God" at the term of a series of highly articulated stages of personal striving, marked at its more advanced levels by the dispensation of certain equally well defined graces from God. From these authors one can elicit some generalized notions about the structure of the Sufi "way" (tariqa), as it had come to be called. Their treatment is rarely theoretical, however, since the works in question generally illustrate their points rather than argue or explain them.

The path to perfection began, of course, with a "conversion," a turning through repentance from the ways of the world toward a consciousness of God. This was, by common consent, the first of the "stations" (maqamat), and was followed by a series of similar stages: scrupulosity of conscience with regard to moral action, self-restraint from even legitimate pleasures, voluntary poverty, patience, abandonment to God, and, finally, the most perfect station, that of divine complaisance, where the striver is in perfect conformity with God's will.

These stations are the fruits of the mystic's own exertions and are akin to the steps along the Christians' *via purgativa*. But once they are achieved, the Sufi's further spiritual progress depends not so much on personal effort as on the benevolent and gracious mercy of God, who bestows the various "states" (ahwal) on the soul. Here too the way is carefully mapped. The Sufi theoreticians distinguished between the states of love, fear, hope, longing, intimacy, tranquillity, contemplation, and certainty. These were by their very nature transitory, as was the culmination of the Sufi's striving and the terminus of the way, unification with God.

The Sufi's transport was a transient state, a brief exaltation into the presence of God. For some it was a unique and almost random event, but it is clear that in Islam many pious souls aspired to this state and they took well-defined and even scholastic steps to attain it. The convert to Sufism was regarded as a mere novice and was placed under the direction of a sheikh already accomplished in the spiritual life. At first that elder may simply have been a skilled and experienced director of souls, but eventually that ideal was replaced, as it was in Eastern Christianity, by the notion of a charismatic guide, a "spiritual father" who possessed the gift of divine grace. For the Muslim no less than the Christian, progress through the stations began as a jihad, a struggle against one's worldly inclinations that reflected the ascetic tradition of the earliest Sufism. The *sheikh* led the novice through the stations by means of exercises like the examination of conscience, meditation, and the constant repetition of God's name. Obedience was expected to be prompt and total.

The spiritual master introduced the novice into two of the most common practices of Sufism, what were called "recollection" (*dhikr*) and the "hearing" (*sama*). The term dhikr has its spiritual, internal sense of recollecting God's name (Quran 18:24; 33:41) and his blessings, but its more common form in Sufism is the ritual repetition of set formulas, notably the Muslim profession of faith or of the ninety-nine "Beautiful Names of God." The dhikr was generally a community exercise, though it could be performed privately, and it was preceded by the tariqa's distinctive litany, or wird, the poetical prayers composed by the founder. The recollection was performed in rhythmical unison by the brethren, and it was often accompanied by controlled breathing, as was the Jesus prayer used to the same end in Eastern Christianity.

The objective of the dhikr was the praise and worship of God, but there was a practical end as well, the achievement of the ecstatic state of annihilation (*fana*), which was for the Sufi a natural antecedent of union with the Divine. There was also often an elaborate ritual of singing and dancing with which the dhikr might be commingled. This sama, as the latter was called, was a virtual "spiritual concert," and though it was highly characteristic of certain Sufi associations such as the celebrated whirling dervishes who followed the teachings of the Persian mystic Jalal al-Din Rumi (1207–1273) at Konya in Turkey, the practice was not everywhere approved or accepted. There were extravagances, to be sure, in these rituals, and more than a few traditional and conservative Muslims were scandalized at what had become, on the eve of modern times, highly theatrical performances rather than spiritual exercises.

SALVATION

The Sufis were attempting nothing other than to anticipate in this life what every Muslim hoped for in the next. All monotheists share the notion of salvation, which both Jews and Christians parse as redemption, being saved from a parlous state, whereas Muslims think of it in terms of an individual's saving himself in a morally neutral universe. God will judge, and those who have chosen wickedness will be punished, while those who have chosen the good will be rewarded, though always and everywhere there hovers the question of predestination. But for the Christians and Jews, redemption is quite a different matter. For Jews it is primarily Israel that will be redeemed: God's people will be freed at last of the subjugation imposed on them by the hostile Gentile world. For the Christian, incontrast, the emphasis rests heavily on individual redemption. The individual has fallen under the subjugation of sin — a legacy of Original Sin — and at the End Time will share at last in the full redemptive act begun with Jesus' death on the cross. In Judaism and Islam, God simply grants salvation; in Christianity, Jesus became the Redeemer by his sacrificial death. The Quran does not cast the future hope of humankind in terms of either redemption or salvation. What is promised is rather "prosperity" (*falah*), a term that occurs often in the Quran and refers to success in both this world and the next. Say your prayers, the Quran advises, and "perhaps you will prosper" (62:10). Muhammad and his followers are counseled to "strive" — the root is the same as that of jihad — "with their possessions and themselves, for them await good things: they are the prosperous ones" (9:88).

This form of salvation is not for Muslims alone. According to the Quran (30:30), all humans are born with a sense of God's "original religion" (*fitra*), as it has been called. Fitra is a difficult quranic word, but it appears clarified in a Prophetic tradition: "Every infant is born according to the fitra, then his parents make him a Jew or a Christian or a Zoroastrian." Many thought this meant that everyone comes into the world a *Muslim*, at least in the sense that Abraham was, and then are "perverted" by parents into other beliefs. If not gifted with revelation, one has but to look at the signs (*ayat*) that God in his mercy has strewn across the universe to understand his uniqueness and generosity (30:20–25). But for Muslims there is a special guidance: the Quran (2:185), with its own clear ayat—a word that soon came to refer to the Quran's individual verses. The Book also characterizes itself as a *furqan*, a "criterion." This too is a difficult word, but its contexts suggest that the entire range of its values is germane here: criterion, revelation, salvation. The Quran is then, in its own words, both a guide and the instrument of salvation, since, as we have just seen, the end for humans is the generous endowment of prosperity, the successful reaping of rewards in this life, and an entry into the Garden that is God's reward to the just in the Afterlife.

The End and What Follows

The corollary of "this world" (*al-dunya*) so despised by the ascetic is "the next world" or, more properly, "the End" (*al-akhira*), which the mystic attempts to anticipate. From the perspective of the three monotheistic communities, this "end" is understood in two related, and sometimes conflicting, senses. It refers in the first instance to the end of the individual: what, if anything, occurs to a person immediately after death. It is a starkly personal and individual concern. But the three faiths are also, and perhaps even more thoughtfully and fretfully, concerned with the End Time, the absolute finale to God's plan for the cosmos, and what might lie beyond. There was, as it turned out, a great deal beyond. The End will mark only the end of history; beyond "The Day" and "The Hour" of the End Time stretches eternity, not the mere prolongation of time but an entirely new dimension of being. Eternity is a state or condition, and although theology undertook to explain in what it consisted, "eternity" simply pronounces of itself that it has no beginning or end. Humans will enter it in progress.

The End Time was and remains a complex affair for Jews, Christians, and Muslims, with an elaborate and articulated scenario for the series of acts that will constitute it. Its formal production design began with the visionary apocalypses of post-Exilic Judaism when privileged individuals were permitted to espy the future. The subsequent reports of these journeys into the Beyond, Jewish, Christian, and Muslim, were filled with circumstantial details of events and their sequences, of topography, of personalities, and even of dialogue. It was left to later and more generally sober theologians and jurists to put some order into these visionary recitals, to filter out elements that proved useless or unacceptable, and to try to incorporate other and older details that had somehow been overlooked. By their own Middle Ages, all three monotheistic communities had a relatively coherent idea of what would occur at the End Time, a schema or scenario for the more literal-minded, a vivid picture for those who took their instruction from preachers, poets, or the walls of churches.

END TIME SCENARIOS

The End, that is, the term of historical time, the Judgment rendered by God on his creation either individually or collectively, and the Requital meted out in consequence are the three main acts of most eschatological scenarios, each enlarged with illustrative, instructive, or even entertaining detail. The End is extended backward to embrace a prelude that might be called Signs: how do we know when the End will come? "No man knows the day or the hour," as the Quran (33:63; 79:42–44) and the other Scriptures warn, but a great many believers have spent a great deal of time calculating it nonetheless. There will be perturbations of nature and perturbations of the spirit, and to the latter belong the false messiahs, false Christs, and the Muslims' "Deceiver." Loose ends are to be tied up: Enoch and Elijah must return to suffer death, to whom the Muslims would add Jesus, who only "seemed" to die on the cross (4:157). For the Christians, Israel must be converted, in history, before Act 2 can begin. The climax comes with the defeat of God's enemies—here the Messiah and Mahdi figures are in evidence—followed by the destruction of the world, the great conflagration in which the material cosmos perishes.

Before the Judgment proper can begin, the resurrection of the dead must occur, a prodigious and troubling event. It is then that the wicked and the good, the sheep and the goats, the "companions of the right hand and the companions of the left hand" (Quran 56:8–9) will be solemnly summoned to God's tribunal, their virtues and vices spelled out—angels have been recording these in books (82:10–12)—and judgment rendered. It is in fact no different from what was decreed for each individual at the moment of death; now, however, God's justice is vindicated to all. The judgment itself is swelled by the desire to make certain that no heroes and particularly no enemies of God go unnoted. This is a time for settling some very human scores since the enemies of God often live up the street or in the house next door, as is graphically illustrated by the Quran, where one unhappy Meccan, Abu Lahab, is consigned by name to hell in sura 111.

Acts 1 and 2 of the eschatological drama are broad canvases for painters and poets; Act 3, "Punishments and Rewards," has ample graphic space as well, but it became more precisely the scratch pad for the theologians and jurists who there, in the midst of the cool running waters of Paradise and raging flames of Hell, had to explain how any of this could happen.

THE MUSLIM DEAD

The drama begins with death. The rituals surrounding death and the dead are simple ones in Islam. The body of the deceased is ritually washed and wrapped in a shroud, some brief funeral prayers (*janaza*) are said in a mosque immediately after the canonical salat, and the interment—cremation, which is traditionally forbidden in Judaism and Christianity, is likewise not countenanced in Islam—takes place as quickly as possible, sometimes on the very day of death. The Quran says nothing of this; its attention is directed almost exclusively to the larger stage of the *yawm al-din*, the Day of Judgment, as it is called in both Arabic and Hebrew.

In the face of this quranic silence on what happens between death and the Judgment, the events that follow an individual Muslim's death unfold in a somewhat confused fashion in the literature on the subject. It is due in part to the freedom of the popular imagination to cast details into that silent vacuum and in part to the difficulty of reconciling what is called in Christianity the "General" and the "Particular" Judgment. All Muslim accounts do agree that the hour of death, what immediately precedes and follows an individual's passing, is a painful and troubled time, rendered even more difficult by the widespread belief that Satan makes a particular effort to persuade the believer to desert the faith just before dying.

At death, the spirit (*ruh*) or soul (*nafs*) — to the chagrin of the philosophers, the two words are often used together or interchangeably in these accounts — leaves the body. At once a moral distinction is discernible. The soul of the believer slips easily from the body and is escorted by white-clad angels through the seven heavens, pausing, much in the manner of the Jewish "Palaces" accounts, to deliver the appropriate password to the guardian of each sphere, until it reaches the Throne of God, though not God's own presence. According to some accounts, the souls of the sinner and the unbeliever attempt to make the same ascent but they are turned back. But at some point, the souls of both the believer and sinner must be returned to the cadaver in order to undergo the ordeal called the "Punishment of the Tomb."

There are suggestions but no clear warrant for this ordeal in the Quran. The hadith, however, describe in graphic terms the violent scrutiny, indeed a test of faith, given the newly dead, who are ordered to "sit up" by two mysterious angels, Munkar and Nakir. The "torment of the grave" is affirmed as dogma in various Muslim creeds, chiefly because it was challenged by Islam's early rationalists, the Mutazilites, who choked on the notion of punishments being visited on a dead body. The traditionalists had reluctantly to concede, relying on a puzzling quranic remark — "Thereof We created you and thereto We return you, and thence we bring you forth a second time" (20:55) — that God had in fact to reunite the soul once more with the body for the verse to make sense. Finally, the newly deceased is confronted by two other figures, one attractive and fragrant, the other repellent and malodorous, who represent the good and evil done during life.

Note: The Muslim notion of a grave ordeal may have had rabbinic origins. Early on the rabbis held that the bodies of the newly dead experienced pain, chiefly, it appears, for "purgatorial" purposes, namely to atone for sins committed during life (BT Sanhedrin 47b). Thereafter the "Pains of the Grave" became synonymous with the "Judgment of the Grave." And the judgment is a "public" one: an angel causes the dead souls to assume bodily forms so that they may be recognized by the other dead. The punishments are exacted by angels, either the single Angel of Death or a group of five such, and they exactly fit the sins being punished, whether of the lips, the eyes, the ears, or the limbs.

At the end of the ordeal, the appropriate chastisements are meted out to those who deserve them — a kind of purgatorial process for those who in the end will not deserve hell — and, for the faithful, the fitting rewards, a foretaste in the tomb itself of the pains of Gehenna and the pleasures of Paradise. Then, according to most accounts, a sleep comes upon the dead until the Final Hour, the Resurrection, and the Judgment.

THE COSMOLOGY OF THE OTHER WORLD

It was in the Valley of Jehosephat, on the eastern side of the city of Jerusalem, that all three traditions placed the site of the Last Judgment, one of the events that would unfold in the great eschatological drama at the far edge of time and the near edge of eternity, and the Kaaba would be miraculously transported to Jerusalem to witness it. The localization of the rest of those events was somewhat more problematic and depended on how the dramatists viewed the world and its parts. The ancients shared two views of the universe, what may be termed a "popular" and a "scientific" version. On a popular level, the earth was thought of as a circular but flat surface, surrounded at its rim by a body of water, which the Greeks called Ocean, and was covered with a vault in which were the planets and the stars. Mythical lands and places, like the Garden of

Eden, the Happy Isles, or the Elysian Fields, could be placed at the remote and imperfectly known outer edges of the inhabited world, much in the way, for example, that Muslims located Eden in Sri Lanka. Places of punishment, the various "hells" often connected with fire, were located beneath the earth. Their point of entry was in some doubt among the pagans — Virgil's *Aeneid* popularized the region around Lake Avernus in southern Italy — but the monotheist tradition fixed it in the Valley of Hinnom (Heb. *Ge Hinnom* > "Gehenna," the Quran's *Jahannam*), the place south of Jerusalem that had once served as the city's smoldering and malodorous garbage dump.

The site of the place of reward was a more complex question, however. There were two competing, sometimes conflicting, and sometimes harmonized versions of where the virtuous would find their final rest. The older, more physical notion was that it would take place in the pristine utopia of Eden, the untroubled Garden of Adam and Eve. And if the Original Sin committed there led to Paradise lost — *paradis* is the familiar Persian loanword for "park" — the blameless could hope to find rest in Paradise regained. Many Jews and early Christians believed, and so too all Muslims still believe since that image of the Garden (*janna*), together with many of its physical details, is deeply embedded in the Quran and Muslims' visions of the Afterlife that have been shaped by the Quran.

The Quran introduces two forms or levels of Paradise. Sura 55 says that "for those who fear to stand before God, there are two Gardens" (v. 46), and shortly after (v. 62) adds, "on this side [or possibly "above"] these are two more Gardens." By one reckoning, then, there are four Gardens for "the blessed," and the Muslim commentators proceeded to work out the details. The *Book of the States of the Resurrection*, an anonymous medieval manual for the Afterlife, numbers seven in all, probably to render them symmetrical to the seven heavens of the traditional Ascension. The sixth of them is called Firdaws, "Paradise," and the seventh and highest, the "Garden of Eden." "This is the capital of the Garden," it adds, "and is higher than all the other Gardens."

A HEAVENLY JOURNEY

There was no place for such a terrestrial Eden in the scientific view of the universe to which the monotheists were all eventually introduced. In this model God dwelled out in the timeless space beyond the seventh heaven, and the notion of bliss for the believers was slowly transformed from restoration to the happiness of our pristine state into a desire to dwell with God, and, as the mystics thought, even to anticipate this good fortune by gazing on God in this life. To reach God's domicile required a perilous journey outward and upward. Second Temple Jews began to lay out the itinerary of the soul's voyage through the spheres to the Throne of God, and eventually this became a staple of meditation, and expectation, among Jewish, Christian, and Muslim mystics alike. The return to God and the enjoyment of his presence was an increasingly attractive prospect for the virtuous. It was reinforced by the notion that the soul, the immortal spiritual soul whose existence and identity emerged from contact with Greek philosophical theories, had originated in the heavens and at birth had descended through the spheres, acquiring in its descent the various astral influences. This premise made astrology, which attempted to read those influences, endlessly fascinating to ancient and medieval men and women of all faiths. The dead, then, did not merely "go to heaven"; they were returning to their original home.

Multistoried versions of heaven and hell made their formal appearance in monotheism in the Jewish apocalypses of the post-Exilic era, but what began there within a journey as a frame tale more often reappeared, particularly in the rabbis' homiletic tales, as simple exposition. The anonymous rabbinic narrator simply described the Garden and Gehenna, and in ever increasing detail. Dante's celebrated tour of heaven, hell, and purgatory represents the continuation of the "journey" tradition in Christianity, but the true sequel to the heavenly journeys of the postbiblical era, and perhaps even the source, as some have suggested, from which Dante derived both the model and many of the details of his *Commedia*, is the trope of the celestial journeys that first appears in the Quran and had a luxuriant afterlife in Islam.

A heavenly journey stands at the very heart of Muslim spirituality. The prototype is Muhammad's own Ascension (*miraj*) into heaven in the course of the famous Night Journey that carried him from Mecca to Jerusalem, thence to the highest heaven and back to his native city, all in the course of a single night. The Quran does no more than allude to it, but the journey, and particularly the Prophet's transit through the heavens, quickly became the stuff of Muslim legend. It soon showed up in enlarged form in the biographies of the Prophet. Eventually there were freestanding treatises devoted entirely to the Ascension of the Prophet—it would have been the translation of one such into Italian that possibly fell into the hands of Dante—and Muslim artists, despite the prohibition against images, found the Ascension a rich ground for illustration.

In its original quranic setting, the story of the Night Journey and the Ascension was perhaps intended to explain the divine origins of Muhammad's revelations, and so it continued to do. But as the story became enlarged, it also included a glimpse into hell and its inhabitants, either on the Prophet's way to Jerusalem or from the vantage point of the third heaven. In its later versions, the seven heavens of the standard cosmology no longer house Muhammad's prophetic predecessors as they had in the earliest accounts but were now populated by a great variety of angelic spirits. The Muslim exploration of heaven had begun.

THE QURANIC ESCHATON

The Quran preaches the Final Judgment in as vivid terms as the New Testament and the Jewish Apocrypha, though there is no clear evidence that it was believed to be imminent, or that Muhammad was in any sense its herald, as Jesus was thought to be. Like its Christian and Jewish counterparts, the Muslim eschaton unfolded in a series of acts, connected at the near end to each individual's death and judgment and at the far end to a universal Day of Judgment (*yawm al-din*) or Day of Resurrection (*yawm al-qiyama*). At "the hour," a trumpet will sound and the world will be rolled up like a scroll. At the second call of the trumpet, the dead will issue forth from their graves and be reunited with their bodies. The great judgment, the Reckoning (al-hisab), will follow: each mortal's book of deeds will be read and assessed, the deeds weighed. The just will be granted the Garden, more properly, Jannat Adan, the "Garden of Eden"; the wicked, Jahannam, or Gehenna. The Quran averts to this judgment scene often in the early suras, and though the pictures of the End are vivid and detailed, they are impressionistic rather than schematic; Jahannam is only one of seven different names for hell in the Quran, for example. The later exegetical tradition often enhanced the details in an imaginative fashion, while the jurists and theologians, as we have seen, who also had a considerable body of hadith on the subject to account for, attempted to reduce the Quran's eschatological "snapshots" to a systematic account. What exactly went on at the End, and in what order, was never precisely settled, but jurists devoted considerable attention to the events, particularly those with political implication, that preceded the End, and to the question of intercession — whether it was possible for the human living, or perhaps just the dead saints, to intervene on behalf of the sinner at the Judgment.

INTERCESSION IN ISLAM

The Quran warns strongly against counting on any assistance before God's tribunal: "If you ask forgiveness for them seventy times, God will not forgive them because they have rejected God and His apostle" (9:50). And again, of the Day of Judgment, "the wrongdoers will have no friend or intercessor to make things easier" (40:19). Indeed, the general principle is stated with great clarity: "Beware of the day when no soul can give satisfaction for another, and no compensation taken for it, and they will not be helpful" (2:45; cf. 2:123). These verses seem to be directed toward unbelievers, that they should not count on some last-minute assistance to save them from damnation. Another set of verses takes on another expectation: the gods worshiped by the pagan Meccans have no power, either in life or in death. "No intercessor will they [the dead sinners] have from among those they have associated with God" (30:13). "Shall I take gods besides Him?" the pagan is made to say. "If the Merciful One intends some adversity, their intercession will profit me nothing" (36:23).

Those points are made with respect to the unbelievers; it does not mean that the faithful should lose hope. There is, as it turns out, the strong possibility of intercession (*shafaa*) at the Day of Judgment on behalf of those who have submitted but have nonetheless sinned. The Quran repeats again and again that such intercession occurs only when and if God allows it (20:109; 34:22). It is not said who enjoys that privilege of intercession—the angels perhaps—but the Muslim tradition was quick to extend it to the greatest among them, the Prophet Muhammad, who on God's orders was granted special favors (17:79; 93:5), including, it was thought, the power of intercession. The hadith fleshed out the modalities. Muhammad is portrayed as praying for the dead, and the custom remained normative among Muslims. Another tradition has all the earlier prophets ceding their powers of intercession to Muhammad, and he, in turn, exercises them on behalf of the members of the Muslim community. What followed was simply a jurists' debate on how far those intercessory powers extended. For serious as well as light sins? On behalf only of those who repented (the Christian position on intercession) or for all sinners? In the end, the traditionalists supplied what became the normative answers: Muhammad will intercede for all sinners and for all sins.

THE VISION OF GOD AND OTHER REWARDS OF PARADISE

The expectation of enjoying a "vision" of God or more simply of "seeing" God is doubtless biblical in its origins. The intimate, even familiar portrait of God in Genesis surely enhanced such a hope, and even the awesome encounters of Moses with his Lord in Exodus, while underlining the privilege, and dangers, of such occasions, reinforced rather than ruled out the possibility. To experience God in such a direct fashion is a theme that exalted and troubled a narrow circle of mystics and their critics, but its occurrence in the Afterlife was the hope of all believers.

The notion of seeing God, even in the Afterlife, was problematic on numerous scores. It reeked, to be sure, of "embodying" God, what the Muslims called *tajsim*, the grossest form of anthropomorphism. Even if the expression "face of God" or "seeing God" was softened into something more acceptable like "being" or "living" in the "presence of God," the troublesome issue "similitude" (*tashbih*), of reducing God to human categories, did not disappear. But whereas the traditionalists fought the notion of a vision of God for the living—the enemy here were Sufis like Ibn al-Arabi who claimed that privilege for themselves during their lifetime—they simply acceded when it came to the reward of the blessed. Both Scripture and tradition were too strong and clear for any Christian or Muslim to resist the conclusion that in eternity the righteous will "be with God," however that might be explained.

The early suras of the Quran, which were attempting to move pagans to "conversion," provide abundant details on the rewards and punishments that will follow the Reckoning, with a distinct emphasis on the subjective state, blissful or painful, of the individual. The rewards of the blessed are chiefly couched in terms of the pleasures of the Garden of Eden, or simply, the Delight. The Meccan chapters of the Quran spell them out in detail: the blessed will recline on couches, dine on fruits, and imbibe the otherwise forbidden wine, served by the much discussed (chiefly by Christian polemicists) virginal houris (the "dark-eyed ones") of Paradise (43: 70–73; 44:54; 55:46–78; 56:11–39, etc.). Later, in the Medina revelations, there is a noticeable shift in emphasis toward the enjoyment of God's "approval" (*ridwan*) as the ultimate reward of the believers (9:72). In one key verse, however, there appears to be an allusion to an actual vision of God in the Afterlife: "On that Day the faces of some will shine, looking toward their Lord" (75:22–23). Another (83:15) states that "that Day shall they (the transgressors) be veiled."

Numerous hadith fill in the details of life in the Garden, many of them in highly literalistic terms. The blessed will "visit" God every Friday, escorted into the Presence, the men by Muhammad and the women by Fatima, and passing on their way the various pieces of cosmic furniture that the tradition had located there, the heavenly Kaaba (52:4), for example, and the "Guarded Tablet" (85:22), the prototype of the Quran. Finally, "the veil is lifted" and God appears to the faithful, shining "like the full moon."

The blatant anthropomorphism of these scenes caused uneasiness in some quarters, as might be imagined. The Mutazilites, Islam's early rationalists, simply read the "looking toward their Lord" verse in another way to eliminate the spatial implications of "turning" and the physical one of "seeing." There was further relief to those anxieties in a hadith where Muhammad reports God as saying, "I have prepared for My servants what no eye has ever seen nor ear heard nor human heart ever felt." This provided a welcome rejection of all similitude and enabled the majority of Muslims to embrace the reward of a "vision of God," even though, like many Christian theologians, they could not quite explain it. It was in this form that the Beatific Vision took its place in various Muslim creeds: "The faithful will see Him in Paradise, with their bodily eyes, but without making comparisons (between Him and us) and without 'howness' (*kayfiyya*)," that is, the need to explain.

ARE THE MARTYRS IN PARADISE?

Islam no less than Christianity has a martyr tradition, and for much the same reason. Both communities were early on faced with a sometimes violent hostility, the Christians from the Roman Empire, the Muslims from the hostile Quraysh of Mecca. For a long time the Christians put up no resistance to their Roman persecutors and so became "witnesses" (*martyres*) to their faith by their willingness to suffer and die rather than deny it. Those witnesses almost immediately became the objects of veneration both by liturgical cult — rites were celebrated at their tombs — and by reason of the special intercessory powers they were believed to have with God. These are the hallmarks of the Christian saint, a person thought to be "in heaven," as the Christian would put it, or "in Paradise," as a Muslim would prefer to think of it.

The mistreatment of the Muslims at Mecca appears to have claimed no lives, but once it was revealed that forceful resistance to forceful oppression was legitimate for a Muslim (22:39–40), there began to be Muslim "witnesses" (*shuhada*; sing. *shahid*), believers who shed their blood or gave their lives for their faith. It is in that very political context that the Quran addresses the issue, after the Medina Muslims had suffered a reversal at arms and several had died. There were those who were against the resistance to the Quraysh — the Quran calls them hypocrites — and who mocked those who had died in the fighting. "Do not think of those who were slain in the way of God as dead," the Quran says at that point. "No, they are alive and have provision with their Lord" (3:169; cf. 2:154), which was taken to mean that they were with God in Paradise. The Book goes on: "Those they have left behind, who have not yet joined them in their bliss, (the martyrs) glory in the fact that they have no fear nor cause to grieve."

There are differences between the Christian and Muslim attitudes toward martyrdom, however. Christian martyrdom was an act of personal heroism, whereas its Muslim counterpart, however personal and however heroic, was a political act, that is, it occurred in the context of what the Muslim jurists were already defining as a holy war (*jihad*). The Muslim martyr was also of necessity a mujahid, a holy warrior. The second difference was in the recognition granted the martyr. In Christianity both the recognition and the acknowledgment of the martyr quickly became, like many other things in the Church, highly formalized. The Christian martyrs were exemplars, of course, but chiefly during the great persecutions, and once the persecutions were suspended, then abolished, Christian exemplarism shifted quickly to the "confessors," the men and women who "witnessed" to their faith by a lifetime of virtue. The martyrs meanwhile became more simply saints, the blessed in heaven whose intercessory powers rather than whose heavenly joys — which tend to be highly spiritualized in Christianity in any event — became the focus of the cult. There was no suspension of persecution in Islam. Those who resisted

Islam, and continue to resist Islam, are in effect its persecutors, and those who defend Islam and its Abode by "striving in the way of God" are mujahideen. Those who perish in the act were and are martyrs. The cults that developed around them—are martyrs traditionally buried in their bloody garments, for example—were (and are) popular, unofficial, and highly varied.

The theology of Islamic martyrdom is clear: the martyr-mujahid will enjoy Paradise and its pleasures as surely as his Christian counterpart. Yet during most of the history of the Abode of the Islam, martyrdom was praised but only rarely urged in Sunni circles, where persecution was scarcely an issue, whereas jihad, as we have seen, was often a highly problematic concept. Among Shiites, however, who have suffered unmistakable persecution at the hands of their Sunni brethren and where there is a distinct and fostered martyr culture centering around the figure of the seventh-century Imam Husayn, martyrdom has had a far stronger appeal. Some branches of the Ismaili Shiites, for example, recruited young men, whom they first drugged—the term "assassin" itself may come from the Arabic for "hashish-crazed"—and in that state allowed them a staged but highly realistic taste of Paradise, complete with actors and props, and then sent off on missions of assassination. These were the *fidaiyun*, "those who sacrificed themselves," Islam's lethal kamikazes turned against other Muslims of a different persuasion.

A SAVIOR RETURNS

As the jurists and theologians read the evidence for the approach of the End Time, the Muslim community will be riven with schism and sectarianism. God will send relief, however, in the form of the Mahdi, the Guided One who will be a man of Muhammad's house—he too will be named Muhammad ibn Abdullah—and he will unite Islam. The notion is not quranic: Muhammad could hardly have foreseen the breadth of his community, much less that it would suffer from schisms, and the mortal and dead Prophet could scarcely serve as his own Messiah. Rather, the belief seems to have arisen in the schismatic civil wars of the first Islamic century and to have had its origin in the same circle that eventually matured into Shiism. According to the Shiites, the Mahdi would indeed be someone from Muhammad's house: a descendant of the Imam Ali. If the Mahdi was a Shiite notion, it was soon embraced by Sunnis, not as a certification of the Alids in this life but as an expectation of help from the Prophetic House at the End Time. What precisely that help would be depended, as it did in Judaism, on what form of the eschatological scenario one was reading. Enough Muslims read it in political terms to make the Mahdi an even more potent symbol of insurrection or apocalyptic revolution than the Messiah was for Jews.

The next act in the eschatological drama will begin with the coming of the Antichrist, the Deceiver (al-Dajjal), who will introduce another reign of terror that will last until the appearance of Jesus, who, according to the Quran was taken up into heaven alive and must return to earth to suffer death. On his return, he will slay the Antichrist, and then the Final Judgment depicted in the Quran will take place.

The swirl of messianic expectation in mid-eighth-century Islam was as real perhaps as that which roiled Palestinian Judaism in the first century. Umayyad extravagance, joined to growing doubts about the legitimacy of the new dynasty and its pretensions, provoked the Islamic reaction, Greek and Roman oppression the Jewish one, to which were added doubts about the Hasmonaean kings, the Herodians who succeeded them, and even, in some quarters, the high priesthood of the temple. Palestinian political and religious unrest ended in two ill-fated insurrections against Rome, the second of which had a distinct messianic aura surrounding its leader Bar Kokhba. Muslim dissatisfaction came to term in what came to be called the Abbasid Revolution of 750, though this latter turned out to be no more than the replacement of one caliphal dynasty by another that rode to power in the wake, or on the promise, of Alid messianism, which had become focused on one of Ali's sons, Muhammad ibn al-Hanifiyya.

SHIITE MESSIANISM

Early on in Shiism, supporters of the cause of Ali's family pinned their hopes for a restoration chiefly on two branches of his descendants. One was the line of Muhammad ibn al-Hanifiyya ("son of the Hanifite woman"), the offspring of Ali and one of his tribal wives, and the other was either Hasan or Husayn, the sons of Ali's union with Muhammad's daughter Fatima. Though the Shiite claims did not achieve their original goal of putting an Alid on the caliphal throne, the Alid connection that passed, by a kind of political sleight of hand, from Ibn al-Hanifiyya's son Muhammad to the first of the Abbasids bolstered the latter's claims to legitimacy as head of the umma. But for all that, it was rather the scions of the Ali-Fatima line who came to rule the Shiite roost, not in the sense that they ever wielded actual political power but insofar as they controlled and shaped the movement called Shiism in both its Ismaili and its Imami varieties.

But the shadowy Ibn al-Hanifiyya was more than a pretender to political power: he appears to have been among the earliest in Islam to be regarded as the Mahdi, a figure believed to be the divinely appointed individual who would preside over the final triumph of Islam. Behind him stood perhaps the prototype of Ali himself, whom many of his followers believed would one day return to guide the community. Indeed, some of Ali's followers denied that he had died at all. Whatever the metaphysics that stood behind this belief — early on the notion current in Shiite extremist groups was that Ali was in some manner divine — was the conviction that the Imam, eventually, the last Imam, would return to his community spread among Shiites of all shades of belief.

Whether dead or disappeared, the reappearance of the Shiite Imam was a return from another dimension of one who had once been alive. The sentiment is parallel to the post-Exilic Jewish (and eventually Islamic) beliefs about Elijah or Enoch. The growth among Shiites of the conviction that the last Imam, whether the seventh or the twelfth, had gone into concealment and would one day return is the plausible result of two factors: a first, denial of the death of a revered leader, which was apparently squelched in the case of Muhammad but persisted in the case of Ali; and second, what can be called in a general fashion "messianic expectation." Messiahs are born of despair, in particular a despair that political processes, or even, more generally, historical processes, can never achieve the desired end. In the Muslim case, it was likely engendered by the failure of the Abbasid Revolution to restore one of the "People of the House," always understood as uniquely the Alid branch of the Prophet's house, to the Imamate. The Abbasids, having unseated the Umayyads, declined to yield the Imamate to an Alid, and the Shiites took their disappointed hopes to another place. The Hidden Imam had gone, concealed in another dimension and so safe from the Abbasid authorities. But he will one day return as Messiah to restore the true Islamic dispensation.

The expected return of Jesus, who underwent his own concealment when he was taken up, glorified but unmistakably in a physical condition, from the slopes of Olivet to his Father in heaven (Acts 1:6–14), was postponed within one generation of Christians from the immediate future to the indefinite future. This transformation of expectation may have occurred even more quickly among the Shiites. By the ninth and tenth centuries, hope for an imminent restoration of an Alid as the head of the umma had all but disappeared in Shiite circles. The believers settled in for the long haul toward the eschaton, and those who were impatient enough to start counting down the days and years to the End Time, and so the return of the Imam, were warned to refrain from such dangerous exercises.

Note: Impatience sometimes triumphed, however. Though concealed, the Hidden Imam, or Imam of the Ages, as he was also called, provides ongoing direction to the Shiite community, as we have already seen. More than counsel, his somewhat more direct intervention has been spectacularly invoked—and was believed to have occurred—at two moments in modern Shiite history. The first was in the Iranian Constitutional Revolution of 1906–1911 when the Shiite ulama announced that opposition to the new constitution was tantamount to taking up arms against the Hidden Imam. The same recourse was taken in 1979 in the Iranian Revolution. This time there was a more particular focus. The Ayatollah Khomeini (d. 1989) was universally recognized as a spokesman of the Imam, and by enthusiasts even as the Imam himself, returned at last to "fill the world with justice and righteousness," or, if not the world, at least the new Islamic Republic of Iran.

THE MAHDI

From somewhere in that same terrain of hopes and disappointment the Sunnis found their own explanation of an End Time savior. He is called *al-mahdi*, or the Divinely Guided One. "Mahdi" did not begin its career as an eschatological epithet; indeed, any number of prominent figures in early Islam were so characterized for their saintliness or upright conduct, and one Abbasid caliph — the Umayyads went by their ordinary names but the Abbasids much preferred throne-titles to mere names — assumed al-Mahdi as his throne-name, and another al-Hadi, or "the Divinely Guiding One," without any notable eschatological implication. The first association of that characterization with the End Time was apparently connected with Jesus, whom the Muslims expected to return not merely to succumb to the mortal necessity of death — his tomb is prepared next to Muhammad's at Medina — but, much as the Christians believed, to initiate the final stage in the history of the cosmos. In the Muslim version of that scenario, *al-mahdi* was simply a characterization of the Jesus of the *parousia*. But Jesus was a mythic personality and, as noted, pious and disappointed Muslims of the mid–eighth century required more concrete and more immediate relief. A Mahdi-prince was projected into the immediate present, a historical rather than an eschatological messiah, to right present wrongs and to inaugurate a more authentic Islam.

Sunnis, like the Shiites, placed their hopes in the Abbasids, the first for relief, the second for fulfillment. Both were disappointed, and while the Shiites had their own candidates standing in the wings in the person of the Alid Imams, the Sunnis had none. There was no need, then, for either a concealment or a return: the Sunni Mahdi was simply postponed to the indefinite eschaton, not as Jesus—though some continue to maintain that Jesus and the Mahdi are one and the same—but next to Jesus, and subsequent Muslim scenarios of the End Time preferred to assign separate roles to the Mahdi and to Jesus.

Like the Jews' Messiah, the Mahdi has not lost all his political potency in his postponement to the End Time. At various times and in various places persons have come forth to announce that *they* were the awaited Mahdi. In modern times, the "restoration of Islam" has most often been pursued in the context of forming an Islamic state or throwing off foreign domination over a Muslim population. The most famous modern representative of the type remains Muhammad Ahmad, who revealed his identity as the Mahdi in the Sudan in 1881 and convinced enough Muslims of the truth of his claims to lead an insurrection against the British that destroyed one British army under General Charles Gordon at Khartoum in 1885 and required another under General Arthur Kitchener to put it down in 1889.

Reflections after a Breakfast

"THE ARABS have their Bible," King Alfonso X advised his Castilian subjects in the mid–thirteenth century, "which was translated from the Hebrew." The king, *salva majestate ejus*, was wrong, but his intentions were good, and his information in one respect was not so very far from the truth. The Quran was indeed "from the Hebrew," although not translated, in the ordinary sense of that word, either by or for Muhammad. But some manner of translation had assuredly taken place between the Scripture of the Hebrews and the audience that heard Muhammad proclaim the Word of God in Arabia in the seventh century of our era, a transfer of the spiritual goods of one established monotheist community into another that was struggling to come into being. Muhammad was aware of the transfer, as were some of his audience, and a number of them accused him of spiritual larceny.

In 1832 a German Jewish scholar, Abraham Geiger, reopened the question in a more secular mode. "What Did Muhammad Take from the Jews?" was the title of his doctoral dissertation, and the same provocative question has been asked from his day to this. The answers have varied from "nothing," as most Muslims would vigorously contend, to "a great deal," as many non-Muslims would equally vigorously argue. But none would say "everything." Muhammad's putative Jewish teacher would hardly have instructed him on the exalted status of Jesus and the Virgin Mary, which the Quran proclaims confidently and often. Christians took note of that latter fact, and many could only imagine that Muhammad had once been a Christian, perhaps even a cleric, who fabricated the Quran out of the Old and New Testaments as an imposture.

Neither supposition has been entertained here, either in its extreme forms — that Muhammad had a Jewish teacher or was himself a failed Christian — or in its mitigated versions — that he was somehow influenced by local Christians or, more plausibly, by contemporary Arabian Jews. Nor has it been suggested that Muhammad concocted a synthesis of the two older monotheist faiths. Such an approach, with its powerful reductionist appeal, does nothing to enhance our understanding of the profound originality of Islam or of its prophet. Whether its source was God or, equally wondrously, the startlingly prophetic insight of a religious poet-genius, the foundation of Islam, its Scripture, was laid down by a single individual. The Bible and the New Testament are clearly community projects elaborated over decades or centuries by individuals with only an uncertain connection with their subject or subjects. The Quran, in contrast, proceeded from the mouth of Muhammad, and his alone, over a rather precisely measured interval of twenty-two years. Even on the Muslim supposition that the Book was sent to him from on high, the community of Muslims, the umma, that issued from it was clearly Muhammad's creation, shaped and guided by his powerful will, tended to by his infinite care, and sustained by his extraordinary courage and determination.

Theologically Christianity rests uniquely on Jesus' redemptive work, whereas Muhammad's theological role in Islam — he was merely a messenger or a warner, he insisted — was quite secondary. But Christendom owes considerably less to Jesus of Nazareth than Islamdom — the social and political body that came forth from the preaching of the Quran — did to Muhammad, without whom it would be unthinkable. Judaism may be unfathomable without Abraham and Moses, but they are powerful characters in a story, role-players in the foundation haggadah of the Jews, whereas Muhammad is a full-bodied individual who rises persuasively above his "story."

We are newly aware of Islam, but only because of our aversion to history, compounded by a secular disinclination to take religion seriously as a cause of anything. But many earlier generations of Jews and Christians and almost as many generations of Europeans have been vividly aware of the worshipers of Allah and the devotees of the Quran. It was the message of Islam that persuaded vast numbers of Jews and Christians from Iran to Spain to abandon their ancestral faith and embrace this new — or was it merely pristine? — version of monotheism. Muslim swords and Muslim galleys dominated, and often terrified, the Mediterranean basin from the eighth to the sixteenth century; Muslim merchants controlled international trade for extensive periods; Muslim artisans surpassed their European counterparts in techniques and materials; and Muslim intellectuals supplied many of the works and much of the energy and curiosity that reignited philosophical and scientific studies in the new university centers of Europe. By the sixteenth century, however, that picture began dramatically to change. Both Islam and Muslims dropped down behind the political and religious horizons of Europe. It has taken oil, Zionism, and Muslim Fundamentalism to bring them rushing back in the twentieth century and, more urgently, in the twenty-first.

What has returned to Western consciousness under the name of "Islam" appears both exotic and threatening. It has seemed so on occasion in the past as well, though somewhat more threatening than exotic perhaps. It is a small matter to predict that eventually it will look less exotic to us as well since increasing numbers of Muslims now live in "Christian" societies of the West, and they in turn are assimilating in much the same fashion that Jews did in Europe and America in the nineteenth century. Islam too will one day pass as a "Western" religion, just as its two monotheist siblings do. As for the threat, it is as real as fanaticism can make it. Fanaticism runs deep into the DNA of all three monotheist communities, but with least restraint in Islam, which from the beginning has recognized no sovereignty other than God's, whereas Jews and Christians have had to accommodate to, and, more recently, be constrained by the secular states that are now their masters. The fanaticism of monotheism embodied in a society that is both a church and a state has been and remains a dangerous threat in a world that no longer seems willing to accept religion as a just cause of war or any other form of violence.

This book has proposed no solutions because it has identified no problems. It has attempted rather to trace for Jews and Christians the spiritual and political bloodlines of Islam, working from etiology rather than behavior. It is an odd enterprise perhaps for someone who sat at his own breakfast table and watched in horrified disbelief the destruction by Muslim fanatics of part of the life and fabric of New York City. My chief reaction on that terrible day was one of profound sadness at the loss to me personally and to the noble enterprise that is America, but sadness too at the sure knowledge of the hate and misunderstanding that prompted the act and the equal portion of each that would surely follow in its wake.

I have spent half of my professional life trying to explain the hate and unravel the misunderstanding that pervades religious history and the other half attempting to describe the joy and sublimity that has often accompanied the worship of God. I have done it the same way I have tried to do it here, by laying bare both the causes of hate and the reasons for the misunderstanding. It still seems to me the only worthwhile way of coming to terms with both the evil and the good that humans do in the name of God.

Index